SPORT PILOT CHECKRIDE GUIDE
A guide to passing the FAA Practical Flight & Oral Exam

A guide to get your Sport Pilot or Sport Pilot Instructor Certificate for

Airplane • Weight-Shift Control
Powered Parachute

by Paul Hamilton

Aviation Supplies & Academics, Inc.
Newcastle, Washington

Sport Pilot Checkride: A Guide to Passing the FAA Practical Flight and Oral Exam to get your Sport Pilot or Sport Instructor Certificate for Airplanes, Weight-Shift Control, and Powered Parachute Light-Sport Aircraft
by Paul Hamilton

Aviation Supplies & Academics, Inc.
7005 132nd Place SE
Newcastle, Washington 98059-3153
Internet: www.asa2fly.com
Email: asa@asa2fly.com

Visit the ASA website often (**www.asa2fly.com**) to find Updates posted due to FAA regulation and procedural revisions that may affect this book.

Printed in the United States of America

09   08   07   06   9   8   7   6   5   4   3   2   1

ASA-F2F-CKRIDE
ISBN   1-56027-592-8
         978-1-56027-592-3

Library of Congress Cataloging-in-Publication Data:

Hamilton, Paul
    Sport pilot checkride : a guide to passing the FAA practical flight and oral exam to get your sport pilot or sport instructor certificate for airplane, weight-shift control, and powered parachute light-sport aircraft / by Paul Hamilton.
        p.   cm.
    ISBN-13: 978-1-56027-592-3 (pbk.)
    ISBN-10: 1-56027-592-8 (pbk.)
    1. Airplanes—Piloting. 2. Air pilots—Licenses—United States. 3. Flight training. I. Title.

    TL710.H28 2006
    629.132'52—dc22
                                2006001954
02

CONTENTS

Part 3
Instructor Checkride Guide **169**

INTRODUCTION

About This Book

This book prepares you for the last step in obtaining sport pilot or sport instructor privileges to fly or teach in light-sport aircraft: the practical test, or checkride.

You should use this book to prepare for your practical test. Use a pencil to cross off areas that do not apply to you. Modify the checklists to fit you and your specific aircraft. By purchasing this book, you have copyright permission to photocopy the checklists or flight log in this book for use during your checkride; this book is meant to be used as a tool.

The Sport Pilot Practical Test Standards book (FAA-S-8081-29, -30, or -31 depending on which aircraft you fly) specifies the areas in which knowledge and skill must be demonstrated by the applicant before issuance of a pilot certificate or rating. This book has been designed to evaluate a pilot's knowledge of those areas. It contains questions and answers organized into 10 main divisions that represent those areas of knowledge required for the practical test.

Although the checkride usually begins with an evaluation of your paperwork and then proceeds to the oral questioning and concludes with the flight, at any time during the checkride the examiner may ask questions pertaining to any of these subject areas.

Description of Part 1, "Getting to the Checkride"

This section lays out the specific steps you must go through to acquire your sport pilot and sport instructor privileges. It also describes how to add a category, class, or make/model/set of aircraft to your existing pilot or instructor certification. It tells you who you need to see and the steps you must take to acquire the signoffs, endorsements and/or certificate you want. *Sport Pilot Checkride* simplifies the FAA system to provide you with specific steps to achieve your goal.

Description of Part 2, "Guide to the Sport Pilot Checkride"

This section is a guide to passing the FAA practical test that includes testing of two specific areas:

- Aeronautical knowledge, which is demonstrated through oral questioning.
- Aeronautical skill, which is the "flight test."

The first part of this section, "Preparation for Preflight," has Task checklists and typical questions the examiner may ask you, along with the information you need to respond with. This is generally considered the oral questioning portion of the practical test.

Following the Preparation section and starting with "Preflight Procedures" through "Post-flight Procedures," are sections covering the information and checklists you can use during the aeronautical skill test. This is considered the flight test guide for the practical test. Checklist use is recommended throughout your checkride, as well as when operating as a licensed sport pilot.

Throughout this section there are specific areas to study for Fixed Wing Airplane, Weight-Shift Control, Powered Parachute, Instructors, and also for different equipment for specific systems. You study only the areas that apply to the aircraft you intend to fly (i.e., your own, and the one in which you will take the checkride).

Description of Part 3, "Instructor Checkride Guide"

This is additional information for the instructor practical test. Sport instructor applicants need to read both Parts 2 and 3 of this book. During the instructor practical, the examiner can ask all the sport pilot questions; however, the instructor should have a higher level of correlation knowledge, plus have the additional ability to:

- Demonstrate knowledge,
- Discuss common errors,
- Demonstrate and explain,
- Analyze and correct mistakes.

Therefore this guide has further questions that may be asked during the instructor checkride. Part 3 is specifically intended for instructors studying for their practical, and should be ignored by the sport pilot applicant.

Supplemental Readings

This book may be supplemented with other study materials, as noted in parentheses after each question—for example: (FAA-H-8083-25). The abbreviations for these materials and their titles are listed below. Be sure to use the latest revision of these references when preparing for the test. You should cross-reference with the Appendix as it details which portions of the books apply to sport pilot and which apply to sport pilot instructors.

14 CFR Part 1	*Definitions and Abbreviations*
14 CFR Part 43	*Maintenance, Preventive Maintenance, Rebuilding, and Alteration*
14 CFR Part 61	*Certification: Pilots, Flight Instructors, and Ground Instructors*
14 CFR Part 71	*Designation of Class A, B, C, D and E Airspace Areas*
14 CFR Part 91	*General Operating and Flight Rules*
NTSB Part 830	*Notification and Reporting of Aircraft Accidents and Incidents*
AC 00-6	*Aviation Weather*
AC 00-45	*Aviation Weather Services*
*AC 61-65	*Certification: Pilots and Flight Instructors*
AC 61-67	*Stall and Spin Awareness Training*
AC 61-84	*Role of Preflight Preparation*
*AC 61-98A	*Currency and Additional Qualification Requirements for Certificated Pilots*
FAA-H-8081-29, -30, -31	*Sport Pilot Practical Test Standards*
FAA-H-8083-3	*Airplane Flying Handbook*
FAA-H-8083-25	*Pilot's Handbook of Aeronautical Knowledge*
FAA-P-8740-2	*Density Altitude*
AIM	*Aeronautical Information Manual*
POH	Pilot Operating Handbook
AFM	*FAA-Approved Airplane Flight Manual*
NACO	National Aeronautical Charting Office
FAR/AIM	Includes regulations and AIM applicable to sport pilots
VFM-HI	*Visualized Flight Maneuvers Handbook*
F2F-W2F	*Weather to Fly for Sport Pilots* DVD and booklet
F2F-L2F	*Learn to Fly* DVD and booklet (use the aircraft applicable to you)
F2F-PF	Preflight [your aircraft] DVD and booklet (use the aircraft applicable to you)
F2F-SPORT	*Sport Pilot: Choosing the Light-Sport Aircraft That's Right for You* DVD and booklet
TP-SPORT	*Sport Pilot Test Prep*
SPT	*Seaplane Pilot* by Dale DeRemer (for seaplane class ratings)
CON-GEAR	*Conventional Gear: Flying a Taildragger* by David Robson (for taildragger operations)

These references are for sport instructors.

Most of the publications listed above are available from ASA and aviation retailers nationwide.

Part 1 **Getting to the Checkride**

Find an Examiner

You will need to see an FAA Aviation Safety Inspector (ASI) or a Designated Pilot Examiner (DPE) to obtain your FAA student, sport pilot, or sport pilot instructor certificate to fly light-sport aircraft (LSA). The hierarchy of the sport pilot system from FAA personnel to civilian pilots is as follows:

Aviation Safety Inspector (ASI)—FAA personnel who can administer all practical and proficiency tests. Can issue student, sport pilot and instructor certificates.

Designated Pilot Examiner (DPE)—A civilian representing the FAA who can issue sport pilot certificates. This person is classified as a Sport Pilot Examiner (SPE) and can issue certificates to students and sport pilots. Sport Pilot Instructor Examiners (SPIE) can also issue sport pilot instructor certificates. Each DPE reports to FAA personnel, the Principle Operations Inspector (POI).

Certified Flight Instructors (CFI)—Instructors who can instruct, endorse, and provide proficiency checks for sport pilots and sport pilot flight instructors. They cannot issue student or sport pilot certificates.

Sport Pilot—Pilot who holds an FAA certificate and exercises sport pilot privileges. Able to fly light-sport aircraft; make/model/set endorsed with logbook signoff.

Using a Driver's License for Medical Eligibility

If an FAA medical has been revoked, denied or suspended, you must obtain a special issuance to use a driver's license as the medical eligibility. Any limitations on your driver's license or FAA medical must be followed.

Continued

The Steps to Follow

These are the steps you need to follow to get where you want to be, starting with where you are now. Follow along in the flow charts below that provide the specific steps to achieve your objective. All the variations on sport pilot and instructor applicants are shown in the flow charts. Decide which one applies to you, then follow the corresponding chart:

To be a Sport Pilot and fly Light Sport Aircraft

- New or existing ultralight pilot without an FAA pilot certificate.
- Pilot with an FAA pilot license, recreational or higher, wanting to fly light-sport aircraft.

To be a Sport Pilot Flight Instructor (Sport Pilot CFI)

- New pilot or existing ultralight instructor without an FAA instructor certificate (CFI).
- An existing Certified Flight Instructor (CFI) who wants to instruct in LSA.

To add category/class and make/model/set

- For sport pilots, private pilots (and higher), and instructors

Pilot Candidates Without FAA Flight Certificate

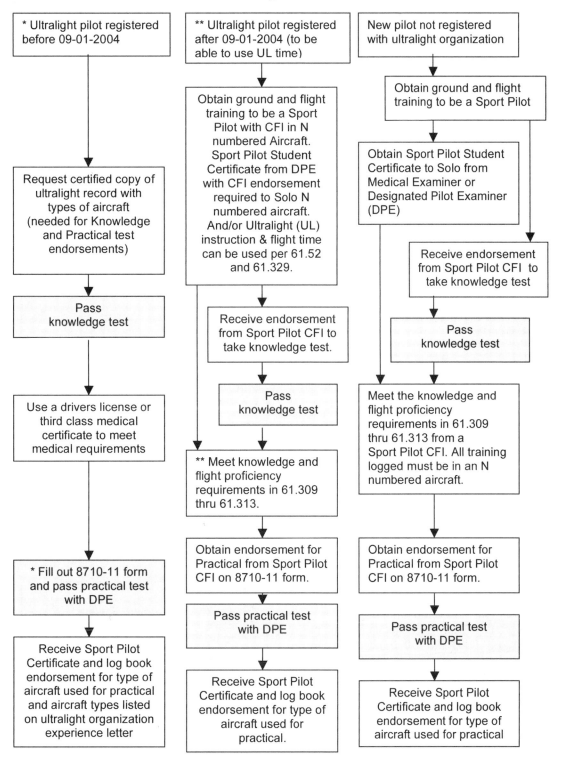

| * Ultralight pilot registered before 09-01-2004 | ** Ultralight pilot registered after 09-01-2004 (to be able to use UL time) | New pilot not registered with ultralight organization |

* Ultralight pilots can use their ultralight experience to meet the aeronautical experience specified in §61.313 until January 31, 2007 for the practical test.

** Ultralight pilots can use their logged ultralight experience but must meet the aeronautical experience requirements specified in §61.313. Training and endorsement by a sport pilot CFI 60 days before the practical test must be logged/endorsed per "Prerequisites for Practical Tests" §61.39(a)(6). The practical test must be completed before January 31, 2007 to utilize ultralight experience.

Pilots With FAA Certificate (Recreational or Higher) Who Want to Fly LSA (with or without a medical)

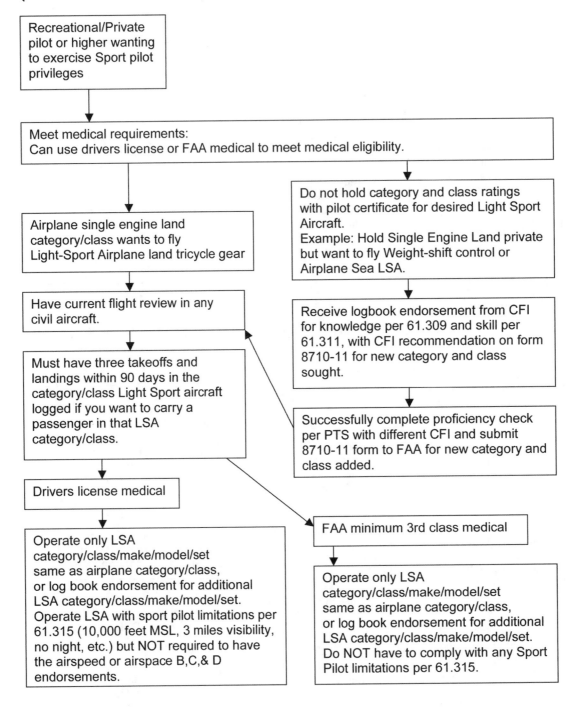

Recreational/Private pilot or higher wanting to exercise Sport pilot privileges

Meet medical requirements:
Can use drivers license or FAA medical to meet medical eligibility.

Airplane single engine land category/class wants to fly Light-Sport Airplane land tricycle gear

Do not hold category and class ratings with pilot certificate for desired Light Sport Aircraft.
Example: Hold Single Engine Land private but want to fly Weight-shift control or Airplane Sea LSA.

Have current flight review in any civil aircraft.

Receive logbook endorsement from CFI for knowledge per 61.309 and skill per 61.311, with CFI recommendation on form 8710-11 for new category and class sought.

Must have three takeoffs and landings within 90 days in the category/class Light Sport aircraft logged if you want to carry a passenger in that LSA category/class.

Successfully complete proficiency check per PTS with different CFI and submit 8710-11 form to FAA for new category and class added.

Drivers license medical

FAA minimum 3rd class medical

Operate only LSA category/class/make/model/set same as airplane category/class, or log book endorsement for additional LSA category/class/make/model/set. Operate LSA with sport pilot limitations per 61.315 (10,000 feet MSL, 3 miles visibility, no night, etc.) but NOT required to have the airspeed or airspace B,C,& D endorsements.

Operate only LSA category/class/make/model/set same as airplane category/class, or log book endorsement for additional LSA category/class/make/model/set. Do NOT have to comply with any Sport Pilot limitations per 61.315.

Pilots (Not Currently CFI) Who Seek Flight Instructor Certificate

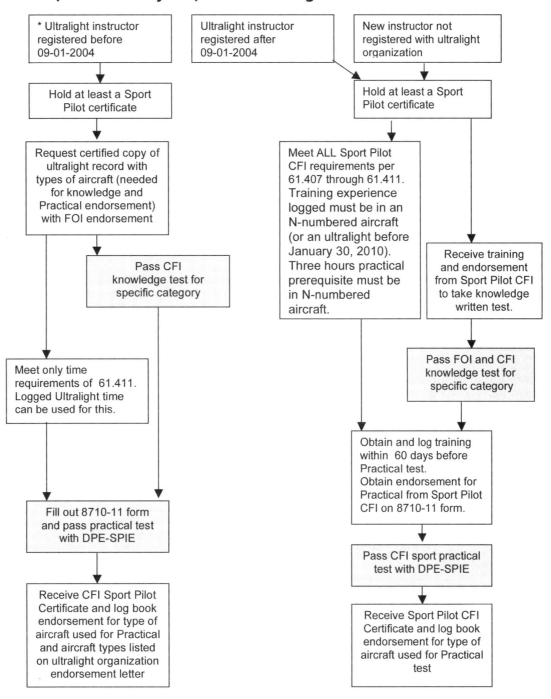

* Ultralight instructors can use
  ultralight experience until
  January 31, 2008.

CFIs Seeking Privileges to Train Sport Pilots and Sport Pilot CFIs in LSA

You hold current CFI certificate with a specific category/class rating (use single engine airplane as example)

Medical eligibility
- Drivers license or
- FAA medical certificate

Want to instruct in different LSA category/class LSA set than that listed on CFI certificate (such as airplane sea, Weight-shift control, Powered parachute, etc.)

Want to instruct in similar LSA set as airplane category/class rating held on CFI certificate

Be a pilot in the set aircraft desired

Flight review current per 61.56 and currency per 61.57

Receive a logbook endorsement for training as specified per 61.409 for additional LSA in category/class/make/model/"set" by qualified instructor

To provide training in LSA, five hours PIC in same category/class/make/model/set, is required per 61.415

Train only in S-LSA (or appropriate E-LSA until 2010) per 61.411 experience.

Successfully complete a proficiency check with an instructor other than who provided training per 61.409, receive logbook endorsement from this instructor, and submit form 8710-11

Aviation 3rd class medical – Do NOT have to comply with any Sport Pilot limitations per 61.315.

Drivers license medical- Operate LSA with sport pilot limitations per 61.315, but NOT required to have the airspeed or airspace B,C,& D endorsements

Comply with all Sport Pilot CFI privileges per 61.413, limitations per 61.415, and record keeping per 61.423

For Sport Pilots and Instructors

Categories
- Airplane
- Weight Shift
- Powered Parachute

Classes
- Land
- Sea

Distinct Category/Classes
- Airplane Single engine Land ASEL
- Airplane Single Engine Sea ASES
- Weight-shift Control Land WSCL
- Weight-shift Control Sea WSCS
- Powered Parachute Land PPL
- Powered Parachute Sea PPS

↓

* Need two CFIs to add a new category/class

↓

CFI 1 Recommendation
Receive training on aeronautical knowledge and skill per § 61.309 and § 61.311 for the additional light-sport aircraft category/class.

Receive logbook endorsement from this authorized instructor.

Get CFI recommendation on the FAA Form 8710-11 for proficiency check.

↓

CFI 2 Proficiency Check
Successfully complete a proficiency check from an authorized instructor other than the instructor who provided training and recommendation

Receive a logbook endorsement from the instructor who conducted the proficiency check for the additional category/class. This instructor will fill out the proficiency check area on the 8710-11 and send the form to the FAA.

○ The 8 Airplane sets are
- Less than 87 KCAS Vh
  1. Tricycle gear
  2. Tailwheel
  3. Float equipped
  4. Ski equipped
- Greater than 87 KCAS Vh
  5. Tricycle gear
  6. Tailwheel
  7. Float equipped
  8. Ski equipped

○ The 3 Weight-Shift Control sets are
  1. Tricycle gear
  2. Float equipped
  3. Ski equipped

○ The 4 Powered Parachute sets are
- Square wing
  1. Land
  2. Sea
- Elliptical Wing
  3. Land
  4. Sea

Note: Airplane recreational/private pilots are qualified for both airspeed sets, ultralight pilots qualify for the below 87 knots, new students qualify for the speed aircraft they are trained in

↓

To add a new set of aircraft

↓

Only one CFI needed

Receive and log ground and flight training from an authorized instructor in a make and model of light-sport aircraft that is within the same set of aircraft as the make and model of aircraft.

Receive a logbook endorsement from the authorized instructor who provided training in the aircraft certifying proficiency to operate the specific make and model of light-sport aircraft.

* Check current regulations because the FAA may change the CFI 2 to DPE in the near future.

Part 2 **Guide to the Sport Pilot Checkride**

Preparation for the Checkride

It is very important to prepare and be ready for the checkride, or "Practical Test." The FAA Sport Pilot Practical Test Standards (PTS) is the principal document used for the practical test. The additional study materials are the sources for the information basis for all the aeronautical knowledge and skill required in the PTS.

This Part 2 follows the organization of the PTS and is your main guide to preparing for the specific tasks listed there. The following items are provided for each PTS task:

- Tips to prepare for the task, make it easier to pass the test, and show your instructor you are prepared

- Checklists you can use for your test

- Typical examiner questions with answers to help with the oral questioning part of the exam

Prerequisites

Before reading this section, be sure you've read Part 1 and figured out the specific steps you need to do and who you need to see, obtained all the required training, flight time experience, completed the FAA Knowledge Exam, and obtained a recommendation and/or endorsement from your flight instructor.

Obtain the specific "Practical Test Standards" for the aircraft you intend to fly as a sport pilot:

- FAA-S-8081-31 for Weight-Shift Control and Powered Parachute

- FAA-S-8081-29 for Airplane, Gyroplane, and Glider

The Sport Pilot PTS must be used as a study guide in addition to this book, as specific PTS task details are not repeated here.

Referencing the PTS, decide what specific tasks you will be tested on:

- Applicants without an FAA pilot certificate will take the complete Practical Test from beginning to end as specified for each area of operation.

- Applicants wishing to add category class privileges with an existing FAA pilot certificate will follow the procedures in the PTS "Additional Privileges Task Table" for a proficiency check.

- Applicants who want to add a set of aircraft within a category/class will study areas added for the new set of aircraft to obtain a logbook signoff.

Getting Started Checklist

☐ Study the materials listed on Page ix in the Introduction. (Use of this book assumes you understand and are proficient in all the questions in the *Sport Pilot Test Prep* book as well.)

☐ Read and understand the "Practical Test Standards" booklet including the "Introduction." It is very important to read this "PTS Introduction." Important information is contained there and is not repeated in this book. A very important aspect of the 17 pages of critical information contained in the PTS introduction are the "Special Emphasis Areas" which are applied throughout the checkride. **If you fail any of these Special Emphasis Areas during one of the tasks, you fail that task. Therefore, always apply these throughout your flight and while demonstrating all the tasks:**

- procedures for positive exchange of flight controls;
- stall and spin awareness (if appropriate);
- collision avoidance;
- wake turbulence and low-level windshear avoidance;
- runway incursion avoidance;
- controlled flight into terrain (CFIT);
- aeronautical decision making/risk management;
- checklist usage.

How to Schedule the Test

Complete all the prerequisites and call an examiner. They can be found on this FAA webpage:

> http://www.faa.gov/licenses_certificates/airmen_certification/sport_pilot/

What to Expect from Your Examiner

When you call the examiner you will be asked some questions to make sure you are prepared for the test. This is to make sure you do not show up unprepared or without the proper documentation.

You should have the following information at hand:

Name _____ Telephone _____

Address _____

Instructors' Names and Telephone numbers _____

Certificate, rating, or privilege sought _____

Retest (Yes / No)   Yes: FAX copy

Aircraft make and model _____ Time _____

N Numbered Aircraft _____

Location of test—time and date _____

Class of airman medical certificate or valid U.S. driver's license (if applicable) _____

Valid knowledge test results passed (if applicable) _____

Aircraft—certificates, logbooks, and equipment _____

FAA Form 8710-11, Airman Certificate and/or Rating Application—Sport Pilot, completed and (if required) signed by instructor _____

Special considerations—drug convictions or other _____

Identification—Photo/signature ID _____

Flight time records and requirements _____

Required endorsements _____

Are you familiar with the PTS _____

PTS checklist of required equipment _____

Fee will be discussed with payment obligation _____

You may be asked to complete the following and bring to the practical test:

Cross-country to be planned (if applicable) _____

Weight-and-balance computations _____

Aircraft performance computations _____

Flight planning facilities/FSS telephone numbers _____

What to Expect For Your Checkride

Start of practical pretest evaluation and briefing. Examiner and applicant introductions conducted in comfortable facilities (location will be established when you schedule the checkride), away from distractions such as cell phones ringing, passersby, etc. Examiner reviews all the supplied paperwork and aircraft to ensure all required materials are present to perform a practical test. The examiner will make sure the applicant is aware of the Sport Pilot PTS tolerances required for the test.

Aeronautical knowledge oral portion of checkride. Once the examiner determines aircraft, pilot, and paperwork is in order, the agreed-to fee is collected and the examiner announces "the test has begun." The oral portion time will vary between examiners, from simple powered parachutes to more complex high-speed airplanes, and in the knowledge and proficiency the applicant has. You should expect from 2 to 4 hours of oral questioning for the practical.

Aeronautical skill flight portion of test. After the oral portion is completed and the applicant exhibits sufficient knowledge, the flight portion of the test begins. Depending on how far you must fly to get to a suitable area for the test, the flight portion can last from 40 minutes to over an hour. Oral questioning will continue throughout this section. Your examiner will distract you to make sure you can focus on competently flying the aircraft during the test. Typically, the examiner will tell you if you did not complete any task successfully—so no news is good news.

Continued

End of practical. There are three (3) possible ways the practical can conclude.

1. *Successful outcome.* The examiner will fill out the Sport Pilot Temporary Airman's Certificate and give you a logbook endorsement after the flight portion of the test.

2. *Test is temporarily halted.* A Letter of Discontinuance is written if the test was stopped for reasons such as bad weather, inoperative aircraft, physical impairment/sickness of examiner or applicant. Examiner documents what was successfully completed and provides you with a letter which allows you to finish the test with the examiner later, or continue the test with a different examiner.

3. *Unsuccessful outcome.* If any task is not completed successfully, the examiner will issue a "Pink Slip" (FAA form 8060-4) indicating what portion of the test was unsatisfactory. If during the test the examiner does announce the task just performed was not completed successfully, you may continue the test in order to evaluate your proficiency for all the remaining tasks, even though the outcome will still be a pink slip.

Applicant's Practical Test Checklist

This checklist comes from the PTS, but is modified to include additional items and tools to help you pass the Practical Test.

Use This Checklist for Appointment With Examiner:

Examiner's Name_____ Phone _____

Location _____

Date/Time _____

Acceptable Aircraft

- ☐ Aircraft Documents: Airworthiness Certificate, Registration
- ☐ Certificate, and Operating Limitations
- ☐ Aircraft Maintenance Records
- ☐ Aircraft Logbook Record of Inspections
- ☐ Airworthiness Directives/Safety Directives
- ☐ Pilot's Operating Handbook or FAA-Approved Flight Manual or
- ☐ Manufacturer's Operating Instructions

Personal Equipment

- ☐ Current Aeronautical Charts for home area and location of practical test if different
- ☐ Flight Log sheets
- ☐ Current Airport/Facility Directories (A/FD) or appropriate airport publications
- ☐ Flight computer (mechanical E6-B or electronic CX-2 Pathfinder) and plotter to plan a cross-country flight
- ☐ Current FAR/AIM book tabbed to sport pilot regulations and procedures
- ☐ This "Sport Pilot Checkride" book to use included checklists

A note about using reference materials during the practical test: You can bring in any reference materials you want for the checkride. However, if you must refer to them for every question asked, the examiner may doubt you actually know the material. Reference materials should be used only if you do not know the answer or if the examiner wants specific details you cannot remember. Don't use the materials to get through and pass the entire test, but only as a reference if you need it. You should be able to pass the practical without ever having to refer to them; however, demonstrating your ability to research and locate an answer to a question is second only to understanding the correct response to begin with. It is certainly better than simply answering, "I don't know"—an unsatisfactory reply which would probably result in the dreaded "pink slip."

Personal Records

☐ Identification—Photo/Signature ID

☐ Current student pilot certificate with solo and cross-country endorsements or any other FAA pilot certificate (ultralight pilots might not have any student or pilot certificate).

☐ Logbook with all applicable time recorded, instructor endorsements, plus 3 hours flight training 60 days before practical test. (Ultralight pilots registered before September 1, 2004 with ultralight organization endorsement letter do not need logbook or 3 hours training prior to practical test. Ultralight organization letter is used for aeronautical knowledge and skill.)

☐ Current medical certificate or current and valid driver's license

☐ Completed FAA Form 8710-11 with instructor's recommendation. (Recommendation is not required for ultralight pilots registered before September 1, 2004.)

☐ Original Airman Knowledge Test Report*

☐ Examiner's Fee (if applicable)

---

* Make sure you have reconciled any missed questions on your Airman Knowledge test report. This should be done by the recommending CFI per §61.39(a)(6)(iii). To reconcile your incorrect answers, follow these easy steps:

1. Match the missed questions code on the test report with the code in the ASA Sport Pilot Test Prep book, in "Cross Reference B" in the back of the book. This provides you with the possible missed question numbers.

2. Find the possible missed-question page numbers by looking them up in "Cross Reference A" (in the back of the same book).

3. Locate the missed-questions and read about the correct answers in the main part of the Test Prep book. Tab those pages with your missed questions, to be able to quickly explain to the examiner that you have researched and understood the correct concepts and answers for those questions.

Part 2 Guide to the Sport Pilot Checkride

I. PREFLIGHT PREPARATION — ORAL QUESTIONING

A. Certificates and Documents

This section covers paperwork, pilot privileges, limitations, and requirements.

Tips

- Use checklists to account for the pilot and aircraft documents.
- Ask to see copies of the aircraft documents ahead of time, if you are taking the test in an aircraft other than the one you trained in.
- Locate the documents in the aircraft in which you will be taking the test to ensure they are there.
- If using a medical certificate instead of a valid U.S. driver's license, review the details in §61.23.

Pilot Checklist

- ☐ Sport pilot certificate (must have in physical possession during flight).
- ☐ Driver's license or third class medical (must have in physical possession during flight).
- ☐ Logbook with appropriate endorsements (for aircraft make/model/set and planned operations for the flight, in physical possession during flight, plus current flight review per §61.56 and flight experience per §61.57 to carry a passenger).
- ☐ Flight information such as aeronautical charts and A/FD (for flight area and airports as well as diversion airports and airspace, in aircraft during flight).
- ☐ Flight plan and navigation log should be in aircraft for cross-country flights.

Aircraft Checklist

- ☐ Airworthiness certificate must be displayed in the aircraft (printed on salmon-colored paper for all LSA).
- ☐ Aircraft registration must be in aircraft for flight.
- ☐ Pilot's Operating Handbook (POH) or Aircraft Flight Manual (AFM), markings/ placards or operating procedures and limitations for aircraft must be in aircraft for flight. This includes aircraft performance with weight and balance capabilities and limitations.
- ☐ Aircraft annual (condition inspection for experimental airplane)/100-hour inspection (commercially-operated airplane) logbook entries — must be current, and must be consulted, but does not have to carried on aircraft.
- ☐ Weight-and-balance plus performance calculations for complete flight including fuel burned, must be calculated and should be in the aircraft for the flight.

. . . .

Questions—Certificates and Documents

For All Aircraft

1. **What are the eligibility requirements for a general sport pilot certificate to fly a light-sport aircraft?** (14 CFR 61.303, 61.305, 61.307, 61.309, 61.311, and 61.313)

   I must:

   a. Be at least 17 years of age.

   b. Be able to read, speak, write, and understand the English language.

   c. Have a valid U.S. driver's license or hold at least a current third class medical certificate.

   d. Receive the required ground and flight training endorsements.

   e. Meet the aeronautical experience requirements.

   f. Pass the required knowledge exam and practical tests.

2. **What are the privileges of a sport pilot certificate?** (14 CFR 61.315)

   I can:

   a. Act as pilot-in-command of a single or two-place LSA with a logbook endorsement from a qualified flight instructor for a specific make and model of aircraft.

   b. Share the operating expenses of a flight with a passenger, provided the expenses involve only fuel, oil, airport expenses, or aircraft rental fees. I must pay at least half the operating expenses of the flight.

   c. Fly in Class E and G airspace. I can fly in Class B, C and D with a proper logbook endorsement.

   d. Fly when the flight or surface visibility is 3 statute miles or better and I have a visual reference to the surface.

   e. Fly within operating limitations placed on the airworthiness certificate of the aircraft being flown, endorsement in my logbook, and any other limit or endorsement from an authorized instructor.

   f. Fly during the daytime and below 10,000 feet MSL.

   g. *(Airplane only)* Fly an aircraft with speed range I have been authorized to fly, above or below 87 knots. To fly a set in the additional speed range 87 knots CAS or above, I need a logbook endorsement from an authorized instructor.

3. **What are the limitations of a sport pilot certificate?** (14 CFR 61.315)

   I can **not** fly—

   a. with a passenger or property for compensation, hire or a furtherance of a business.

   b. in Class B, C or D airspace without additional training, meeting the requirements of 61.325, and a CFI endorsement in my logbook.

   c. with more than one passenger, at night, or above 10,000 feet MSL.

d. *(Airplane only)* Fly an aircraft with a V_H that exceeds 87 knots CAS, unless I receive training, an endorsement for this set of aircraft, meeting the requirements of §61.327.

e. outside the U.S. without prior authorization from the country in which I seek to operate.

f. to demonstrate the aircraft in flight to a prospective buyer as an aircraft salesperson.

g. in a passenger-carrying airlift sponsored by a charitable organization.

h. contrary to any restriction or limitation on my U.S. driver's license, or any restriction or limitation imposed by judicial or administrative order, when using my driver's license to satisfy a requirement.

i. while towing any object.

j. as a pilot/flight crewmember on any aircraft for which more than one pilot is required by the type certificate of the aircraft or the regulations under which the flight is conducted.

4. With respect to certification, privileges, and limitations of sport pilots, define the terms "category," "class," "type," "make/model" and "set." (14 CFR §1.1)

Category. A broad classification of aircraft such as airplane, weight-shift control, powered parachute, gyroplane, glider, lighter-than-air.

Class. A broad classification within a category having similar operating characteristics; i.e., airplane land and sea, weight-shift control land and sea, powered parachute land and sea.

Type and make/model are the same. A specific make and model of aircraft that do not change its handling or flight characteristics; i.e., Cosmos Phase II, Air Borne Streak, Flight Design CT, Challenger, Quicksilver MX, Drifter, Air Creation GTE, Powrachute Pegasus, Piper J-3 Cub, North Wing Apache, etc.

Set. Aircraft that share similar performance characteristics—similar airspeed and altitude operating envelopes, similar handling characteristics, and the same number and type of propulsion systems.

The 8 airplane sets are:

Less than 87 KCAS V_H
1. Tricycle gear
2. Tailwheel
3. Float-equipped
4. Ski-equipped

Greater than 87 KCAS V_H
5. Tricycle gear
6. Tailwheel
7. Float equipped
8. Ski equipped

The 3 weight-shift control sets are:
1. Tricycle gear
2. Float equipped
3. Ski equipped

The 4 powered parachute sets are:
Square wing
1. Land
2. Sea
Elliptical wing
3. Land
4. Sea

5. **What are the currency requirements for a sport pilot?**
(14 CFR 61.56 and 61.57)

Sport pilot currency requirements are the same as a recreational or private pilot.

a. Within the preceding 24 months, must have accomplished a flight review given in an aircraft for which that pilot is rated by an authorized instructor and received a logbook endorsement certifying that the person has satisfactorily completed the review.

b. To carry passengers, a pilot must have made, within the preceding 90 days three takeoffs and landings as the sole manipulator of flight controls of an aircraft of the same category and class and, if a type rating is required, of the same type. If the aircraft is a tailwheel airplane, the landings must have been made to a full stop in an airplane with a tail wheel. If the aircraft is a weight-shift control, or a powered parachute, the landings must have been made to a full stop in that particular set of aircraft.

6. **What are the medical eligibility requirements for a sport pilot to fly LSA?**
(14 CFR 61.303)

The pilot must—

a. have either a valid U.S. driver's license or a third class medical airman certificate.

b. (if applicable) not have a most-recently issued medical certificate denied, suspended or revoked, or Authorization for a Special Issuance of a Medical Certificate withdrawn.

c. not know or have reason to know of any medical condition that would make the pilot unable to operate LSA in a safe manner.

7. **If a pilot changes his/her permanent mailing address and fails to notify the FAA Airmen Certification branch of the new address, how long may the pilot continue to exercise the privileges of his/her pilot certificate?** (14 CFR 61.60)

30 days after the date of the move.

8. **What documents are required to be on board an aircraft prior to flight?**
(14 CFR 91.203 and 91.9)

A irworthiness Certificate

R egistration Certificate

O perating limitations (usually in the POH)

W eight and balance data for flight

9. **What documents must be with me as PIC of the aircraft during taxi and flight?** (14 CFR 61.3)

a. Current driver's license or medical certificate

b. Valid pilot certificate

c. Logbook or flight records with endorsement for the make and model aircraft I am authorized to fly. This allows me to fly other makes and models within the same set of aircraft.

10. What type of aircraft does the sport pilot certificate allow you to fly? (14 CFR 61.317–61.323)

My sport pilot certificate does not list aircraft category and class ratings. When I successfully pass the practical test for the certificate, regardless of the LSA privileges I seek, the FAA will issue me a sport pilot certificate without any category and class ratings. The FAA will provide me with a logbook endorsement for the category, class, and make/model of aircraft in which I am authorized to act as PIC throughout this practical test, allowing me to fly other make and models within the same set of aircraft.

11. What type of LSA are you authorized to fly? (14 CFR 61.319–61.323)

Once I hold a sport pilot certificate I may operate any make and model of LSA in the same category and class, and within the same set of aircraft as the make and model of aircraft for which I have received an endorsement:

Airplanes sets — tailwheel, nosewheel, float, and ski; additional logbook endorsements are required for V_H speeds above 87 CAS.

Weight-shift control/land — all in the same set, with additional sets of sea- and ski-equipped.

Powered parachutes/land sets — elliptical wings and square wings, plus additional sets for sea.

12. When will an aircraft registration certificate expire? (FAA-H-8083-25)

When any of the following occur:

a. The aircraft is registered under the laws of a foreign country.

b. The registration of the aircraft is canceled at the written request of the holder of the certificate.

c. The aircraft is totally destroyed or scrapped.

d. The ownership of the aircraft is transferred.

e. The holder of the certificate loses U.S. citizenship.

f. 30 days have elapsed since the death of the holder of the certificate.

13. What type of flight time must be documented and recorded by all pilots, typically in a logbook? (14 CFR 61.51)

a. The training and aeronautical experience used to meet the requirements for a certificate, rating, or flight review.

b. The aeronautical experience required for meeting the recency of flight requirements of Part 61.

14. What are the ratings that may be placed on a sport pilot certificate? (14 CFR 61.5)

There are no ratings on the sport pilot certificate. Category/Class/Make/Model are logbook endorsements.

15. What requirements must be met when conducting a flight review? (14 CFR 61.56)

A flight review, sometimes called a biennial flight review or BFR, consists of a minimum of 1 hour flight training and 1 hour ground training, including a review of the current Part 91 general operating and flight rules; also, a review of those maneuvers and procedures that, at the discretion of the person giving the review, are necessary for the pilot to demonstrate the safe exercise of the privileges of the pilot certificate.

• •

B. Airworthiness Requirements

This section covers ensuring your aircraft is in condition for safe flight.

Tips

- Use checklists to account for aircraft documents.
- Ask to see copies of the aircraft documents ahead of time, if you are taking the test in an aircraft other than the one you trained in.
- There are differences between Special Light-Sport Aircraft (S-LSA), Experimental Light-Sport Aircraft (E-LSA), and FAA standard category aircraft. You will be responsible for answering the questions for the type of aircraft you own and will fly for the checkride.
- For E-LSA aircraft, you can cover-up and label "inoperative" the instruments you do not want to be tested on, or remove instruments you do not want to be tested on.

Aircraft Checklist

☐ Aircraft logbooks with proper maintenance intervals documented. This includes any aircraft or safety directives (owner or operator must keep these records).

☐ Instruments, systems and equipment are present and functional for sport pilot privileges and the flight plan with diversions.

☐ Minimum instruments required for the checkride are those needed to measure the PTS task tolerances:

- Airplane—altitude and airspeed
- Weight-shift control—altitude and airspeed
- Powered parachute—altitude only (unless the examiner determines this is not needed for the test)

☐ An ELT is required for all airplane category aircraft except during training.

☐ Communications equipment required:
- If the test is to be conducted with the examiner in the aircraft, communications will be required between the applicant and the examiner unless other arrangements are approved by the examiner.
- Capabilities to broadcast out and receive are required if the applicant is testing for the privilege to operate in Class B, C and D airspace.
- Capabilities to receive broadcasts from the examiner are required in a single-seat test, so the examiner can provide instructions from the ground for the applicant to perform the tasks in the aircraft.

☐ S-LSA must have manufacturer required instruments and equipment as specified in the POH/AFM.

☐ A Letter of Authorization from the FAA may be required to operate the aircraft if the pilot wants to fly with inoperative equipment the manufacturer recommends as required for flight.

☐ For E-LSA, the pilot must determine if instruments or equipment in operation is acceptable to operate aircraft safely.

☐ FAA certified standard category aircraft must have the instruments for which the aircraft was originally certified.

. . . .

Questions—Airworthiness Requirements

1. **Who is responsible for ensuring that an aircraft is maintained in an airworthy condition?** (14 CFR 91.403)

   The owner or operator of an aircraft is primarily responsible for maintaining an aircraft in an airworthy condition.

2. **After aircraft inspections have been made and defects have been repaired, who is responsible for determining if the aircraft is in an airworthy condition?** (14 CFR 91.7)

   The pilot-in-command is responsible for determining if the aircraft is in safe condition for flight. The pilot-in-command shall discontinue the flight when unairworthy mechanical, electrical, or structural conditions occur.

3. **What records or documents should be checked to determine that the owner or operator of an aircraft has complied with all required inspections and airworthiness directives?** (14 CFR 91.405)

   The maintenance records—aircraft and engine logbooks. Each owner or operator of an aircraft must ensure that maintenance personnel make appropriate logbook entries indicating the aircraft has been approved for return to service.

4. What is the regulation concerning the operation of an aircraft that has had alterations or repairs which may have substantially affected its operation in flight? (14 CFR 91.407)

No person may operate or carry passengers in any aircraft that has undergone maintenance, preventative maintenance, rebuilding, or alteration that may have appreciably changed its flight characteristics or substantially affected its operation in flight until an appropriately rated pilot:

a. flies the aircraft;

b. makes an operational check of the maintenance performed or alteration made;

c. logs the flight and the aircraft flight characteristics in the aircraft records.

5. What is an Airworthiness Certificate and how long does it remain valid? (FAA-H-8083-25)

An Airworthiness Certificate is issued by the FAA only after the aircraft has been inspected and found to meet the requirements of 14 CFR, and is in a condition for safe operation.

The certificate must be displayed in the aircraft so that it is legible to passengers and crew whenever the aircraft is operated, and it may be transferred with the aircraft except when sold to a foreign purchaser. Special airworthiness certificates remain in effect as long as the aircraft receives the required maintenance and is properly registered in the U.S.

6. What is the difference between an S-LSA airworthiness certificate and an E-LSA certificate? (14 CFR 21.190 and 21.191)

a. S-LSA are manufactured and sold ready-to-fly under a new certification without Part 23 compliance, but they must meet an industry ASTM consensus standard. Aircraft under this standard may be used for sport, recreation, flight training, and aircraft rental.

b. There are three kinds of E-LSA:

   • Kit-built, built from plans, or assembled out-of-the-box per manufacturer's specifications. This type of aircraft must be the same design as an S-LSA. It can be used for sport and recreation and flight instruction for the owner of the aircraft.

   • The existing fleet of ultralight trainers and fat ultralights (single-place, but weigh too much to be an ultralight) which will be transitioned to E-LSA. These aircraft must be transitioned to the E-LSA category no later than January 31, 2008.

   • An existing S-LSA that has been modified and removed from S-LSA status.

7. What is "preventive maintenance"? (FAA-H-8083-25)

"Preventive maintenance" means simple or minor preservation operations and the replacement of small standard parts not involving complex assembly operations. Certificated pilots may perform preventive maintenance on any aircraft owned or operated by them.

8. What is an LSA repairman certificate with an inspection rating?
(14 CFR 65.107)

As owner of an E-LSA, you may take a 16-hour course on performing a condition inspection annually on the aircraft to verify it is airworthy. This rating is not applicable to S-LSA or FAA standard category certified aircraft.

9. What is an LSA repairman certificate with a maintenance rating?
(14 CFR 65.107)

This certifies mechanics can repair/maintain, and can work on S-LSA and E-LSA after taking what is known as the 120-hour course for airplanes, 104 hours for weight-shift control and powered parachute class privileges. They may perform 100-hour and annual condition inspections for E-LSA and S-LSA aircraft. They cannot do inspections or perform maintenance on FAA standard category certified aircraft.

10. What are the required maintenance inspections when an aircraft is used for training or hire? (14 CFR 91.327)

In addition to the annual condition inspection, a 100-hour inspection by an A&P mechanic, an approved repair station, or a person holding an LSA repairman certificate with a maintenance rating is required.

11. What preventative maintenance may the owner of a LSA perform?
(14 CFR Part 43 Appendix A)

Note: It is not necessary to memorize all of these 32 approved preventative maintenance items, but rather to understand what they are and where to find this detailed list (Part 43 Appendix A). Some typical maintenance items are in bold type.

(1) Removal, installation, and repair of landing gear tires.

(2) Replacing elastic shock absorber cords on landing gear.

(3) Servicing landing gear shock struts by adding oil, air, or both.

(4) Servicing landing gear wheel bearings, such as cleaning and greasing.

(5) Replacing defective safety wiring or cotter keys.

(6) Lubrication not requiring disassembly other than removal of nonstructural items such as cover plates, cowlings, and fairings.

(7) Making simple fabric patches not requiring rib stitching or the removal of structural parts or control surfaces. In the case of balloons, the making of small fabric repairs to envelopes (as defined in, and in accordance with, the balloon manufacturers' instructions) not requiring load tape repair or replacement.

(8) **Replenishing hydraulic fluid in the hydraulic reservoir.**

(9) Refinishing decorative coating of fuselage, balloon baskets, wings tail group surfaces (excluding balanced control surfaces), fairings, cowlings, landing gear, cabin, or cockpit interior when removal or disassembly of any primary structure or operating system is not required.

(10) Applying preservative or protective material to components where no disassembly of any primary structure or operating system is involved and where such coating is not prohibited or is not contrary to good practices.

Continued

(11) Repairing upholstery and decorative furnishings of the cabin, cockpit, or balloon basket interior when the repairing does not require disassembly of any primary structure or operating system or interfere with an operating system or affect the primary structure of the aircraft.

(12) Making small simple repairs to fairings, nonstructural cover plates, cowlings, and small patches and reinforcements not changing the contour so as to interfere with proper airflow.

(13) Replacing side windows where that work does not interfere with the structure or any operating system such as controls, electrical equipment, etc.

(14) Replacing safety belts.

(15) Replacing seats or seat parts with replacement parts approved for the aircraft, not involving disassembly of any primary structure or operating system.

(16) Troubleshooting and repairing broken circuits in landing light wiring circuits.

(17) Replacing bulbs, reflectors, and lenses of position and landing lights.

(18) Replacing wheels and skis where no weight and balance computation is involved.

(19) Replacing any cowling not requiring removal of the propeller or disconnection of flight controls.

(20) **Replacing or cleaning spark plugs and setting of spark plug gap clearance.**

(21) Replacing any hose connection except hydraulic connections.

(22) Replacing prefabricated fuel lines.

(23) **Cleaning or replacing fuel and oil strainers or filter elements.**

(24) Replacing and servicing batteries.

(25) Cleaning of balloon burner pilot and main nozzles in accordance with the balloon manufacturer's instructions.

(26) Replacement or adjustment of nonstructural standard fasteners incidental to operations.

(27) The interchange of balloon baskets and burners on envelopes when the basket or burner is designated as interchangeable in the balloon type certificate data and the baskets and burners are specifically designed for quick removal and installation.

(28) The installations of antimis fueling devices to reduce the diameter of fuel tank filler openings provided the specific device has been made a part of the aircraft type certificate data by the aircraft manufacturer, the aircraft manufacturer has provided FAA approved instructions for installation of the specific device, and installation does not involve the disassembly of the existing tank filler opening.

(29) Removing, checking, and replacing magnetic chip detectors.

(30) Removing and replacing self-contained, front instrument panel-mounted navigation and communication devices that employ tray-mounted connectors that connect the unit when the unit is installed into the instrument panel, (excluding automatic flight control systems, transponders, and microwave frequency distance measuring equipment (DME)). The approved unit must be designed to be readily and repeatedly removed and replaced, and pertinent instructions must be

provided. Prior to the unit's intended use, and operational check must be performed in accordance with the applicable sections of Part 91.

(31) Updating self-contained, front instrument panel-mounted Air Traffic Control (ATC) navigational software databases (excluding those of automatic flight control systems, transponders, and microwave frequency distance measuring equipment (DME)) provided no disassembly of the unit is required and pertinent instructions are provided. Prior to the unit's intended use, an operational check must be performed in accordance with applicable sections of Part 91.

For S-LSA and FAA Standard Category Aircraft (as indicated) Only

1. Who can inspect, maintain, repair, perform conditions inspections annually and 100-hour inspections on S-LSA? (14 CFR 65.107)

An FAA certificated airframe and powerplant mechanic (A&P), or an FAA authorized repair station can do maintenance, preventative maintenance, and alterations to S-LSA and FAA standard category aircraft.

LSA repairman certificate with a maintenance rating can also perform this work. This requires taking a training course of 120 hours in the airplane category, 104 hours for weight-shift or powered parachute, or 80 hours for glider or lighter-than-air. An A&P certificate counts towards these LSA requirements, but additional training on the specific category of aircraft is required.

2. Can a pilot conduct flight operations in an aircraft with known inoperative equipment? (14 CFR 91.213(d))

Yes, under specific conditions—the instruments must be:

a. not required by the manufacturer for safe operation;

b. removed or placarded;

c. recorded in the aircraft log as inoperable; and

d. the pilot-in-command determines the inoperative instrument does not cause or constitute a hazard to the safe flight of the aircraft.

3. What are the procedures to follow when using 14 CFR 91.213(d) for deferral of inoperative equipment? (FAA-H-8083-25)

The pilot determines whether the inoperative equipment is required by type design, the regulations, manufacturers specifications, or ADs. If the inoperative item is not required, and the airplane can be safely operated without it, the deferral may be made. Then the pilot removes or deactivates the inoperative item, and places an inoperative placard near the appropriate switch, control, or indicator. If deactivation or removal involves maintenance (removal always will), it must be accomplished by certificated maintenance personnel. For example, if the position lights (installed equipment) were discovered to be inoperative prior to a daytime flight, the pilot would follow the requirements of §91.213(d).

4. What are the required maintenance inspections for S-LSA aircraft?
(14 CFR 91.327)

   a. Annual condition inspection—within the preceding 12 calendar months.

   b. 100-hour inspection is required if the aircraft is used for hire (including training and rental).

5. If an aircraft has been on a schedule of inspection every 100 hours, under what condition may it continue to operate beyond the 100 hours without a new inspection? (14 CFR 91.409)

The 100-hour limitation may be exceeded by not more than 10 hours while en route to a place where the inspection can be done. The excess time used to reach a place where the inspection can be done must be included in computing the next 100 hours of time in service.

6. What is the difference between a condition inspection annually and a 100-hour inspection? (14 CFR Part 43)

There is no difference, when comparing the content of an annual condition inspection with that of a 100-hour inspection. However, only an LSA repairman with a maintenance rating or a qualified A&P mechanic can perform annual condition inspections on LSA. Only A&P mechanics or repair stations can perform these inspections on FAA standard category aircraft.

7. A sport pilot should be capable of locating the required maintenance and equipment inspections in the aircraft and engine logbooks. What should these include? (14 CFR 91.207, 91.215, 91.405, and 91.413)

   a. Annual condition inspection.

   b. ELT inspection (12 calendar months), if applicable.

   c. ELT battery expiration date, if applicable.

   d. Transponder certification (24 calendar months), if applicable.

   e. Compliance with applicable ADs and manufacturer's directives.

8. What are some of the responsibilities an aircraft owner has pertaining to aircraft documents, maintenance and inspections of their aircraft?
(FAA-H-8083-25)

Aircraft owners must:

   a. Have a current Airworthiness Certificate and Aircraft Registration in the aircraft.

   b. Maintain the aircraft in an airworthy condition including compliance with all applicable ADs and manufacturer's directives.

   c. Ensure maintenance is properly recorded.

   d. Keep abreast of current regulations concerning the operation of that aircraft.

   e. Notify the FAA Civil Aviation Registry immediately of any change of permanent mailing address, of the sale or export of the aircraft, or of the loss of citizenship.

9. **What are "Special Flight Permits" and when are they necessary?**
(14 CFR 91.213 and 14 CFR 21.197)

A Special Flight Permit may be issued for an aircraft that may not currently meet applicable airworthiness requirements but is capable of safe flight, and are typically issued for the following purposes:

a. Flying an aircraft to a base where repairs, alterations or maintenance are to be performed, or to a point of storage.

b. Delivering or exporting an aircraft.

c. Production flight-testing new-production aircraft.

d. Evacuating aircraft from areas of impending danger.

e. Conducting customer demonstration flights in new-production aircraft that have satisfactorily completed production flight tests.

10. **How do you obtain a "Special Flight Permit"?** (FAA-H-8083-25)

Assistance and the necessary forms may be obtained from the local Flight Standards District Office (FSDO) or Designated Airworthiness Representative (DAR).

11. **What are ADs and whom do they apply to?** (FAA-H-8083-25)

An AD is the medium the FAA uses to notify aircraft owners and others of unsafe conditions that may exist because of design defects, maintenance, or other causes, and to specify the conditions under which the product may continue to be operated. ADs are regulatory in nature, and compliance is mandatory for S-LSA and FAA standard category certified aircraft. ADs are highly recommended for E-LSA. It is the aircraft owner's or operator's responsibility to ensure compliance with all pertinent ADs.

For All Fixed Wing and other Aircraft that have an ELT

1. **What is an "ELT"?** (AIM Glossary)

Emergency Locator Transmitter—A radio transmitter attached to the aircraft structure which operates from its own power source on 121.5 and 243.0 MHz. It aids in locating downed aircraft by radiating a downward-sweeping audio tone, 2–4 times a second. It is designed to function without human action after an accident. It can be operationally tested during the first 5 minutes after any hour.

2. **Is an ELT required on all aircraft?** (14 CFR 91.207)

An ELT is required for all aircraft except the following:

a. Aircraft engaged in training operations conducted entirely within a 50-nautical-mile radius of the airport from which such local flight operations began.

b. Aircraft engaged in design and testing.

c. New aircraft engaged in manufacture, preparation and delivery.

d. Aircraft engaged in agricultural operations.

e. Aircraft equipped to carry not more than one person.

f. Weight-shift control and powered parachutes.

3. When must the batteries in an ELT be replaced or recharged, if rechargeable? (14 CFR 91.207)

Batteries used in ELTs must be replaced (or recharged, if the batteries are rechargeable):

a. When the transmitter has been in use for more than 1 cumulative hour; or

b. When 50 percent of their useful life (or, rechargeable batteries, 50 percent of their useful life of charge), has expired.

Note: The new expiration date for replacing (or recharging) the battery must be legibly marked on the outside of the transmitter and entered in the aircraft maintenance record. This date indicates 50% of the battery's useful life.

For E-LSA

1. Who can perform maintenance on an E-LSA? (14 CFR 91.319)

Just as with all experimental aircraft, anyone can perform maintenance on an E-LSA. If training is taking place in an E-LSA, and the aircraft is being rented, it needs a 100-hour inspection.

2. Is an E-LSA 100-hour inspection required? (14 CFR 91.319)

No. A 100-hour inspection is only required for E-LSA that are operated for hire.

3. Who may perform an annual condition inspection on an E-LSA? (14 CFR 65.107)

The E-LSA owner may obtain a repairman certificate with an inspection rating via a 16-hour training course specifically for the aircraft he/she owns; or, a nonowner LSA repairman with a maintenance rating, an A&P, or an FAA authorized repair station can perform this inspection.

4. What is the difference between an annual condition inspection and a 100-hour inspection for an E-LSA? (14 CFR Part 43)

The only difference is who is allowed to perform these inspections. The owner of the aircraft can perform the condition inspection annually if he has a 16-hour LSA repairman certificate with an inspection rating.

If someone other than an owner is hired to perform these inspections, he/she must be a qualified LSA repairman with a maintenance rating, an FAA-approved repair station, or an A&P mechanic to perform a 100-hour inspection.

5. **What are the requirements for operating an E-LSA with inoperative equipment?** (14 CFR 91.319)

   The pilot-in-command determines if the aircraft is safe to operate with inoperative equipment.

6. **If an aircraft has been on a schedule of inspection every 100 hours, under what condition may it continue to operate beyond the 100 hours without a new inspection?** (14 CFR 91.409)

   The 100-hour limitation may be exceeded by not more than 10 hours while en route to a place where the inspection can be done. The excess time used to reach a place where the inspection can be done must be included in computing the next 100 hours of time in service.

Additional Instructor Question

1. **What additional maintenance procedures are required for training in LSA?** (14 CFR 91.319)

   Each operator flying an S-LSA or E-LSA issued under §21.191(i)(1) may not conduct flight training for compensation or hire in an aircraft which that person provides unless within the preceding 100 hours of time in service the aircraft has been inspected by a certificated repairman (LSA) with a maintenance rating, an appropriately rated mechanic, or an appropriately rated FAA repair station in accordance with inspection procedures developed by the aircraft manufacturer or a person acceptable to the FAA; or just received an inspection for the issuance of an airworthiness certificate in accordance with 14 CFR Part 21.

• •

C. Weather Information

Pilot capabilities and aircraft limitations are weighed against weather considerations to determine whether or not to fly.

Tips

- Use the Weather to Fly for Sport Pilots DVD and companion book system.
- Fill out the sport pilot logbook with weather predictions and show to examiner you have done your preflight weather preparation.
- Print out the METAR observations and TAF forecasts decoded to aid in answering METAR or TAF decoding questions.

Checklist
Information Resources

Regional Weather

Fronts
☐ warm   ☐ cold   ☐ approaching   ☐ past   ☐ none
☐ current warm air mass   ☐ current cold air mss

Pressure systems
☐ high   ☐ low   ☐ high and low   ☐ standard

Isobars
☐ close   ☐ far   ☐ none

Jet stream
☐ close   ☐ far   ☐ north   ☐ south   ☐ overhead

Local Conditions

Moisture
☐ high   ☐ some clouds   ☐ low

Wind and Upper Air
☐ windy   ☐ moderate   ☐ calm
values (winds aloft forecast) _____

Stability (lapse rate)
☐ stable (1°C/1000)   ☐ standard (2°C/1000)
☐ unstable (3°C/1000)   ☐ highly unstable (4°C/1000)

Barometer
☐ high   ☐ low   ☐ steady   ☐ rising   ☐ falling

Site observations

Name/airport ID/location/altitude/terrain features _____

_____

Winds and Cycles
☐ average speed   ☐ direction   ☐ gusts   ☐ cycle length (if applicable)

Mechanical turbulence potential
(Building, tree, bush, mountain or other terrain feature directly up wind 10 times height, closer the worse)
☐ none   ☐ some   ☐ high

Clouds and overall sky
☐ hazy/stable   ☐ stratus clouds   ☐ cumulus clouds
☐ wind clouds   ☐ clouds moving, estimated speed _____

Whether to fly?

Pilot prediction
☐ calm air   ☐ windy   ☐ smooth   ☐ bumpy
Explain predicted expected changes during the flight _____

Pilot capabilities for predicted conditions
☐ capable   ☐ questionable   ☐ not capable

Aircraft limitations for predicted conditions
☐ capable   ☐ questionable   ☐ not capable

Physical condition
☐ good   ☐ marginal   ☐ not good

Mental attitude
☐ good   ☐ marginal   ☐ not good

Whether to fly decision
☐ go   ☐ no go

• •

Questions—Weather Information

1. **How much does the temperature drop for every 1,000 feet increase in altitude from sea level, for standard atmosphere?** (F2F-W2F)

   $2°C$

2. **What is the primary factor that creates weather?** (F2F-W2F)

   Temperature creating heat exchange.

3. **What are the typical weather patterns we see from warm and cold fronts?** (F2F-W2F)

   Warm fronts move slower with drizzly weather, cold fronts move faster with vertical clouds and more dynamic weather.

4. **What are the basic weather characteristics of high and low pressure systems?** (F2F-W2F)

High pressure produces good weather and low pressure produces dynamic or bad weather.

5. **What are isobars on a surface analysis map and what do they tell you?** (F2F-W2F)

Constant pressure lines on a surface analysis map that provide a look at the regional wind potential.

6. **What is the significance of the jet stream?** (F2F-W2F)

Its position provides general weather characteristics and creates possible areas of high winds.

7. **How do you interpret the direction for wind readings?** (F2F-W2F)

Wind readings are always given with reference to where the wind is coming from.

8. **What are the winds aloft forecast tables?**

Predicted wind direction, speed, and temperature at increasing altitudes from weather stations.

9. **What are the winds aloft forecast tables used for?**

To look at the upper air predictions for cross-country planning. They are an important factor in determining pilot capabilities and aircraft limitations.

10. **What does the wind normally do with increasing altitude?** (F2F-W2F)

Wind speed typically increases with altitude because of the friction of the ground.

11. **What factors establish your wind limitations?** (F2F-W2F)

Aircraft limitations, pilot capabilities in specific aircraft, and bump tolerance.

12. **What is the most important reason to avoid severe turbulence at low altitudes?** (F2F-W2F)

You could lose control and hit the ground.

13. **When is the best time of day to fly if you want the best chance for smooth conditions?** (F2F-W2F)

Mornings after sunrise.

14. **It is early morning just after sunrise. There are predicted high winds for the day 3,000 feet above you, but the air is perfectly still in an open field on the ground. What weather conditions would you expect?** (F2F-W2F)

High winds will probably reach the ground sometime during the day as the inversion dissipates from surface heating and winds above.

15. **When a cloud is forming during the cumulus growth stage, what happens to the air under the cloud?** (F2F-W2F)

There is a continuous updraft.

16. **What are downdrafts from thunderstorms created by?** (F2F-W2F)

Rain and the cooling of the air as the water melts and evaporates.

17. **What do downdrafts create when they hit the ground?** (F2F-W2F)

Gust fronts.

18. **What three factors are necessary to create towering cumulus or thunderstorms?** (F2F-W2F)

Instability, high moisture content in the air, and lifting of air.

19. **What is the dewpoint spread and what does it mean?** (F2F-W2F)

The dewpoint spread is the difference between the current temperature and dewpoint temperature. It helps you predict at what altitude clouds will form.

20. **What does high relative humidity mean?** (F2F-W2F)

An area of significant moisture in an air mass, combined with other factors, can create "its own weather"— that is, produce a separate microclimate within the air mass.

21. **It has been raining for a day and the barometer starts to rise, what does this indicate?** (F2F-W2F)

The weather should start to improve.

22. **Why do you call a flight briefer before each flight?** (F2F-W2F)

To see if there are any Notices to Airmen (NOTAMs) or Terminal Flight Restrictions (TFRs) that you should know about for your flight, and also get weather conditions.

23. **What does it mean if there are no clouds in the sky?** (F2F-W2F)

There is not enough moisture in the air for clouds to form.

24. **What do clouds tell you about the air?** (F2F-W2F)

Clouds provide some visual reference about what the air is doing. Cumulus clouds indicate the air is unstable with vertical air movement; stratus clouds indicate generally stable air with not much vertical movement at cloud level.

25. **What do towering cumulus clouds indicate?** (F2F-W2F)

Strong vertical air currents with gust fronts and turbulence.

26. **When will clouds form?** (F2F-W2F)

When there is moisture in the air and the air temperature hits the dew point.

27. What do wind and cumulus clouds indicate about the air? (F2F-W2F)

The air currents will be challenging and should be approached with caution.

28. What are the three stages of a thunderstorm? (F2F-W2F)

Cumulus updraft, mature cloud-forming rain, and rain downdraft dissipation stage.

29. How do mountains affect airflow? (F2F-W2F)

Mountains can cause turbulence or unpredictable winds from heating, cooling, and mechanically changing wind flow.

30. What type of terrain would cause the most turbulent air at noon? (F2F-W2F)

Mountains or dark areas that gather heat.

31. What type of terrain would have the smoothest air to fly over at noon? (F2F-W2F)

Green meadows, swamps, or lakes.

32. Where will mechanical turbulence be found and how does it affect your flight? (F2F-W2F)

Mechanical turbulence can be found downwind, in the wind shadow of mountains, buildings or trees—typically 7 to 10 times the object's height—and can cause a loss of control or stall if not avoided.

33. When will mechanical turbulence be the worst? (F2F-W2F)

In high winds.

34. What is a wind rotor? (F2F-W2F)

Rotating air behind a large object (i.e., a big building, a hill or mountain) in higher winds.

35. Why do high deserts generally have more extreme weather than rolling hills in the plains? (F2F-W2F)

This is because temperature difference between day and night is great.

36. What unique characteristics in the midwest cause extreme weather, such as thunderstorms and tornadoes? (F2F-W2F)

This happens when warm moist air from the tropics meets the cold air from the north.

37. When can fog form and how does it affect you as a pilot? (F2F-W2F)

Fog can form when the surface air cools to the dew point or moisture is added to the air close to the ground. It can affect our ability to aviate by restricting visibility to the ground.

38. What is the best way to observe the surface wind before you take off? (F2F-W2F)

Look at the windsock ahead of you in the middle of the runway.

39. If you are on the ground or in the air and do not have a windsock available, what is the best way to measure the velocity of the air? (F2F-W2F)

Observe the trees, water, flags or smoke using the "Sport Pilot Wind Observation" table (*see* Page 32 of DVD booklet).

40. What variations in wind velocity would produce moderately bumpy conditions? (F2F-W2F)

The wind varying more than 10 MPH in less than 3-second intervals.

41. It is early in the morning. Your research with the winds aloft forecast predicted the wind to be 20 MPH 3,000 feet above you, but the windsock and trees show no wind. What is the most probable situation? (F2F-W2F)

You are in the morning inversion and the wind is probably blowing above you.

42. What are the most important factors in determining whether to fly (that is, the go/no-go decision)? (F2F-W2F)

Aircraft limitations, pilot capabilities, physical shape, mental attitude.

43. How do you determine density altitude? (F2F-W2F)

Look at the local conditions for pressure, temperature, humidity, and MSL altitude.

44. You have determined there is a 15 MPH wind from the north and you have determined this is within your aircraft and pilot capabilities. You plan on doing an out and return. Your choices are to head out to the north or south. Which direction would you fly your first leg for best fuel management? (F2F-W2F)

To the north.

45. You flew the day before and your altimeter was reading 2,300 feet when you landed. The next morning it reads 2,900 feet. What is the most probable cause? (F2F-W2F)

The air pressure has dropped significantly.

46. You are climbing at full throttle RPM. You normally have a 600 feet per minute climb rate, but your vertical speed indicator is reading only 100 feet per minute climb rate. You sense you are not climbing very fast. What is the most probable situation related to weather? (F2F-W2F)

You are flying in air that is descending at 500 feet per minute.

47. What speed does the GPS indicate? (F2F-W2F)

Ground speed.

48. **You are flying at 2,000 feet MSL, 10 miles from, and flying directly towards the ocean. Your indicated airspeed is 40 MPH and your GPS is reading 55 MPH. Do you have a headwind or a tailwind? (F2F-W2F)**

You have a 15 MPH tailwind.

49. **You are at full throttle trying to climb over a mountain range so you can proceed to your safe landing area. The air is bumpy with your vertical speed indicator reading up to 1,500 feet per minute up and as low as 200 feet per minute down. What is your best option?**

Try to stay in the updrafts to use the lifting air to help you climb; or, turn back if you feel these conditions exceed your aircraft or pilot capabilities.

50. **What is the safest way to operate when flying in the mountains?**

Stay high over the ridges, avoid the valleys and account for sinking air.

51. **What is your best safety procedure for flying in gusty winds?**

Always be actively controlling the aircraft with ample speed near the ground.

52. **You have come back to your landing area later than you wanted because a headwind is stronger than you expected. You are coming in for final approach and all of a sudden it gets really turbulent. It appears that you might fly into the bushes along side the runway because of a sudden side gust. What should you do?**

Do a go-around and assess the situation for another landing or fly to another spot.

53. **Where do you find the internet FAA Aviation weather services available for preflight planning?**

The FAA weather services website, www.aviationweather.gov/

54. **What are METAR and TAF reports?**

METAR is an abbreviation for the "Aviation Routine Weather Observations" facility at a weather site, similar to what you would see if you were there. TAF stands for "Terminal Area Forecasts," which are predicted conditions at weather stations.

55. **What are the FAA aviation weather services available for regional, local, and enroute weather?**

Regional weather, for cross-country and generalized local conditions:

- *prognostic charts* (provide national map of *predicted* fronts, pressure systems, and isobars; predict up to 48 hours ahead).
- *weather depiction charts* provide national *observed* (similar information to the prognostic charts, but more depicted from a pilot's point of view — *actual* observed flying conditions on a national scale; current observations, not predictions).

- *low-level significant weather prognostic charts* provide national map of *predicted* conditions similar to the pilot's point of view of actual flying conditions in the future.
- *surface analysis charts* provide *observed* surface conditions such as wind, visibility, pressure systems, sky cover.
- *radar summary charts* provides heavy precipitation and predicts their movement (this is not weather that sport pilots should be flying in or near).
- *severe weather outlook chart (AC)* is *predicted* severe weather.
- *area forecasts (FA),* an overview of large area *predicted* to be used between reporting stations.

Local and specific airport weather:

- Weather briefing at 800-WX-BRIEF (992-7433).
- METAR *observed* conditions and TAF *predicted* conditions at major and more remote airports and locations.
- Smaller airports have AWOS (Automated Weather Observing System) of *observed* conditions; ATIS (Automatic Terminal Information System) provides larger airports important terminal information plus weather observations; AWOS at smaller airports or ASOS (Automated Surface Observation System) generally at larger airports *observed* conditions; for all these automated weather reports, aircraft frequencies can be obtained on the sectional map and A/FD, with telephone numbers in the A/FD.

Enroute weather, typically used for long cross-country flights:

- EFAS (Enroute Flight Advisory Service, or "Flight Watch"), call sign FLIGHT WATCH at frequency 122.0; here you can provide PIREP (pilot weather reports) and hear inflight updates for your route.
- Some navigation stations and air traffic control frequencies broadcast weather advisories:
  — AIRMETs (WA) warn of hazards, primarily to small aircraft.
  — SIGMETs (WS) and convective SIGMETs (WST) warn of hazards to all aircraft; these would be considered severe hazards to smaller aircraft.

56. How do you do your weather analysis to determine whether or not you are going to fly?

Get on the internet and look at the regional weather, see if there are any fronts, threatening low pressure systems, or tight isobars in the area or approaching. Then look at the specific local conditions, winds aloft forecast, stability, and general predictions for the area. METAR observations and TAF forecasts are also evaluated for surface conditions. Look outside to verify the internet forecasts. If all looks good, make the decision to drive to the airport based on this analysis. Upon arrival, observe the air and clouds to make the final decision of whether to fly.

57. What are your weather limitations and what are the conditions where you will make the no-go decision to fly?

Note that these are generic examples not for any specific aircraft, but typical tolerances for the aspiring sport pilot applicant. No one answer is correct, but answers can be used as a guideline for your specific pilot capabilities and aircraft limitations. You should have a specific checklist that covers the following areas for takeoff, en route, and destinations:

- visibility
- stability and time of day flying
- upper air velocity
- surface air velocity

My limitations are:

Airplane with V_S above 87 knots—

Bad visibility, no afternoon flying if there are severe thunderstorms predicted, winds aloft forecasts of enroute altitudes 30 knots or more, or surface wind conditions over 15 knots for any landing area or 12-knot crosswind component for any landing area.

Airplane with V_S below 87 knots—

Bad visibility, no afternoon flying if there are thunderstorms predicted, winds aloft forecasts of enroute altitudes 20 knots or more, or surface wind conditions over 12 knots for any landing area or 8-knot crosswind component for any landing area.

Weight-shift control with large wing—

Bad visibility, no afternoon flying if there are thunderstorms predicted, winds aloft forecasts of enroute altitudes 20 knots or more, or surface wind conditions over 15 knots for any landing area or 12-knot crosswind component for any landing area.

Powered parachute—

Bad visibility, no afternoon flying unless it is stable, winds aloft forecasts of enroute altitudes 10 knots or more, or surface wind conditions over 6 knots for any landing area or 4-knot crosswind component for any landing area.

D. Cross-Country Flight Planning

Flight planning for flying away from your local airfield.

The least stringent requirements, in which the least navigation competency is required, are for a powered parachute without a magnetic compass or a GPS, where the applicant is testing for privileges to operate in Class E and G airspace. Airplanes navigating with a magnetic compass, preparing for operations in the set of aircraft above 87 knots, and/or for operations in Class B, C and D airspace, will need a higher competency in navigation principles and instruments. **However, all pilots must have a basic understanding of how to perform cross-country pilotage, accounting for the wind and calculating fuel burn to make sure to not run out of fuel.**

Tips

- Have a current sectional chart for the area where you are taking the test plus one for your home field/airport and understand all the airspace within 1 hour flight time from each takeoff airport.

- Use the sectional chart (particularly the legend) to help you with any questions regarding airspace or cross-country.

- Get a cross-country task to work on before you arrive at your checkride. Fill out a flight on the "Flight Planning and Navigation Log" table below to show you know how to plan a flight.

- Fill out a flight plan with FAA Form 7233-1 for your test (included in this section), since you will be required to simulate a VFR flight plan.

- The examiner will ask questions according to the type of equipment in the aircraft in which you will be taking the test; therefore if you will be taking the test in an aircraft other than your own, ask the examiner ahead of time what equipment that aircraft has. Also, try to get a task from the examiner, to work on ahead of time.

- If you are being tested in your own E-LSA or S-LSA aircraft, you may label any equipment "inoperative" that you do not want to be tested on, or do not need for the test, as long as the aircraft manufacturer does not include it as equipment necessary for safe flight.

- If you are being tested for operations in Class B, C and D airspace, either a magnetic compass or GPS will be required for direction and headings.

- Use the CX-2 electronic flight computer for answering the more complicated questions for flight planning—it is much faster and easier than the E6-B sliderule type, and also is more accurate.

Continued

Checklist

☐ Compute distance, time, and fuel considering wind and aircraft capabilities.

☐ Use appropriate aeronautical charts considering airspace and terrain for planned flight with diversions.

☐ Use appropriate A/FD with operating procedures and communication frequencies (if required and radio equipped in the aircraft) for planned flight with diversions.

☐ Select easily identifiable enroute visual checkpoints as primary navigation system using aeronautical charts.

☐ Program GPS waypoints and/or destination and cross-check with aeronautical charts before takeoff, if so equipped.

☐ Check for NOTAMs and TFRs for flight plan area with diversions.

☐ Complete navigation log and file flight plan if needed (included later in this chapter).

Flight Planning and Navigation Log

Use the following steps with the "Flight Planning and Navigation Log" table to plan a flight for your test. Use additional sheets if necessary for more route segments.

1. Safe altitude—Minimum altitude you must fly to be above any terrain features.

2. Altitude—Cruising flight altitude.

3. Indicated airspeed—Cruising indicated airspeed (knots or MPH).

4. True airspeed—Indicated airspeed (knots or MPH) corrected for pressure altitude.

5. Winds aloft forecast—Wind speed, direction and temperature at the cruising altitudes.

6. Distance—Miles (statute or nautical) for the segment.

7. Course in degrees—True direction aircraft travels for flight segment.

8. Heading in degrees—direction the aircraft is pointed after correction for crab angle:

   a. True heading calculated; and

   b. Magnetic heading for compass navigation (in the western U.S. with easterly heading, subtract variation from true heading; in eastern U.S. with westerly variation, add for magnetic heading). Any aircraft deviation must also be included in this calculation.

9. Ground speed—Speed over the ground accounting for wind effects. Actual ground speed can be read directly from GPS during flight.

10. Time en route—Distance divided by ground speed.

11. a. Fuel burned per leg—fuel consumption multiplied by time.

    b. Fuel burned total—totaled for all legs.

12. Longitude and latitude—Coordinates for GPS input if needed.

13. ATC Radio frequencies—Frequencies: UNICOM, CTAF, or ATC (if operating in or near Class B, C, or D airspace).

14. Verify performance—Calculate and verify weight and balance for all aspects of the flight and takeoff and landing distances for intended and diverted airports.

Flight Planning and Navigation Log

	Route Segment 1		Route Segment 2		Route Segment 3	
Departure location ID _____	Checkpoint ID		Checkpoint ID		Checkpoint ID	
	Planned	Actual	Planned	Actual	Planned	Actual
1. Safe altitude		X		X		X
2. Altitude						
3. Indicated airspeed						
4. True airspeed						
5. Winds aloft forecast						
6. Distance		X		X		X
7. Course in degrees		X		X		X
8. a. True heading b. Magnetic heading		X		X		X
9. Groundspeed						
10. Time to checkpoint						
11. a. Fuel burned per leg b. Fuel burned total						
12. Longitude and latitude						
13. ATC radio frequencies _____						
14. Verify performance						

FAA Flight Plan

The following is the FAA flight plan form for flying cross-country. This is advised for any flights away from the local airport for search and rescue to locate you if you do not arrive at the destination.

File flight plan with Flight Service Station (FSS) in person or by phone (can use 1-800-WX-BRIEF) at least 30 minutes before your estimated departure time.

FAA Flight Plan
Form 7233-1 (8-82)

U.S. DEPARTMENT OF TRANSPORTATION FEDERAL AVIATION ADMINISTRATION **FLIGHT PLAN**	(FAA USE ONLY)	☐ PILOT BRIEFING ☐ VNR ☐ STOPOVER		TIME STARTED	SPECIALIST INITIALS

1. TYPE VFR IFR DVFR	2. AIRCRAFT IDENTIFICATION	3. AIRCRAFT TYPE/ SPECIAL EQUIPMENT	4. TRUE AIRSPEED KTS	5. DEPARTURE POINT	6. DEPARTURE TIME PROPOSED (Z) ACTUAL (Z)	7. CRUISING ALTITUDE

8. ROUTE OF FLIGHT

9. DESTINATION (Name of airport and city)	10. EST. TIME ENROUTE HOURS MINUTES	11. REMARKS

12. FUEL ON BOARD HOURS MINUTES	13. ALTERNATE AIRPORT(S)	14. PILOT'S NAME, ADDRESS & TELEPHONE NUMBER & AIRCRAFT HOME BASE 17. DESTINATION CONTACT/TELEPHONE (OPTIONAL)	15. NUMBER ABOARD

16. COLOR OF AIRCRAFT	CIVIL AIRCRAFT PILOTS, FAR 91 requires you file an IFR flight plan to operate under instrument flight rules in controlled airspace. Failure to file could result in a civil penalty not to exceed $1,000 for each violation (Section 901 of the Federal Aviation Act of 1958, as amended). Filing of a VFR flight plan is recommended as a good operating practice. See also Part 99 for requirements concerning DVFR flight plans.

FAA Form 7233-1   (8-82)   **CLOSE VFR FLIGHT PLAN WITH**_____ **FSS ON ARRIVAL**

1. Check the VFR box since all sport pilot flights are VFR.

2. Use full N-number registration.

3. Indicates aircraft type (AirB/Trike) and any special electronic equipment onboard that has an alphabetical code such as a transponder or GPS.

4. Enter computed true airspeed for cruise.

5. Enter departure airport identifier and name (RNO/Reno).

6. Insert proposed departure time and actual in UTC.

7. Enroute estimated cruise altitude considering winds and terrain.

8. Planned route of flight using place names and intersections shown on aeronautical charts.

9. Name of airport and city.

10. Estimated time en route.

11. Insert any relevant remarks such as changes in cruise altitude.

12. Fuel on board based on usable in tank converted to hours and minutes (should be from departure point to first intended stop with 30 minutes reserve at normal cruise).

13. Alternate airports or landing locations in case of diversion or weather.

14. Pilot name/address etc.

15. Number of people on board (1 or 2).

16. Color of aircraft (main colors for visual identification of top surface and fuselage).

17. Destination contact telephone (include phone at your destination or your mobile phone number).

Important: At the end of your flight, ensure the flight plan has been closed with the nearest FSS, or request an FAA facility such as ATC in the tower, to relay your cancellation to FSS.

• •

Questions—Cross-Country Flight Planning

For All

1. What are three common ways sport pilots navigate?

a. Pilotage (by reference to visible landmarks);

b. Dead reckoning (by computing direction and distance from a known position);

c. Global positioning system (GPS).

2. What types of aeronautical charts are available for use in VFR navigation? (AIM 9-1-4)

Sectional Charts—Designed for visual navigation. One inch equals 6.86 nautical miles. They are revised semiannually, except for most Alaskan charts, which are revised annually. These are typically used for sport pilot planning and navigation.

VFR Terminal Area Charts (TAC)—TACs depict the Class B airspace. While similar to sectional charts, TACs have more detail because the scale is larger. One inch equals 3.43 nautical miles. Charts are revised semiannually, except in Puerto Rico and the Virgin Islands where they are revised annually.

World Aeronautical Charts (WAC)—WACs cover large land areas for navigation by moderate speed aircraft operating at high altitudes. Because of a smaller scale, WACs do not show as much detail as sectionals or TACs, and therefore are not recommended for pilots of low speed, low altitude aircraft. One inch equals 13.7 nautical miles. WACs are revised annually except for a few in Alaska and the Caribbean, which are revised biennially.

VFR Flyway Planning Charts—This chart is printed on the reverse side of selected TAC charts. The coverage is the same as the associated TAC. They depict flight paths and altitudes recommended for use to bypass high traffic areas.

3. What are lines of latitude and longitude? (FAA-H-8083-25)

Circles parallel to the equator (lines running east and west), or parallels of latitude, enable us to measure distance in degrees latitude north or south of the equator. Meridians of longitude are drawn from the North Pole to the South Pole and are at right angles to the equator. The "Prime Meridian," which passes through Greenwich, England, is used as the zero line from which measurements are made in degrees east and west to 180°. The 48 conterminous states of the United States lie between 25 degrees and 49 degrees north latitude and between 67 degrees and 125 degrees west longitude.

4. Before attempting a cross-country flight, a pilot will need to know how to make common calculations for time, speed, distance, amount of fuel required, as well as basic wind calculations. Solve the following:

Time, speed and distance problems:

a. **How fast are you going if you travel 30 NM in 25 minutes?**

b. **How much time does it take to travel 84 NM at 50 knots? What will the time be?**

c. **How far will you travel in 51 minutes at 30 MPH?**

a. 72 knots

b. 1 hour, 40 minutes

c. 25.5 statute miles

Fuel consumption problems:

a. **How much fuel will burn if you fly 1 hour 27 minutes at a fuel rate of 3.3 gallons per hour?**

b. **What is your fuel rate if you burn 8 gallons 2 hours, 13 minutes?**

c. **What is the endurance if you burn 9.8 gallons in 4.2 hours?**

a. 4.8 gallons

b. 3.6 gallons per hour

c. 2 hours, 20 minutes

True airspeed problems:

a. **If altitude is 9,800 feet, temperature is 0°C, and IAS is 50, what will the TAS be?**

b. **If IAS is 60, altitude is 6,000 feet, and the temperature is 20°C, what will the TAS be?**

c. **If the temperature is 40°F, the IAS is 65, and the altitude is 9,500 feet, what will the TAS be?**

a. 58.5 TAS

b. 67.6 TAS

c. 76.2 TAS

Density altitude problems:

    a. If pressure altitude is 1,500 feet and the temperature is 35°C, what will the density altitude be?

    b. If pressure altitude is 5,000 feet and the temperature is -10°C, what will the density altitude be?

    c. If the pressure altitude is 2,000 feet and the temperature is 30°C, what will the density altitude be?

    a. 4,100 feet

    b. 3,100 feet

    c. 4,100 feet

Conversion problems:

    a. 100 nautical miles = _____ statute miles

    b. 4 quarts oil = _____ pounds

    c. 15 gallons fuel = _____ pounds

    d. 80°F = _____ °C

    e. 20 knots = _____ miles per hour

    a. 115 SM

    b. 7.5 pounds

    c. 90 pounds

    d. 26.6°C

    e. 23 MPH

Groundspeed and heading problems:

    a. If wind direction is 220, wind speed is 030, true course is 146, and TAS is 60, what will ground speed and true heading be?

    b. If wind direction is 240, wind speed is 025, true course is 283 and TAS is 70, what will ground speed and true heading be?

    c. If wind direction is 060, wind speed is 030, true course is 036 and TAS is 50, what will ground speed and true heading be?

    a. Ground speed is 44, true heading is 175.

    b. Ground speed is 50, true heading is 269.

    c. Ground speed is 21, true heading is 050.

5. Be capable of locating the following items on a sectional chart:

Abandoned airports
Air Defense Identification Zone (ADIZ)
Airport elevation
Alert Area
Class B airspace
Class C airspace
Class D airspace
Class D airspace ceiling
Class E airspace (without operating control tower)
Class E airspace (controlled airspace 700 foot floor)
Class E airspace (controlled airspace 1,200 foot floor)
Class E airspace extensions to Class D airspace
Class G airspace
CTAF
Flight Service Station frequencies
Glider operating area
Hard surfaced runway airports
Maximum elevation figures
Military airports
Military Training Routes
Non-hard surfaced runways
Nontower controlled airport
Obstructions above 1,000 feet AGL
Obstructions below 1,000 feet AGL
Parachute jumping area
Private airports
Prohibited area
Restricted area
Runway length
Special VFR not authorized (sport pilots cannot use SVFR)
UNICOM frequencies
Victor airways
Visual checkpoints
Warning area
LSA equipped with magnetic compass: isogonic lines

Additional chart identification for operations in Class B, C and D airspace

Approach control frequencies
ATIS (automated terminal information service)
No fixed-wing special VFR available
Airports with a rotating beacon
Airports with lighting facilities
Airports with services
Part-time lighting

Pilot controlled lighting
TRSA (Terminal Radar Service Area) if available
TWEB (transcribed weather broadcast)
HIWAS (hazardous in flight advisory service)

For aircraft equipped with VOR navigation equipment:
- VORTAC (VHF omni-directional range/tactical air navigation)
- Non-directional radio beacons

6. How much fuel do you need on board? (14 CFR 91.151)

During the day, you must be able to fly to the first point of intended landing, and assuming normal cruising speed, to fly after that for at least 30 minutes.

7. When operating an aircraft under VFR in level cruising flight at an altitude of more than 3,000 feet above the surface, what rules apply concerning specific altitudes flown? (14 CFR 91.159)

When operating above 3,000 feet AGL but less than 18,000 feet MSL on a magnetic course of 0° to 179°, fly at an odd-thousand-foot MSL altitude plus 500 feet. When on a magnetic course of 180° to 359°, fly at an even-thousand-foot MSL altitude plus 500 feet.

For Aircraft Equipped with a GPS

1. What is GPS? (AIM Glossary)

Global Positioning System—a space-based radio positioning, navigation, and time-transfer system. The system provides highly accurate position and velocity information, and precise time, on a continuous global basis to an unlimited number of properly equipped users. The system is unaffected by weather, and provides a world-wide common grid reference system. The GPS concept is predicated upon accurate and continuous knowledge of the spatial position of each satellite in the system with respect to time and distance from a transmitting satellite to the user. The GPS receiver automatically selects appropriate signals from satellites in view and translates these into three-dimensional position, velocity, and time. System accuracy for civil users is normally 100 meters horizontally.

2. How do you navigate using a GPS?

You set a waypoint, which is a destination for a complete route, or a segment of a route, and select "go to" this waypoint. The GPS provides you a direct route to the waypoint. It tells you if you are on the direct route, or deviating from the direct route.

3. What calculations does the GPS provide you while en route?

a. Ground speed, accounting for headwind and tailwind components.
b. Time to the waypoint accounting for headwind or tailwind components.
c. True course to the waypoint.

4. What are the benefits of navigating with GPS?

GPS is a simple, accurate and reliable navigation system outdating all other aviation navigation technologies that can help you easily find specific locations better than any other navigation system available. Common GPS have moving maps with roads and landmarks to aid in navigation. Advanced top-of-the-line aviation GPS include databases with airspace, search for nearest airport and services available there, and terrain warning functions, eliminating much of the inflight workload during a cross-country flight.

5. Can GPS be used as the only means of navigation for sport pilots?

No. A sport pilot must use pilotage along with GPS for navigation during a cross-country flight.

For Aircraft Equipped with a Magnetic Compass

1. What is an "isogonic line"? (FAA-H-8083-25)

Shown on most aeronautical charts as broken magenta lines, isogonic lines connect points of equal magnetic variation. They show the amount and direction of magnetic variation, which from time to time may vary.

2. What is "magnetic variation"? (FAA-H-8083-25)

Variation is the angle between true north and magnetic north. It is expressed as east variation or west variation depending upon whether magnetic north (MN) is to the east or west of true north (TN), respectively.

3. How do you convert a true direction to a magnetic direction? (FAA-H-8083-25)

To convert true course or heading to magnetic course or heading, note the variation shown by the nearest isogonic line on the sectional chart. If you are in the eastern U.S., then variation is west—add. If you are in the western U.S., variation is east—subtract.

Remember: East is Least (Subtract)   West is Best (Add)

4. What is "magnetic deviation"? (FAA-H-8083-25)

Because of magnetic influences within the airplane itself (electrical circuits, radios, lights, tools, engine, magnetized metal parts, etc.) the compass needle is frequently deflected from its normal reading. This deflection is called deviation. Deviation is different for each aircraft, and also varies for different headings of the same aircraft. For S-LSA, the deviation value may be found written on a deviation card located in the aircraft.

E. National Airspace System

Sport Pilots typically fly out of nontowered airports and in uncontrolled (Class G) or lightly-controlled (class E) airspace. You need to have a full understanding of the complete National Airspace System (NAS)—how to recognize what airspace is where, what and where you can operate as a Sport Pilot, and what limitations, communications or equipment requirements will apply to the airspace you intend to fly in.

Tips

- Decide if you are going to be tested on the basic sport pilot Class E and G airspace, or seek an endorsement to operate with additional sport pilot privileges in airspace that uses an operating control tower (Class B, C or D).

- Make it clear to your examiner whether you are seeking additional airspace privileges, or simple operation in uncontrolled Class G airspace and controlled Class E airspace.

- Sport pilots operate in simple Class E and G airspace. The main difference between the two is cloud clearances for visibility.

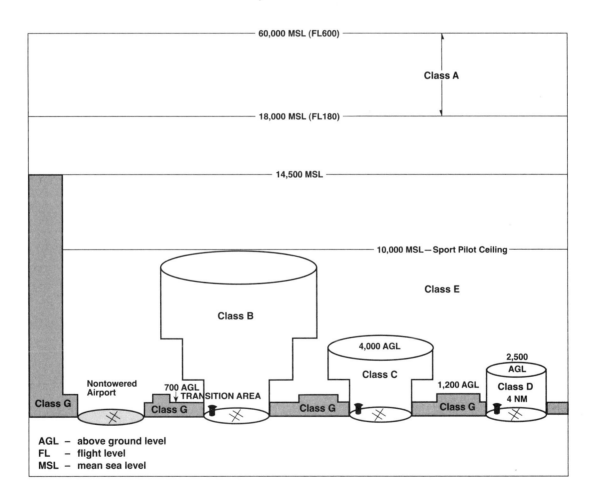

Checklist

☐ Have a sectional chart available for all the areas you'll be flying to while taking the practical test—starting from where the test begins, and into any other chart areas where you will be flying to.

☐ Have a handy kneeboard with cloud clearances specific to sport pilots with you for your oral and flight test to help you remember details.

☐ Go to the "Legend" on the front of the chart to identify any airspace and markings.

Note: If further airspace explanations are needed for the airspace and operating procedures, these are explained in 14 CFR §§91.126 and 91.127 for Class E and G airspace. Sections 91.133 through 91.145 describe other special airspace operations.

☐ Chapter 3 of the AIM has a helpful explanation of airspace.

• •

Questions—National Airspace System

Class E and G Airspace

1. What type of airspace are sport pilots allowed to operate in?
(14 CFR 61.325, 91.129, 91.130, and 91.131)

Sport pilots are allowed to fly in Class E (controlled) and Class G (uncontrolled) airspace, and can fly in Class B, C, and D airspace with additional training and a logbook ensorsements. No operations are allowed in Class A airspace which is above 18,000 feet MSL.

2. How is Class E airspace identified on a sectional?
(AIM 3-2-6, 14 CFR 71.71, NACO)

Class E airspace is most airspace above 1,200 feet above ground level (AGL) when no markings are shown on a sectional. The soft side of shaded magenta on a sectional shows the lower floor of Class E airspace dropping to 700 feet AGL around airports. The dashed magenta line drops the Class E airspace to the ground for some airports that have large airplanes approaching with instruments.

3. How is Class G airspace identified on the sectional? (AIM 3-3-1, NACO)

Class G airspace is generally not marked on the sectional, and extends from the ground up to 1,200 feet AGL, unless other markings are shown on the sectional dropping controlled airspace below the 1,200-foot AGL level. There are special cases in remote areas where the Class G airspace extends up to 14,500 feet MSL. This is indicated by the hard side of the blue shading encircling these areas.

Class G airspace can also extend higher if marked on a sectional with jagged blue lines.

4. What are the overall rules for sport pilots to operate in all airspace?
(14 CFR 61.315)

a. Minimum 3 miles visibility

b. No night flying

c. Below 10,000 feet MSL only

d. Must have visual reference with ground

e. Communications are required for operation in Class B, C, and D airspace with logbook signoff for this airspace.

5. What is the definition of Class E (controlled) airspace? (AIM 3-2-6)

Generally, if the airspace is not Class A, Class B, Class C, or Class D, and it is controlled airspace, it is Class E airspace.

6. State several examples of Class E airspace. (AIM 3-2-6)

Class E airspace is surface area designated for an airport and configured to contain all instrument approaches.

An extension to a surface area—There are Class E airspace areas that serve as extensions to Class B, Class C, and Class D surface areas designated for an airport. Such airspace provides controlled airspace to contain standard instrument approach procedures without imposing a communications requirement on pilots operating under VFR.

Airspace used for transition—Class E airspace beginning at either 700 or 1,200 feet AGL used to transition to/from the terminal enroute environment.

En Route domestic areas—Class E airspace areas that extend upward from a specified altitude and provide controlled airspace in those areas where there is a requirement to provide IFR en route ATC services but the Federal airway system is inadequate.

Federal airways—The federal airways are within Class E airspace areas and, unless otherwise specified, extend upward from 1,200 feet to, but not including 18,000 feet MSL. It includes the airspace within parallel boundary lines 4 miles each side of the centerline.

Offshore airspace areas—Class E airspace that extend upward from a specified altitude to, but not including 18,000 feet MSL. These areas provide controlled airspace beyond 12 miles from the coast of the United States in those areas where there is a requirement to provide IFR en route ATC services.

Unless designated at a lower altitude—Class E airspace begins at 14,500 feet MSL to, but not including 18,000 feet MSL overlying the 48 contiguous states, including the waters within 12 miles from the coast of the 48 contiguous states; the District of Columbia; Alaska, including the waters within 12 miles from the coast of Alaska, and airspace above FL600, excluding specified areas in Alaska.

7. What are the operating rules and pilot/equipment requirements to operate within Class E airspace? (AIM 3-2-6)

a. Minimum pilot certification—student pilot certificate.

b. No specific equipment requirements in Class E airspace.

c. No specific requirements for arrival or through flight in Class E airspace.

8. Are you required to establish communications with a tower located within Class E airspace? (14 CFR 91.127)

Yes. Unless otherwise authorized or required by ATC, no person may operate an aircraft to, from, through, or on an airport having an operational control tower unless two-way communications are maintained between that aircraft and the control tower. Communications must be established prior to 4 nautical miles from the airport, up to and including 2,500 feet AGL.

9. How is Class E airspace depicted on navigational charts?
(AIM 3-2-6; 14 CFR 71.71; NACO)

Class E airspace below 14,500 feet MSL is charted on sectional, terminal, and IFR enroute low altitude charts. The lateral and vertical limits of all Class E controlled airspace up to but not including 18,000 feet are shown by narrow bands of vignette on sectional and terminal area charts. Controlled airspace floors of 700 feet AGL are defined by a magenta vignette; floors other than 700 feet that abut uncontrolled airspace are defined by a blue vignette; differing floors greater than 700 feet AGL are annotated by a symbol and a number indicating the floor. If the ceiling is less than 18,000 feet MSL, the value (prefixed by the word "ceiling") is shown along the limits of the controlled airspace.

10. How are Class E surface extension areas depicted on navigational charts?
(NACO)

Class E airspace areas that serve as extensions to Class B, Class C, and Class D airspace are depicted by a magenta segmented line.

11. What is the definition of Class G airspace? (AIM 3-3-1)

Class G or uncontrolled airspace is that portion of the airspace that has not been designated as Class A, B, C, D, or E airspace.

12. Are you required to establish communications with a tower located within Class G airspace? (14 CFR 91.126)

Yes. Unless otherwise authorized or required by ATC, no person may operate an aircraft to, from, through, or on an airport having an operational control tower unless two-way communications are maintained between that aircraft and the control tower. Communications must be established prior to 4 nautical miles from the airport, up to and including 2,500 AGL.

13. What are the vertical limits of Class G airspace? (FAA-H-8083-25)

Class G airspace begins at the surface and continues up to the overlying controlled (Class E) airspace, not to exceed 14,500 feet MSL. Class G airspace typically starts at the ground and continues upward to 1,200 feet above the ground, unless other airspace is shown on the sectionals.

14. What is the main difference between Class G airspace and Class A, B, C, D, and E airspace?

The main difference which distinguishes Class G airspace from Class A, B, C, D, and E airspace is the flight visibility/cloud clearance requirements necessary to operate within it because it is near the ground where typical airport traffic would not be operating and less visibility is required there.

15. What are the cloud clearances for Class E airspace? (14 CFR 91.155)

Cloud clearance is 500 feet below, 1,000 feet above, 2,000 feet horizontal.

16. What are the cloud clearances for Class G airspace? (14 CFR 91.155)

Clear of clouds. This allows us to fly right next to the clouds but not in them.

17. What general rules apply concerning traffic pattern operations at non-tower airports within Class E or G airspace? (14 CFR 91.126, 91.127)

Each person operating an aircraft to or from an airport without an operating control tower shall:

a. in the case of an airplane approaching to land, make all turns to the left unless the airport displays light signals or visual markings indicating that turns should be made to the right, in which case the pilot shall make all turns to the right.

b. in the case of an aircraft departing an airport, comply with any traffic patterns established for that airport.

18. What procedure should be used when approaching to land on a runway with a Visual Approach Slope Indicator? (14 CFR 91.129)

Aircraft approaching to land on a runway served by a Visual Approach Slope Indicator (VASI) shall maintain an altitude at or above the glide slope until a lower altitude is necessary for a safe landing.

19. Where is aerobatic flight not permitted? (14 CFR 91.303)

No person may operate an aircraft in aerobatic flight:

a. Over any congested area of a city, town, or settlement;

b. Over an open air assembly of persons;

c. Within the lateral boundaries of the surface areas of Class B, Class C, Class D, or Class E airspace designated for an airport;

d. Within 4 nautical miles of the center line of a Federal airway;

e. Below an altitude of 1,500 feet above the surface; or

f. When flight visibility is less than 3 statute miles.

20. What is "aerobatic flight?" (14 CFR 91.303)

Aerobatic flight means an intentional maneuver involving an abrupt change in an aircraft's attitude, an abnormal attitude, or abnormal acceleration, not necessary for normal flight.

21. When are parachutes required on board an aircraft? (14 CFR 91.307)

Unless each occupant of the aircraft is wearing an approved parachute, no pilot of a civil aircraft carrying any person (other than a crewmember) may execute any intentional maneuver that exceeds:

a. a bank angle of 60° relative to the horizon; or

b. a nose-up or nose-down attitude of 30° relative to the horizon.

This does not apply to:

- flight tests for pilot certification or rating; or
- spins and other flight maneuvers required by the regulations for any certificate or rating when given by a CFI or ATP instructing in accordance with 14 CFR 61.67

Class A, B, C, D Airspace

22. What is Class A airspace and how does it affect sport pilots? (AIM 3-2-2)

Generally, that airspace from 18,000 feet MSL up to and including FL600, including that airspace overlying the U.S. coastal oceans. This is for aircraft flying IFR and does not affect sport pilots because we are not allowed to fly above 10,000 feet MSL.

23. What is Class B airspace and how is it depicted on navigational charts? (AIM 3-2-3)

Class B airspace surrounds the largest airports and is typically where the big jets create significant air traffic. It is charted on sectional charts, IFR en route low altitude charts, and terminal area charts. A solid shaded blue line depicts the lateral limits of Class B airspace.

24. What is Class C airspace and how is it depicted on the navigational charts? (AIM 3-2-4)

Generally, that airspace from the surface to 4,000 feet above the airport elevation (charted in MSL) surrounding those airports that have an operational control tower, are serviced by a radar approach control, and that have a certain number of IFR operations and large passenger jets. It is similar to Class B airspace but generally smaller airports with less air traffic.

A solid magenta line is used to depict Class C airspace, and it is charted on sectional charts, IFR en route low altitude charts, and terminal area charts where appropriate.

25. What is Class D airspace and how is it depicted on the navigational charts? (AIM 3-2-5)

Generally, that airspace from the surface to 2,500 feet above the airport elevation (charted in MSL) surrounding those airports with an operational control tower. The configuration of each Class D airspace area is individually tailored and when instrument procedures are published, the airspace will normally be designed to contain those procedures.

Class D airspace areas are depicted on sectional and terminal charts with blue segmented lines, and on IFR en route low altitude charts with a boxed [D].

26. When a control tower, located at an airport within Class D airspace, ceases operation for the day, what happens to the lower limit of the controlled airspace? (AIM 3-2-5)

During the hours the tower is not in operation, Class E surface area rules, or a combination of Class E rules down to 700 feet AGL and Class G rules to the surface, will become applicable. Check the A/FD for specifics.

27. Will all airports with an operating control tower always have Class D airspace surrounding them? (AIM 4-3-2)

No. Some airports do not have the required weather reporting capability necessary for surface-based controlled airspace. The controlled airspace over these airports normally begins at 700 feet or 1,200 feet AGL and can be determined from visual aeronautical charts.

28. What are the "basic" VFR weather minimums required for operation of an aircraft into Class B, Class C, Class D, or Class E airspace? (14 CFR 91.155)

No person may operate an aircraft, under VFR, within the lateral boundaries of the surface areas of Class C, Class D, or Class E airspace designated for an airport when the ceiling is less than 1,000 feet, and unless the ground visibility is at least 3 statute miles, or if ground visibility is not reported at that airport, then unless flight visibility during landing, takeoff or while operating in the traffic pattern is at least 3 statute miles.

Special Use Airspace

29. What is a "Prohibited Area"? (AIM 3-4-2)

Prohibited areas are certain airspace of defined dimensions identified by surface areas within which aircraft flight is prohibited. Such areas are established for security or other reasons associated with the national welfare.

30. What is a "Restricted Area"? (AIM 3-4-3)

Restricted areas are airspace identified by surface areas within which aircraft flight, while not wholly prohibited, is subject to restrictions. These areas denote the existence of unusual, often invisible, hazards to aircraft such as artillery firing, aerial gunnery, or guided missiles. Penetration of restricted areas without authorization from the using or controlling agency may be extremely hazardous to the aircraft and its occupants.

31. Under what conditions, if any, may pilots enter restricted or prohibited areas? (14 CFR 91.133)

No person may operate an aircraft within a restricted area contrary to the restrictions imposed, or within a prohibited area, unless that person has the permission of the using or controlling agency. Normally, no operations are permitted within a prohibited area and prior permission must always be obtained before operating within a restricted area.

32. What is a "Warning Area"? (AIM 3-4-4)

A warning area is airspace of defined dimensions extending from three nautical miles outward from the coast of the United States, containing activity that may be hazardous to nonparticipating aircraft. The purpose of such an area is to warn nonparticipating pilots of the potential danger. A warning area may be located over domestic or international waters, or both.

33. What is a "MOA"? (AIM 3-4-5)

A Military Operating Area (MOA) consists of airspace of defined vertical and lateral limits established for the purpose of separating certain military training activities from IFR traffic. Pilots operating under VFR should exercise extreme caution while flying within an MOA when military activity is being conducted. The activity status (active/inactive) of MOAs may change frequently. Therefore, pilots should contact any FSS within 100 miles of the area to obtain accurate real-time information concerning the MOA hours of operation. Prior to entering an active MOA, pilots should contact the controlling agency for traffic advisories.

34. What is an "Alert Area"? (AIM 3-4-6)

Alert areas are depicted on aeronautical charts to inform nonparticipating pilots of areas that may contain a high volume of pilot training or an unusual type of aerial activity. Pilots should be particularly alert when flying in these areas. All activity within an Alert Area shall be conducted in accordance with regulations, without waiver, and pilots of participating aircraft as well as pilots transiting the area shall be equally responsible for collision avoidance.

35. What are "Controlled Firing Areas"? (AIM 3-4-7)

Controlled Firing Areas (CFAs) contain activities that, if not conducted in a controlled environment, could be hazardous to nonparticipating aircraft. The distinguishing feature of the CFA, as compared to other special use airspace, is that its activities are suspended immediately when spotter aircraft, radar or ground lookout positions indicate an aircraft might be approaching the area. CFAs are not charted.

36. What is a "National Security Area"? (AIM 3-5-7)

National Security Areas consist of airspace of defined vertical and lateral dimensions established at locations where there is a requirement for increased security and safety of ground facilities. Pilots are requested to voluntarily avoid flying through the depicted NSA. When it is necessary to provide a greater level of security and safety, flight in NSAs may be temporarily prohibited by regulation under the provisions of 14 CFR 99.7.

37. Where can information on special use airspace be found? (AIM 3-4-1)

Special use airspace (except CFAs) is charted on IFR or visual charts and include the hours of operation, altitudes, and the controlling agency.

38. If VFR flight minimums cannot be maintained, can a VFR flight be made into Class B, C, D, or E airspace? (AIM 4-4-5)

No. Sport pilots are not allowed to request a special VFR clearance, which private pilots may use to enter Class B, C, D, or E airspace provided the flight can be made clear of clouds with at least 1 mile visibility.

39. What is an "Airport Advisory Area"? (AIM 3-5-1)

An airport advisory area is the area within 10 statute miles of an airport where a control tower is not operating but where a FSS is located. At such locations, the FSS provides advisory service to arriving aircraft. It is not mandatory that pilots participate in the airport advisory program, but it is strongly recommended they do so.

40. What are "Military Training Routes"? (AIM 3-5-2)

Military Training Routes are developed for use by the military for the purpose of conducting low-altitude, high-speed training. The routes above 1,500 feet AGL are developed to be flown, to the maximum extent possible, under IFR. The routes at 1,500 feet AGL and below are generally developed to be flown under VFR. Routes below 1,500 feet AGL use four-digit identifiers (i.e., IR 1004, VR 1008). Routes above 1,500 feet AGL use three-digit identifiers, (i.e., IR 003, VR 004). IR is for IFR routes and VR is for VFR routes.

41. What is a "TRSA"? (AIM Glossary)

A Terminal Radar Service Area (TRSA) consists of airspace surrounding designated airports wherein ATC provides radar vectoring, sequencing, and separation on a full time basis for all IFR and participating VFR aircraft. Pilot participation is urged but not mandatory.

42. What class of airspace is a "TRSA"? (AIM 3-5-6)

TRSAs do not fit into any of the U.S. airspace classes and are not contained in 14 CFR Part 71 nor are there any operating rules in Part 91. The primary airport(s) within the TRSA become Class D airspace. The remaining portion of a TRSA overlies other controlled airspace which is normally Class E airspace beginning at 700 or 1,200 feet and established to transition to/from the enroute/terminal environment. TRSAs will continue to be an airspace area where participating pilots can receive additional radar services which have been redefined as TRSA service.

Radio Communications Questions

(For aircraft equipped with radios, and for operations in Class B, C or D airspace.)

1. What is the most common type of communication radio equipment installed in general aviation aircraft? How many channels are available? (FAA-H-8083-25)

The most common type of radio is VHF. A VHF radio operates on frequencies between 118.0 and 136.975 MHz and is classified as 720 or 760 depending on the number of channels it can accommodate. The 720 and 760 uses .025 spacing (118.025, 118.050, etc.) with the 720 having a frequency range up to 135.975 and the 760 up to 136.975.

2. What is the universal VHF "emergency" frequency? (AIM 6-3-1)

121.5 MHz; this frequency is guarded by military towers, most civil towers, FSS's, and radar facilities.

3. What bandwidths are used for ground control frequencies? (FAA-H-8083-25)

The majority of ground control frequencies are in the 121.6 to 121.9 MHz bandwidth.

4. What is a "CTAF"? (AIM 4-1-9)

A CTAF (Common Traffic Advisory Frequency) is designated for the purpose of carrying out airport advisory practices while operating to or from an airport without an operating control tower. The CTAF may be a UNICOM, MULTICOM, FSS or TOWER frequency and is identified in appropriate aeronautical publications (including the A/FD and Sectionals).

5. What is "UNICOM," and what frequencies are designated for its use? (AIM 4-1-9)

UNICOM is a non-government communication facility which may provide airport information (such as current wind conditions, runway in use, fuel availability, etc.) at certain airports. Airports other than those with a control tower/FSS on airport will normally use 122.700, 122.725, 122.800, 122.975, 123.000, 123.050, and 123.075 MHz. Airports with a control tower or an FSS on airport will normally use 122.950 MHz.

6. **What does "ATIS" mean?** (AIM 4-1-13)

Automatic Terminal Information Service (ATIS) is the continuous broadcast of recorded noncontrol information in selected high-activity terminal areas. Pilots can use ATIS to learn of the current airport conditions such as ceiling, visibility, temperature, dew point, wind, altimeter, other remarks, and instrument approach and runway in use. Its purpose is to improve controller effectiveness and to relieve frequency congestion by automating the repetitive transmission of essential but routine information.

7. **If operating into an airport without an operating control tower, FSS or UNICOM, what procedure should be followed?** (AIM 4-1-9, Glossary)

Where there is no tower, FSS, or UNICOM station on the airport, use MULTICOM frequency 122.9 for self-announce procedures. MULTICOM is used to provide communications essential to private aircraft.

8. **What frequencies are monitored by most FSS's other than 121.5?** (AIM 4-2-14)

FSS's and supplemental weather service locations are allocated frequencies for different functions; for example, 122.0 MHz is assigned as the Enroute Flight Advisory Service frequency (EFAS) at selected FSS's. In addition, certain FSS's provide Local Airport Advisory on 123.6 MHz. Frequencies are listed in the A/FD. If you are in doubt as to what frequency to use, 122.2 MHz is assigned to the majority of FSS's as a common enroute simplex frequency.

9. **What is "Local Airport Advisory Service"?** (AIM 4-1-9)

Certain FSS's provide Local Airport Advisory service to pilots when an FSS is physically located on an airport without a control tower or where the tower is operated on a part-time basis. The CTAF (usually 123.6) for FSS's that provide this service are found in appropriate aeronautical publications. A CTAF FSS provides wind direction and velocity, favored or designated runway, altimeter setting, known traffic, NOTAMs, airport taxi routes, airport traffic pattern information, and instrument approach procedures. The information is advisory in nature and does not constitute an ATC clearance.

10. **How can a pilot determine what frequency is appropriate for activating his/her VFR flight plan once airborne?**

Two ways:

a. Ask the FSS briefer during the preflight weather briefing.

b. Consult the communications section under flight service for the airport of departure in the A/FD.

11. **What is the meaning of a heavy-lined blue box surrounding a NAVAID frequency?** (Chart Legend)

It indicates that both standard FSS frequencies are available at all altitudes without terrain interference. The standard frequencies are 121.5 and 122.2.

12. **Why would a frequency be printed on top of a heavy-lined box?** (Chart Legend)

This usually means that this frequency is available in addition to the standard FSS frequencies.

13. **What is the meaning of a thin-lined blue box surrounding a NAVAID frequency?** (Chart Legend)

A plain box without frequencies on top indicates that there are no standard FSS frequencies available. These NAVAIDs will have a "no voice" symbol (underline under frequency).

14. **Why would a frequency be printed on top of a thin-lined blue box?** (Chart Legend)

These are the best frequencies to use in the immediate vicinity of the NAVAID site, and will ensure reception by the controlling FSS at low altitudes without terrain interference. They will normally be followed by an "R," which indicates the FSS can receive only on that frequency (you transmit on that frequency). The pilot will listen for a response over the NAVAID frequency.

15. **How can a pilot determine the availability of HIWAS when looking at a VFR Sectional chart?** (FAA-H-8083-25)

NAVAIDs that have HIWAS capability are depicted on sectional charts with an "H" in the upper right corner of the identification box.

16. **What meaning does the letter "T" in a solid blue circle appearing in the top right corner of a NAVAID frequency box have?** (Chart Legend)

A letter "T" indicates that a transcribed weather broadcast (TWEB) is available. A TWEB is a continuous recording of meteorological and aeronautical information broadcast on L/MF and VOR facilities for pilots.

For Pilots Seeking Operations in Class B, C, or D Airspace

Study the questions for the class of airspace you want the endorsement in.

1. Under what conditions may a student sport pilot operate in Class B, C and D airspace? (14 CFR 61.94)

A sport pilot student must receive ground and flight training for:

a. The use of radios, communications, navigation systems and facilities, and radar services.

b. Operations at airports with an operating control tower, to include three takeoffs and landings to a full stop, with each landing involving a flight in the traffic pattern, at an airport with an operating control tower.

c. Applicable flight rules of Part 91 for operations in Class B, C, and D airspace and air traffic control clearances.

d. The specific Class B, C, or D airspace for which the solo flight is authorized, if applicable, within the 90-day period preceding the date of the flight in that airspace. The flight training must be received in the specific airspace area for which solo flight is authorized.

In addition to the above, the student must receive from an authorized instructor who provides the specified training, a logbook endorsement that certifies the student has received that training and is proficient to conduct solo flight in the specific airspace or at the specific airport, in the required aeronautical knowledge areas, and areas of operation specified.

2. What is the definition of Class B airspace? (AIM 3-2-3)

Generally, that airspace from the surface to 10,000 feet MSL surrounding the nation's busiest airports in terms of IFR operations or passenger jets. The configuration of each Class B airspace area is individually tailored and consists of a surface area and two or more layers (some Class B airspace areas resemble a upside-down wedding cakes), and is designated to contain all published instrument procedures once an aircraft enters the airspace.

3. What minimum sport pilot certification is required to operate an aircraft within Class B airspace? (14 CFR 91.131)

No sport pilot may take off or land a light-sport aircraft at an airport within a Class B airspace area or operate within a Class B airspace area unless:

a. The pilot-in-command holds a sport pilot certificate and has met the requirements of 14 CFR 61.325.

b. The aircraft is operated by a student pilot seeking a sport pilot certificate who has met the requirements of 14 CFR 61.94 or 61.95. Certain Class B airspace areas do not allow pilot operations to be conducted to or from the primary airport, unless the pilot-in-command holds at least a private pilot certificate (example: Dallas/Fort Worth International).

4. **What is the minimum equipment required for operations of an aircraft within Class B airspace?** (14 CFR 91.131)

   a. An operable two-way radio capable of communications with ATC on the appropriate frequencies for that area.

   b. A Mode C altitude encoding transponder unless the aircraft was not certificated with an electrical system **and** the ATC provides clearance to proceed without a Mode C transponder.

5. **Before operating an aircraft into Class B airspace, what basic requirement must be met?** (14 CFR 91.131)

   Pilots of arriving aircraft must obtain an ATC clearance from the ATC facility having jurisdiction for that area, prior to operating an aircraft in that area.

6. **What minimum weather conditions are required when conducting VFR flight operations within Class B airspace?** (14 CFR 91.155)

   VFR flight operations must be conducted clear of clouds with at least 3 statute miles flight visibility.

7. **What basic ATC services are provided to all aircraft operating within Class B airspace?** (AIM 3-2-3)

   VFR pilots will be provided sequencing and separation from other aircraft while operating within Class B airspace.

8. **It becomes apparent that wake turbulence may be encountered while ATC is providing sequencing and separation services in Class B airspace. Whose responsibility is it to avoid this turbulence?** (AIM 3-2-3)

   The pilot-in-command is responsible. The services provided by ATC do not relieve pilots of their responsibilities to see and avoid other traffic operating in basic VFR weather conditions, to adjust their operations and flight path as necessary to preclude serious wake turbulence encounters, to maintain appropriate terrain and obstruction clearance, or to remain in weather conditions equal to or better than the basic VFR visibility and cloud clearance requirements.

9. **What are the basic dimensions of Class C airspace?** (AIM 3-2-4)

   Although the configuration of each Class C airspace area is individually tailored, the airspace usually consists of a 5 NM radius core surface area that extends from the surface up to 4,000 feet above the airport elevation, and a 10 NM radius shelf area that extends from 1,200 feet to 4,000 feet above the airport elevation. The outer area radius will be 20 NM, with some variations based on site-specific requirements. The outer area extends outward from the primary airport and extends from the lower limits of radar/radio coverage up to the ceiling of the approach controls airspace.

10. **What minimum equipment is required to operate an aircraft within Class C airspace?** (14 CFR 91.130, 91.215)

Unless otherwise authorized by the ATC having jurisdiction over the Class C airspace area, no person may operate an aircraft within a Class C airspace area designated for an airport unless that aircraft is equipped with the following:

a. A two-way radio.

b. A transponder per §91.215 with automatic pressure altitude reporting equipment with Mode C capability.

11. **When operating an aircraft through Class C airspace or to an airport within Class C airspace, what basic requirement must be met?** (14 CFR 91.130)

Each person must establish two-way radio communications with the ATC facilities providing air traffic services prior to entering that airspace and thereafter maintain those communications while within that airspace.

12. **Two-way radio communications must be established prior to entering Class C airspace. Define what is meant by "established" in this context.** (AIM 3-2-4)

If a controller responds to a radio call with, "(aircraft call sign) standby," radio communications have been established. If the controller responds to the initial radio call without using the aircraft's N-number, radio communications have not been established and the pilot may not enter the Class C airspace.

13. **When departing a satellite airport without an operative control tower located within Class C airspace, what requirement must be met?** (14 CFR 91.130)

Each person must establish and maintain two-way radio communications with the ATC facilities having jurisdiction over the Class C airspace area as soon as practicable after departing.

14. **What minimum weather conditions are required when conducting VFR flight operations within Class C airspace?** (14 CFR 91.155)

VFR flight operations within Class C airspace require 3 statute miles flight visibility and cloud clearances of at least 500 feet below, 1,000 feet above and 2,000 feet horizontal to clouds.

15. **What type of air traffic control services are provided when operating within Class C airspace?** (AIM 3-2-4)

When two-way radio communications and radar contact are established, all participating VFR aircraft are:

a. Sequenced to the primary airport.

b. Provided with Class C services within the Class C airspace and the outer area.

c. Provided with basic radar services beyond the outer area on a workload-permitting basis. This can be terminated by the controller if workload dictates.

16. **Describe the various types of terminal radar services available for VFR aircraft.** (AIM 4-1-17)

    Basic radar service—safety alerts, traffic advisories, limited radar vectoring (on a workload-permitting basis) and sequencing at locations where procedures have been established for this purpose and/or when covered by a letter of agreement.

    TRSA service—radar sequencing and separation service for VFR aircraft in a TRSA.

    Class C service—this service provides, in addition to basic radar service, approved separation between IFR and VFR aircraft, and sequencing of VFR arrivals to the primary airport.

    Class B service—provides, in addition to basic radar service, approved separation of aircraft based on IFR, VFR, and/or weight, and sequencing of VFR arrivals to the primary airport(s).

17. **Where is Mode C altitude encoding transponder equipment required?** (AIM 4-1-19)

    a. At or above 10,000 feet MSL over the 48 contiguous states or the District of Columbia, excluding that airspace below 2,500 feet AGL (not applicable to sport pilots with the 10,000 MSL ceiling.

    b. Within 30 miles of a Class B airspace primary airport, below 10,000 feet MSL.

    c. Within and above all Class C airspace, up to 10,000 feet MSL.

    d. Within 10 miles of certain designated airports, excluding that airspace which is both outside the Class D surface area and below 1,200 feet AGL.

    e. All aircraft flying into, within, or across the contiguous U.S. ADIZ.

    Note: Mode C is not required if the ATC provides clearance in the above areas. The aircraft is not required to have Mode C when the aircraft is certificated without an electrical system (per §91.213b), but must call an hour ahead of time to deviate from ATC procedures (per §91.215(d)(3)).

18. **When operating an aircraft through Class D airspace or to an airport within Class D airspace, what requirement must be met?** (14 CFR 91.129)

    Each person must establish two-way radio communications with the ATC facilities providing air traffic services prior to entering that airspace and thereafter maintain those communications while within that airspace.

19. **When departing a satellite airport without an operative control tower located within Class D airspace, what requirement must be met?** (14 CFR 91.129)

    Each person must establish and maintain two-way radio communications with the ATC facility having jurisdiction over the Class D airspace area as soon as practicable after departing.

20. **Is an ATC clearance required if flight operations are conducted through a Class D arrival extension area?** (AIM 3-2-5 and 3-2-6)

    Arrival extensions for instrument approach procedures may be Class D or Class E airspace. As a general rule, if all extensions are 2 miles or less, they remain part of the Class D surface area (blue segmented line). However, if any one extension is greater than 2 miles, then all extensions become Class E. Class E airspace areas that serve as extensions (magenta segmented line) to Class B, Class C, and Class D surface areas, provide controlled airspace to contain standard instrument approach procedures without imposing a communications requirement on pilots operating under VFR.

21. **What minimum weather conditions are required when conducting VFR flight operations within Class D airspace?** (14 CFR 91.155)

    VFR flight operations within Class D airspace require 3 statute miles flight visibility and cloud clearances of at least 500 feet below, 1,000 feet above and 2,000 feet horizontal to clouds.

22. **What type of air traffic control services are provided when operating within Class D airspace?** (AIM 3-2-5, 5-5-8, and 5-5-10)

    No separation services are provided to VFR aircraft. When meteorological conditions permit, regardless of the type of flight plan or whether or not under the control of a radar facility, the pilot is responsible to see and avoid other traffic, terrain or obstacles. A controller, on a workload-permitting basis, will provide radar traffic information, safety alerts and traffic information for sequencing purposes.

23. **Where can a pilot find information on VFR flyways, VFR corridors, Class B airspace transition routes, and terminal area VFR routes used to transition busy terminal airspace?** (AIM 3-5-5)

    Information will normally be depicted on the reverse side of VFR terminal area charts, commonly referred to as Class B airspace charts.

24. **When may a pilot intentionally deviate from an ATC clearance or instruction?** (14 CFR 91.123)

    A pilot may deviate from an ATC clearance when:

    a. an amended clearance has been obtained,

    b. an emergency exists,

    c. or in response to a traffic and collision avoidance system resolution advisory.

25. As pilot-in-command, what action, if any, is required if you deviate from an ATC instruction and priority is given? (14 CFR 91.123)

Two actions are required of you as PIC:

a. Each pilot-in-command who, in an emergency, deviates from an ATC clearance or instruction shall notify ATC of that deviation as soon as possible (in-the-air responsibility).

b. Each pilot-in-command who is given priority by ATC in an emergency shall submit a detailed report of that emergency within 48 hours to the manager of that ATC facility, if requested by ATC (on-the-ground responsibility).

26. In the event of radio failure while operating an aircraft to, from, through or on an airport having an operational tower, what are the different types and meanings of light gun signals you might receive from an ATC tower? (14 CFR 91.125)

Light	On Ground	In Air
Steady Green	Cleared for Takeoff	Cleared to Land
Flashing Green	Cleared to Taxi	Return for Landing
Steady Red	Stop	Yield, Continue Circling
Flashing Red	Taxi Clear of Runway	Unsafe, Do Not Land
Flashing White	Return to Start	Not Used
Alternate Red/Green	Exercise Extreme Caution	Exercise Extreme Caution

Note: Most pilots find these hard to remember; attach them to your kneeboard or your flight log form.

27. If the aircraft radio fails in flight under VFR while operating into a tower-controlled airport, what conditions must be met before a landing may be made at that airport? (14 CFR 91.126, 91.127, 91.129)

a. Weather conditions must be at or above basic VFR weather minimums;

b. Visual contact with the tower is maintained; and

c. A clearance to land is received.

28. **What procedures should be used when attempting communications with a tower when the aircraft transmitter or receiver or both are inoperative?** (AIM 4-2-13)

Arriving aircraft receiver inoperative:

- Remain outside or above Class D surface area.
- Determine direction and flow of traffic.
- Advise tower of aircraft type, position, altitude, and intention to land. Request to be controlled by light signals.
- At 3 to 5 miles, advise tower of position and join traffic pattern.
- Watch the tower for light gun signals.

Arriving aircraft transmitter inoperative:

- Remain outside or above Class D surface area.
- Determine direction and flow of traffic.
- Monitor frequency for landing or traffic information.
- Join the traffic pattern and watch for light gun signals.
- Daytime, acknowledge by rocking wings. Nighttime, acknowledge by flashing landing light or navigation lights (note: sport pilots may not fly at night).

Arriving aircraft transmitter and receiver inoperative:

- Remain outside or above Class D surface area.
- Determine direction and flow of traffic.
- Join the traffic pattern and watch for light gun signals.
- Acknowledge light signals as noted above.

• •

F. Operation of Systems

Understanding how your aircraft systems work.

Tips

- Study the areas and equipment that apply to your aircraft.
- It is easiest to show as you explain, than to just explain verbally.
- You need to be proficient in the systems of your aircraft, and the systems of the aircraft in which you will be taking the test.

Checklist

Propulsion system

- ☐ Engine (four- or two-stroke)
- ☐ Throttle system (lever, cable, indication)
- ☐ Ignition system
- ☐ Fuel delivery
- ☐ Fuel and air induction — carburetor or fuel injection — carb ice
- ☐ Fuel/gasoline
- ☐ Oil systems
- ☐ Engine instruments
- ☐ Exhaust systems
- ☐ Propellers and reduction drives
- ☐ Torque effects from propeller

Other systems

- ☐ Electric systems
- ☐ Brake systems
- ☐ Ground steering
- ☐ Emergency parachute systems
- ☐ Communications systems

Airplanes: Flight controls

- ☐ Primary — ailerons, rudder or elevator (stabilizer if used instead of elevator)
- ☐ Secondary — Trim systems and flaps
- ☐ Leading edge lift enhancing systems
- ☐ Spoilers (if used)
- ☐ Ground adjustable tabs

Continued

Weight-shift control: Flight control systems

☐ Primary roll and pitch

☐ Trim systems

Powered parachutes: Flight controls

☐ Steering lines and bars

☐ Trim systems

Flight instruments (if applicable)

☐ Airspeed

☐ Altimeter

☐ Vertical speed indicator

☐ Directional

  • Magnetic compass

  • GPS

• •

Questions—Operation of Systems

Not all the questions in Section I.F. are applicable to all pilots. The questions are also broken down further into groups applicable to the different types of engines, the category of aircraft, and even instrumentation. Study the questions that apply to your aircraft, and the one in which you will take the test:

  • All Sport Pilots

  • Four-Stroke Engines only

  • Two-Stroke Engines only

  • Fixed Wing Airplanes (AIR) only

  • Weight-Shift Control (WSC) only

  • Powered Parachute (PPC) only

For All Sport Pilots

1. Describe the landing gear system on this aircraft. (AFM)

The nose wheel landing gear consists of a tricycle-type system with two main wheels and a steerable nose wheel. Tubular spring steel main gear struts—or gas shocks for some aircraft, bungies for others—provide main gear shock absorption. Nose gear shock absorption is provided by a combination air/oil shock strut. This is typical for AIR, WSC and PPC.

2. **Describe the braking system on this aircraft.** (AFM)

They are hydraulically actuated disc-type brakes. A hydraulic line connects the brake actuation to a master cylinder which supplies the hydraulic pressure to the brakes.

or

They are mechanical brakes consisting of a brake pedal or actuation that when pressure is applied, the cable pulls the mechanical brake to the drum or disk brake. This can be the case for a nose wheel, rear wheels, or differential rear wheel system.

Airplanes—There is a brake on the top of each rudder pedal with two master cylinders. By applying pressure to the top of either the pilot's or copilot's set of rudder pedals, the brakes may be applied individually to each main gear wheel. This differential braking can be found on either hydraulic or mechanical brake systems.

3. **How is the power developed by the engine for your aircraft?** (FAA-H-8083-25)

Most small airplanes are powered by reciprocating ("recip") engines made up, in part, of cylinders, pistons, connecting rods and a crankshaft. The pistons move back and forth within the cylinders. Connecting rods connect the pistons to the crankshaft, which converts the back and forth movement of the pistons to a rotary motion. It is this rotary motion that drives the propeller. There are two types of engines used for LSA, the four-stroke and the two-stroke.

4. **What type of engine do you have and what are its typical uses?** (AFM)

Four-stroke engines are typical in automobiles and heavy aircraft, two-stroke engines are typical for high performance motorcycles and snowmobiles, which need an optimum power per weight ratio. Two-strokes have evolved as aircraft engines, delivering optimum performance per pound of engine.

5. **What two things does fuel do for the engine?** (FAA-H-8083-25)

Fuel acts both as an agent for combustion and as an agent for cooling (based on the mixture setting of the engine).

6. **What is a fuel system?** (FAA-H-8083-25)

Basic fuel systems are made to take fuel out of the tank and deliver it to the engine. There are a large variety of fuel system options and designs. All are designed to deliver a clean and reliable supply of fuel to the engine.

7. **What are the two main types of fuel systems that produce pressure in the fuel system?** (FAA-H-8083-25)

Gravity flow—where fuel naturally flows to the carburetor from above.

Pumped system—where the fuel is below the carburetor and must be pumped into the float bowls.

8. How do you determine what type of fuel to use in your engine? (AFM)

Fuel is available in several grades. The proper grade for a specific engine will be listed in the AFM. If the proper grade of fuel is not available, it is possible to use the next higher grade, but a lower grade of fuel should never be used.

If your engine runs on auto gas, aviation fuel may be used if this is the only fuel available—but it should not be used on a consistent basis. Many times you fly into an airport and aviation gas (avgas) is the only fuel available. The extra lead in the aviation fuel is not good for the engine, but can be used as an alternative on a very limited basis.

Regular auto gas is used for many LSA. The engine operator's manual will specify the minimum octane grade to be used.

9. What is detonation and what causes it? (FAA-H-8083-25)

The use of low-grade fuel or a too lean air/fuel mixture may cause detonation, which is the uncontrolled spontaneous explosion of the mixture in the cylinder. Detonation produces extreme heat.

10. What is pre-ignition and what causes it? (FAA-H-8083-25)

Pre-ignition is the premature burning of the air/fuel mixture. It is caused by an incandescent area (such as a carbon or lead deposit heated to a red hot glow) which serves as an igniter in advance of normal ignition.

11. How can fuel be contaminated? (FAA-H-8083-25)

Fuel can be contaminated by water and/or dirt at any step throughout the fueling process.

12. How can fuel be contaminated with water, without you having added water to the tank? What problems could result? (FAA-H-8083-25)

Through bad gas (water in the gas) or through condensation. The air inside the aircraft fuel tanks can cool at night, and this cooling forms water droplets on the insides of the fuel tanks. These droplets then fall into the fuel. To avoid this problem, always fill the tanks completely when parking overnight.

The water can freeze in cold temperatures, anywhere in the fuel supply system, or be inadvertently supplied to the engine when it is expecting fuel. Either situation can cause the engine to stop resulting in an emergency situation.

13. How can water contamination be avoided before flight during your preflight procedures? (FAA-H-8083-25)

Visually check for water contamination using a fuel tester. Many fuel tanks, or fuel lines coming from the tanks have a low point where the heavier water settles to the bottom and can be drained out before each flight. Thoroughly drain all of the aircraft's sumps, drains, and strainers before a flight to eliminate the water that might have collected there.

14. **How can you avoid dirt contamination if the fuel source is sloppy, unknown, or you can visually see dirt in the fuel container?** (FAA-H-8083-25)

   Use a funnel with a strainer. Some strainer funnels are also designed to separate the water from the fuel.

15. **What is a throttle system, how does it work and what does it do?** (FAA-H-8083-25)

   Every aircraft has a throttle lever set to increase engine power and resultant thrust. As the throttle is moved it varies the amount of air and fuel flowing into the cylinders. Opening the throttle and letting more air/fuel into the engine produces more power. Closing the throttle or lowering the amount of air/fuel mixture into the cylinders reduces power. The throttle can open this space via a butterfly valve or sliding valve.

   Each throttle system opening and closing is actuated by the pilot with the throttle lever in the cockpit. All throttle systems should have a friction device so they can be set and left in any position. It is typical to move the throttle forward to add throttle, and move it back to reduce throttle but that isn't the only method—there are many types of throttle actuation systems for different aircraft.

16. **What are the two types of systems to tell you how much fuel you have on board?** (AFM)

   LSA have two types of fuel level indication. Remote fuel sensors provide a gage reading in the cockpit. Visual indications, such as a clear tube, show the fuel level or clear tanks so you can visually see the fuel in the tank.

17. **What is a fuel vent and why is it important?** (FAA-H-8083-25)

   As the fuel level in an aircraft fuel tank decreases, a vacuum would be created within the tank which would eventually result in a decreasing fuel flow and finally engine stoppage. Fuel system venting provides a way of replacing fuel with outside air, preventing formation of a vacuum. Fuel vents can be in the fuel cap for simple systems, or vented elsewhere with a vent line. A vent line allows the vapors from the fuel tank to escape away from heat, sparks, or where they could pose a problem for the occupants.

18. **What is a "fuel strainer"?** (FAA-H-8083-25)

   In gravity flow systems and pumped systems, a strainer is normally installed to keep the larger contaminants that made it into the fuel tank out of the system.

19. **In a pumped system where there is no auxiliary fuel pump, what method is used to get the fuel up to the bowls to start the engine?**

   If no electric fuel pump is installed to accomplish this, a primer bulb is used to fill the carburetor float bowls with fuel before starting.

20. What should be installed when using a primer bulb in case the primer bulb fails?

A bypass is typically installed to keep the fuel flowing in case the primer bulb fails during flight. A valve is shut when the primer bulb is used and opened after the fuel system has been primed. Priming the fuel system with an electric pump or a primer bulb is a typical procedure before you start the engine.

21. Where is a fuel filter normally installed and what does it do?
(FAA-H-8083-25)

A fuel filter is normally installed before the fuel pump and after the primer bulb to strain out any of the smaller fuel contaminants that could plug the jets in the carburetor and stop the engine.

22. What type of fuel filter is preferred if you want to inspect it before flight?

A filter where you can see the screen is preferred so it can be visually checked during a preflight inspection. Cheap paper filters are not recommended.

23. How often are fuel filters typically changed?

Fuel filters are typically changed every 50 hours of operation.

24. For fuel pumped systems, how is the fuel pump driven?

The main fuel pump is normally driven from the engine. Many two-stroke fuel pumps operate pneumatically from the high and low pressures created in the crankcase, with a line connecting the crankcase to the fuel pump. Four-stroke engines usually have a mechanically-driven fuel pump.

25. Explain an electric boost pump or (auxiliary pump) system and operation.
(FAA-H-8083-25)

An electric boost pump is installed in parallel to the main fuel pump to operate in case the main fuel pump fails. This is typically operated during takeoff and landing to ensure the maximum reliability for these critical periods. Boost pumps can be installed on two- and four-stroke engines. A fuel pressure gage is often used to monitor the fuel pressure.

26. How do you start a cold engine? (FAA-H-8083-25)

Engines typically need extra fuel to start when they are cold. This can be accomplished two ways:

a. A primer hand pump has historically been used on four-stroke vintage aircraft engines and also used on two-stroke engines. This pumps raw fuel into the cylinders for starting and can be pumped during cold engine starts until the engine gets up to operational speed.

b. The other option is a choke, or many times it is called an enrichener. This is operated by the pilot with a lever in the cockpit, via a cable to the carburetor, to provide a richer mixture (more gas than normal) to start the cold engine.

27. What are the two types of air/fuel induction systems? (FAA-H-8083-25)

Most light airplane engines use either a carburetor or a fuel injection system to deliver an air/fuel mixture to the cylinders.

28. How does a fuel injection system work? (FAA-H-8083-25)

The fuel is injected either directly into the cylinder or just ahead of the cylinder at the precise time with a control unit. It is atomized (mist) through the discharge nozzles. No carburetor is used. The throttle lever still opens the air passage into the engine, but the fuel control unit provides the metered fuel which is injected directly into the cylinders. Fuel injection systems are used on both four- and two-stroke engines.

29. What does the carburetor do? (FAA-H-8083-25)

Carburetion is the process of mixing fuel and air in the correct proportions to form a combustible mixture. The carburetor vaporizes liquid fuel into small particles and then mixes it with air. It measures the airflow and meters fuel accordingly.

30. How does the carburetor maintain and manage fuel intake? (FAA-H-8083-25)

In a carburetor induction system, the job of the main fuel pumps is to supply the float chamber with fuel. Two-stroke engines also use float-type carburetors—this is called a float bowl instead of a float chamber. As the engine uses this fuel, the float lowers, and opens the fuel inlet needle valve allowing fuel to enter the chamber. When the fuel rises to the specified level the valve closes, stopping the fuel flow. This process maintains the specified fuel level in the float chamber/bowls.

31. How is the fuel mixed with the air in a float-type carburetor?
(FAA-H-8083-25)

It takes in air from the air inlet, flows through a restriction (venturi), which creates a low-pressure area. The pressure difference between the low-pressure area and outside air forces fuel into the airstream where it is mixed with the flowing air, drawn through an intake manifold, and delivered to the engine for combustion.

Carburetors are normally set to deliver the correct air/fuel mixture at sea level. Since air density decreases with altitude, the same amount of fuel is supplied but the amount of air is decreased, delivering a richer mixture with increased altitude.

Many four-stroke engine airplanes have mixture adjustment for this situation requiring continual monitoring and adjustment at different altitudes.

32. What is carburetor ice and how is it formed? (FAA-H-8083-25)

As air flows through a carburetor it expands rapidly. At the same time, fuel forced into the airstream is vaporized. Expansion of the air and vaporization of the fuel causes a sudden cooling of the mixture which may cause ice to form inside the carburetor.

33. What problems can carburetor ice produce? (FAA-H-8083-25)

The formation of carburetor ice may reduce or block fuel/airflow to the engine, thereby reducing needed power.

34. In aircraft susceptible to carburetor icing, what atmospheric conditions create the best chance of ice forming, and how can it be avoided? (FAA-H-8083-25)

The possibility of icing should always be considered when operating in conditions where the temperature is between 20°F and 70°F, and the relative humidity is high. Carburetor heat preheats the air before it enters the carburetor and either prevents carburetor ice from forming, or melts any ice that may have formed.

35. How does carburetor heat affect aircraft performance? (FAA-H-8083-25)

When carburetor heat is applied, the heated air that enters the carburetor is less dense. This causes the fuel/air mixture to become enriched, and this in turn decreases engine output.

During engine run-up prior to departure from a high-altitude airport, the pilot may notice a slight engine roughness not affected by the ignition check, which grows worse during the carburetor heat check. In this case, the air/fuel mixture may be too rich due to the lower air density at the high altitude, and applying carburetor heat decreases the air density even more. A leaner setting of the mixture control may correct this problem.

36. What are the symptoms of carburetor ice and the results of applying carburetor heat? (FAA-H-8083-25)

The first indication of carburetor ice would likely be a decrease in RPM as the air supply is choked off. Application of carburetor heat will decrease air density, causing the RPM to drop even lower. Then, as the carburetor ice melts, the RPM will rise gradually.

37. What systems are more or less susceptible to carburetor ice? (FAA-H-8083-25)

Fuel injection systems do not use a carburetor and are generally considered to be less susceptible to icing than carburetor systems. However, moisture and/or ice at the air filter can be a problem for both carburetor and fuel injection systems.

Two-stroke engines are less susceptible to carburetor icing if the carburetor is close to the combustion chamber and engine, and the carburetor throat larger and is a straight-shot into the engine. Specific installations must be evaluated by the manufacturer to determine icing susceptibility and vary greatly based on specific installation.

38. What is an ignition system, how does it work and what does it do? (FAA-H-8083-25, AFM)

A magneto ("mag") used on most vintage aircraft is a self-contained source of electrical energy, so that even if an aircraft loses total electric power, the ignition system and engine will continue to run. The magneto is a small generator with magnets rotating off the crank or flywheel, around ignition coils which produce the electricity to fire the spark plugs. Points on mechanical systems tell the system when to discharge the high voltage at the precise time to ignite the air/fuel mixture with the spark plug.

Typical vintage aircraft engines produce the required voltage to fire the spark plugs directly and the points are located in the magneto.

Capacitance Discharge Ignition (CDI) is used for most modern LSA. It has no moving parts and is on all modern ROTAX engines. A pickup coil with an electronic box are used to trigger and boost the voltage to the spark plug.

39. What is unique about most aircraft ignition systems? (FAA-H-8083-25)

Many LSA engines have two completely separate ignition systems—two completely separate magneto or CDI circuits. These feed to two separate spark plugs for each cylinder. The main advantages of the dual ignition system are increased safety with reliability and improved engine performance.

When checking for ignition systems prior to flight, the engine should run smoothly when operating with the ignition selector set on "BOTH," and should experience a slight drop in revolutions per minute (RPM) when running on only one or the other system.

40. What is the function of the manual primer, and how does it operate? (AFM)

The manual primer's main function is to provide assistance in starting the engine. The primer draws fuel from the fuel strainer and injects it directly into the cylinder intake ports. This usually results in a quicker, more efficient engine start.

41. What is an engine inlet air system and what is its importance? (FAA-H-8083-25)

All air going into the combustion chamber needs to be filtered to keep out dust, dirt, and other debris. Some two-stroke systems will have an intake silencer chamber between the filter and the carburetor to reduce the engine noise out of the carburetor. Intake silencers reduce the power to the engine slightly and require slightly smaller jetting.

42. What is an exhaust system? (FAA-H-8083-25)

Exhaust systems carry the hot exhaust gasses from the cylinder to a suitable location to exhaust them to the atmosphere.

43. How are the circuits for the various electrical accessories within the aircraft protected? (AFM)

Most of the electrical circuits in an airplane are protected from an overload condition by either circuit breakers or fuses or both. Circuit breakers perform the same function as fuses except that when an overload occurs, a circuit breaker can be reset.

44. The electrical system provides power for what equipment in an airplane? (AFM)

Normally, the following:

Radio equipment, fuel gauges, landing light, taxi light, strobe lights, interior lights, instrument lights, position lights, flaps (maybe), oil temperature gauge, and electric fuel pump (maybe).

45. What does the ammeter indicate? (AFM)

The ammeter indicates the flow of current, in amperes, from the alternator to the battery or from the battery to the electrical system. With the engine running and master switch on, the ammeter will indicate the charging rate to the battery. If the alternator has gone off-line and is no longer functioning, or the electrical load exceeds the output of the alternator, the ammeter indicates the discharge rate of the battery.

46. What function does the voltage regulator have?

The voltage regulator is a device that monitors system voltage, detects changes, and makes the required adjustments in the output of the alternator to maintain a constant regulated system voltage. It must do this at low RPM, such as during taxi, as well as at high RPM in flight. In a 28-volt system, it will maintain 28 volts ±0.5 volts.

47. Why is the generator/alternator voltage output slightly higher than the battery voltage? (FAA-H-8083-25)

The difference in voltage keeps the battery charged. For example, a 12-volt battery would be supplied with 13 to 14 volts.

48. What does the engine oil system do? (FAA-H-8083-25)

Engine lubricating oil not only prevents direct metal-to-metal contact of moving parts, it also absorbs and dissipates some of the engine heat produced by internal combustion.

On a four-stroke engine, if the engine oil level should fall too low, an abnormally high engine oil temperature indication may result. The same would happen on a two-stroke engine if the oil injection system failed or the pilot/operator did not mix the oil in with the gasoline.

On the ground or in the air, excessively high engine temperatures can cause excessive oil consumption (for four-stroke engines), loss of power, and possible permanent internal engine damage.

49. What type of oil should you use for your engine? (AFM)

All engines should use the oil the engine manufacturer recommends. Four-stroke and two-stroke engines use different types of oils and are completely different lubrication systems.

50. What are some indications of high engine temperatures? (AFM)

If the engine oil temperature (for a four-stroke engine) gets too high, the cylinder head temperature gauges have exceeded their normal operating range, or the water temperature for water-cooled engine exceeds limitations.

51. What are some of the causes of high engine temperature? (FAA-H-8083-25, AFM)

If the pilot suspects that the engine is detonating during climb-out, the pilot may have been operating with either too much power and a too lean mixture, using too-low-grade fuel, or operating the engine with an insufficient amount of oil.

52. If high engine temperature or detonation is suspected, what should be the pilot's first action? (FAA-H-8083-25, AFM)

Reducing the rate of climb and increasing airspeed, enriching the fuel mixture (if possible), or retarding the throttle will aid in cooling an engine that is overheating. Most LSA engines have ground-adjustable jets to adjust the mixture for different density altitudes, so the mixture cannot be adjusted during flight.

53. How is engine temperature normally indicated? (FAA-H-8083-25)

Generally, air-cooled engines measure the cylinder head temperature (CHT) with a thermocouple on a washer under the spark plug, and water-cooled engines measure the cooling fluid water temperature entering the engine system with a thermocouple in the water stream. Four-stroke engines may also use oil temperature readings.

54. What type of engines use exhaust gas temperature (EGT)? (FAA-H-8083-25)

Both two- and four-stroke engines use EGT.

55. What is EGT, and what affects it? (FAA-H-8083-25)

This is a measure of the temperature of the gas as it is leaving the cylinder on the way to the exhaust pipe. At constant power settings, higher EGT is the result of a less fuel per air mixture (leaner), and lower EGT means more gasoline per air mixtures. This is a direct reading used to determine proper mixtures at different power levels. You want all your EGT to read about the same from each cylinder.

56. What is the cause of out-of-range EGT readings? (FAA-H-8083-25)

EGT out of range means a problem in the mixture and combustion process.

57. What is an engine cooling system? (FAA-H-8083-25)

Cooling systems are there to maintain the engine temperatures within the manufacturer's operational specifications.

58. What type of engines have an oil cooler?

Only four-stroke engines have the option of an oil cooler.

59. What type of engines can be air-cooled or water-cooled?

Both four- and two-stroke engines have the option of being air- or water-cooled. These systems can use the option of a fan or ram air pressure.

60. How do air-cooled engines provide airflow to cool?

Some air-cooled engines use the airspeed pressure for ram air-cooling to force the air through the cylinder heads with baffles directing the air. This is typical for many classic LSA and modern aircraft also. Faster flight speeds normally create better cooling with this design. Little to no cooling while taxiing provides little ram air pressure through the cooling fins. Opening the cowl flaps increases the cooling airflow; closing the cowl flaps (when an option) decreases the engine cooling.

61. What is a water-cooled engine?

Water-cooled engines run a fluid with an antifreeze/anti-boil solution through passages in the engine out to a separate radiator where air moves through to dissipate the heat picked up on the engine.

62. What engines use a propeller reduction drive?

Many of the vintage engines are designed to operate at a low RPM and can have a direct drive to operate the propeller up to 2,700 RPM. Two-stroke engines can operate up to 6,500 RPM, which is too fast for the propeller to turn because of excessive noise and decreased efficiency. A reduction drive can reduce the propeller RPM for quiet and efficient operation. Modern four-stroke engines operate at higher RPM where reduction gear boxes are used.

63. How are engines that use a prop reduction drive lubricated?

The four-stroke engines use the oil system to lubricate the gear box. The two-stroke gear boxes have a separate oil reservoir to lubricate the gears which must be changed per manufacturer's specified periods.

64. What type of a reduction drive does not need an oil sump for lubrication?

Belt drives are also used as reduction drives and do not need an oil reservoir.

65. If a propeller reduction is 4 to 1, and the engine RPM is 6,500, at what RPM will the propeller be turning?

1,625 propeller RPM.

66. What does a propeller do?

A propeller turns engine power into thrust to propel the airplane through the air.

67. How is a light-sport aircraft propeller pitch adjusted?

The propeller pitch is adjusted on the ground initially to be 300 to 500 RPM less than maximum RPM, and adjusted to not reach maximum engine RPM at maximum level speed of the aircraft.

Four-Stroke Engines

1. **What type of engine does your aircraft have?** (AFM)

   A horizontally-opposed four-cylinder, overhead-valve, water-cooled, carbureted engine. The engine is manufactured by Rotax and rated at 100 HP.

2. **What four strokes must occur in each cylinder of a typical four-stroke engine in order for it to produce full power?** (FAA-H-8083-25)

   The four strokes are:

   Intake—fuel mixture is drawn into cylinder by downward stroke

   Compression—mixture is compressed by upward stroke

   Power—spark ignites mixture forcing piston downward and producing power

   Exhaust—burned gases pushed out of cylinder by upward stroke

3. **How does the carburetor heat system work?** (AFM)

   A carburetor heat valve controlled by the pilot allows unfiltered, heated air from a shroud located around an exhaust riser or muffler to be directed to the induction air manifold prior to the carburetor. Carburetor heat should be used any time suspected or known carburetor icing conditions exist.

4. **What change occurs to the fuel/air mixture when applying carburetor heat?** (FAA-H-8083-25)

   Normally, the introduction of heated air into the carburetor will result in a richer mixture. Warm air is less dense, resulting in less air for the same amount of fuel.

5. **What does the mixture control do?** (FAA-H-8083-25)

   Mixture control regulates the fuel-to-air ratio. Some airplane engines incorporate a device called a mixture control, by which the fuel/air ratio can be controlled by the pilot during flight. The purpose of a mixture control is to prevent the mixture from becoming too rich at high altitudes, due to decreasing air density. It is also used to lean the mixture during cross-country flights to conserve fuel and provide optimum power.

6. **Describe an oil system on a four-stroke engine.**

   Four-stroke engines have a separate oil system to lubricate the engine, same as an automobile. An engine-driven oil pump pressurizes the oil and pumps it through the oil system passages to lubricate the engine. The purpose of the oil system is to:

   • lubricate the moving parts to reduce friction and minimize wear,

   • assist in cooling the engine by taking some of the heat away from the hot parts,

   • carry away contaminants which are then removed during maintenance in the oil filter.

   Some engines have separate oil coolers. Oil pressure and temperature are typical gages to monitor the health of the four-stroke engine.

stroke engine fires on every revolution of the crankshaft making it typically more

Two-Stroke Engines

1. What does two-stroke mean and how is it different from a four-stroke?

Two-stroke engines use the crankcase and the cylinder action simultaneously to achieve all four elements of the Otto cycle in only two strokes of the piston. The oil is mixed with the gas/air mixture, passes through the crankcase providing lubrication and eliminating the separate oil system required for a four-stroke engine. A two-stroke engine fires on every revolution of the crankshaft making it typically more powerful than a four-stroke engine of equivalent size. The lightweight and simplicity make a two-stroke engine an excellent alternative for LSA. They do need more attention but can be used reliably with proper operation and maintenance (O&M) procedures.

2. What are the strokes of a two-stroke engine?

One stroke of the piston is intake and compression and the second stroke is power and exhaust.

3. Does a two-stroke engine have valves?

Two-stroke engines are often known for not having valves. This is partly true. A wide range of valve systems are found on two-stroke engines.

4. What type of valve system does your engine have? (AFM)

There are 3 options for this answer depending on your engine:

One-way pressure inlet valves called spring, reed, or poppet valves, open when the pressure drops within the crankcase, and suck the fuel from the carburetor into the crankcase. Reed valves are open with low pressure and close when the pressure increases. Hirth engines typically use this system.

Mechanical rotary valves are driven off the engine, rotate to provide an opening at the precise time, and can be on the intake and exhaust ports. Rotax 582 and 618 engines use this for an intake valve, and the 618 also has a rotary exhaust valve.

The simplest is no valves at all. All valving is accomplished with transfer ports opened and closed by the piston position as it moves up and down in the cylinder. This is called a "piston ported inlet." The Rotax 503 and lower use this system.

5. Do two-stroke engines have mixture controls?

Normally they do not. However some carburetors do have a mixture adjustment but this is not required for normal operations.

6. Without a carburetor mixture control, what happens when you operate at higher altitudes than normal?

You simply operate at richer mixtures at higher altitudes. If an engine continually operates from a higher altitude airport, the jets are changed to provide the proper mixture at the higher density altitudes. If an aircraft is jetted specifically to a high altitude and/or warm temperatures, and that aircraft goes back to sea level or cold ambient air temperatures, the jets should be changed back to the factory-set sea-level conditions, or too lean a mixture could result, possibly causing engine damage.

7. **How many jetting systems are typically in a two-stroke carburetor?**

    Three jetting systems, depending on engine power typically idle, mid-range, and full power.

    Idle—When the throttle is closed, for engine idling, the throttle valve is closed and the fuel is supplied through the idle (pilot) jet and idle (pilot) air passage. The fuel/air mixture is supplied to the cylinders through the bypass hole.

    Mid-range—As the throttle is advanced and the throttle valve is raised, the fuel is sucked up through the main jet but is controlled by the opening and taper of the jet needle and needle jet. This is effective throughout most of the mid-range operation.

    Full throttle—About half throttle, the main jet size starts to influence the amount of fuel mixed with the air; this effect continues until it is the main influence at the highest throttle settings.

8. **Describe the lubrication system of a two-stroke engine.**

    Two-stroke engines mix the oil with the gas to provide engine lubrication. As the oil/fuel mixture is drawn in through the crankcase, it lubricates the crank, connecting rods and pistons. It is most important to use the oil specified in the POH for the specific engine.

9. **What are the two options for two-cycle oil and fuel mixing?**

    The oil can be automatically mixed with the gas as it is injected into the engine (oil injection) or the oil is premixed with the fuel by the pilot/operator before it is put into the fuel tank.

10. **What is the typical two-stroke premixing ratio?**

    Premixing oil is typically 50 parts gas to 1 part oil (mixing ratio of 50 to 1) unless specified differently in the POH.

11. **Describe an oil injection system.**

    The oil injection system injects the proper amount of oil needed for different power settings which is about 200 to 1 mixture ratio at idle, to 50 to 1 mixture ratio at full power. This reduces carbon buildup in the cylinders, and uses less oil. The operator does not have to measure and premix the oil with the gasoline. The oil tank is filled when needed.

12. **What additional oil systems are used on two-stroke engines?**

    Some two-stroke engines have oil systems for specific systems, such as a rotary valve oil system used on the Rotax 582 and 618.

13. **What are the advantages and disadvantages of premix verses oil injection?**

    Premixing oil rather than oil injection has the advantages of fewer moving parts on the engine, cleaner looking with fewer tanks on top of engine, less weight without carrying the extra oil and system parts, plus less initial expense. Oil injection has the advantages of less oil use, and less carbon buildup due to better oil mixtures at lower RPM.

14. Why is a tuned exhaust system needed for a two-stroke engine?

The length and diameter of the exhaust system is designed to provide a pressure wave that acts as a valve for the exhaust port. After the exhaust has exited the combustion chamber, a precisely timed pressure echo or pressure wave seals the exhaust port so the fuel can enter the combustion chamber and minimize the flow of the fuel out the exhaust.

This tuned exhaust system is important to provide the rated power for the engine. An exhaust system not properly tuned for a two-stroke engine will reduce the engine power significantly and burn more fuel. This requires specific design for each engine. Most packaged engine systems already have tuned systems.

15. What adjustments must be made if an intake silencer is added or removed?

The carburetor must be adjusted. Silencer added is more air restriction and smaller jet required (which has the advantage of less engine noise and quieter operation and the disadvantage of a slight loss in power). Silencer removed requires a larger jet.

Flight Instruments

1. What flight instruments do you have?

Altimeter, vertical speed indicator, airspeed indicator, magnetic compass, GPS (airplanes may also have a ball or inclinometer for rudder coordination).

2. What instruments operate from air pressure and are part of the pitot/static system? (FAA-H-8083-25)

Altimeter, vertical speed, and airspeed indicator.

3. How does an altimeter work? (FAA-H-8083-25)

Aneroid wafers expand and contract as atmospheric pressure changes, and through a shaft and gear linkage rotate pointers on the dial of the instrument.

4. What are the limitations of a pressure altimeter? (FAA-H-8083-25)

a. Nonstandard pressure and temperature; temperature variations expand or contract the atmosphere and raise or lower pressure levels that the altimeter senses.

b. On a warm day the pressure level is higher than on a standard day. The altimeter indicates lower than actual altitude.

c. On a cold day the pressure level is lower than on a standard day. The altimeter indicates higher than actual altitude.

d. Changes in surface pressure also affect pressure levels at altitude:

- Higher than standard pressure—The pressure level is higher than on a standard day. The altimeter indicates lower than actual altitude.

- Lower than standard pressure—The pressure level is lower than on a standard day. The altimeter indicates higher than actual altitude.

High to low or hot to cold, look out below!

5. **Define and state how you would determine the following altitudes:**

Absolute altitude—the vertical distance of an aircraft above the terrain.

Indicated altitude—the altitude read directly from the altimeter (uncorrected) after it is set to the current altimeter setting.

Pressure altitude—the altitude when the altimeter setting window is adjusted to 29.92. Pressure altitude is used for computer solutions to determine density altitude, true altitude, true airspeed, etc.

True altitude—the true vertical distance of the aircraft above sea level. Airport, terrain, and obstacle elevations found on aeronautical charts are true altitudes.

Density altitude—pressure altitude corrected for nonstandard temperature variations. Directly related to an aircraft's takeoff, climb, and landing performance.

Airspeed Indicator

Airspeed measurement is required for airplanes and weight-shift control only. The following 4 questions could be asked if a PPC is equipped with an airspeed indicator:

1. **How does the airspeed indicator operate?** (FAA-H-8083-25)

   The airspeed indicator is a sensitive, differential pressure gauge that measures the difference between impact pressure from the pitot head and undisturbed atmospheric pressure from the static source. The difference is registered by the airspeed pointer on the face of the instrument.

2. **What is the limitation of the airspeed indicator?** (FAA-H-8083-25)

   The airspeed indicator is subject to proper flow of air in the pitot/static system.

3. **What are the errors of the airspeed indicator?**

   Position error—Caused by the static ports sensing erroneous static pressure; slipstream flow causes disturbances at the static port preventing actual atmospheric pressure measurement. It varies with airspeed, altitude and configuration, and may be a plus or minus value.

   Density error—Changes in altitude and temperature are not compensated for by the instrument.

4. **What are the different types of aircraft speeds?** (FAA-H-8083-25)

   Indicated airspeed (IAS)—read off the instrument.

   Calibrated airspeed (CAS)—IAS corrected for instrument and position errors; obtained from the POH or off the face of the instrument.

   True airspeed (TAS)—CAS corrected for nonstandard temperature and pressure; obtained from the flight computer or POH. Usually higher than indicated airspeed at higher altitudes.

   Ground speed (GS)—TAS corrected for wind; speed across ground; use the flight computer to calculate, or a GPS to measure in-flight.

5. **Name several important airspeed limitations not marked on the face of the airspeed indicator.** (FAA-H-8083-25)

Airplane and weight-shift control:

Maneuvering speed (V_A)—the "rough air" speed and the maximum speed for abrupt maneuvers. If rough air or severe turbulence is encountered during flight, the airspeed should be reduced to maneuvering speed or less to minimize the stress on the airplane structure.

Best Angle-of-Climb speed (V_X)—important when a short-field takeoff to clear an obstacle is required.

Best Rate-of-Climb speed (V_Y)—the airspeed that will give the pilot the most altitude in a given period of time.

6. **What airspeed limitations apply to the color-coded marking system of the airspeed indicator?** (FAA-H-8083-25)

Airplane and weight-shift control:

Green arc .... Normal operating range
Lower A/S limit green arc .... V_{S1} (stall speed clean or specified configuration)
Upper A/S limit green arc .... V_{NO} (normal operations or maximum structural cruise)
Yellow arc .... Caution Range (operations in smooth air only)
Red line .... V_{NE} (maximum speed to never exceed, or structural damage could occur)

Airplane only

White arc .... Flap operating range
Lower A/S limit white arc .... V_{SO} (stall speed landing configuration)
Upper A/S limit white arc .... V_{FE} (maximum flap extension speed)

Vertical Speed Indicator

The following 2 questions may be asked if an aircraft is equipped with a vertical speed indicator:

1. **How does the vertical speed indicator work?** (FAA-H-8083-25)

The vertical speed indicator (VSI) is a pressure differential instrument. Inside the instrument case is an aneroid very much like the one in an airspeed indicator. Both the inside of this aneroid and the inside of the instrument case are vented to the static system, but the case is vented through a calibrated orifice that causes the pressure inside the case to change more slowly than the pressure inside the aneroid. As the aircraft ascends, the static pressure becomes lower and the pressure inside the case compresses the aneroid, moving the pointer upward, showing a climb and indicating the number of feet per minute the aircraft is ascending.

2. What are the limitations of the vertical speed indicator? (FAA-H-8083-25)

The VSI is not accurate until the aircraft is stabilized. Because of the restriction in airflow to the static line, a 6 to 9 second lag is required to equalize or stabilize the pressures. Sudden or abrupt changes in aircraft attitude will cause erroneous instrument readings as airflow fluctuates over the static port. Both rough control technique and turbulent air result in unreliable needle indications.

Magnetic Compass

The following 3 questions may be asked if an aircraft is equipped with a magnetic compass:

1. How does the magnetic compass work? (FAA-H-8083-25)

Magnetized needles fastened to a float assembly, around which is mounted a compass card align themselves parallel to the Earth's lines of magnetic force.

2. What limitations does the magnetic compass have? (FAA-H-8083-25)

The float assembly of the compass is balanced on a pivot, which allows free rotation of the card, and allows it to tilt at an angle up to 18 degrees.

3. What are the various compass errors? (FAA-H-8083-25)

Oscillation error—Erratic movement of the compass card caused by turbulence or rough control technique.

Deviation error—Due to electrical and magnetic disturbances in the aircraft.

Variation error—Angular difference between true and magnetic north; reference isogonic lines of variation.

Dip errors:
Acceleration error—On east or west headings, while accelerating, the magnetic compass shows a turn to the north, and when decelerating, it shows a turn to the south.

Remember: ANDS

A ccelerate
N orth
D ecelerate
S outh

Northerly turning error—The compass leads in the south half of a turn, and lags in the north half of a turn.

Remember: UNOS

U ndershoot
N orth
O vershoot
S outh

GPS

The following 2 questions may be asked if an aircraft is equipped with a GPS:

1. **What is a GPS, how does it work, and what information does it provide?**
(FAA-H-8083-25)

The GPS is a satellite-based navigation system. In addition to its navigation capabilities, it provides a direct reading of ground speed, a valuable aircraft instrument reading for the sport pilot. Extensive navigation databases for roads and airports are built into a GPS. A database of roads and airports is best for sport pilots. Top of the line aviation GPS units will tell you what airspace you are in, warn you if you are going to fly into some terrain, and provide detailed information on airports.

The space segment is composed of a constellation of satellites orbiting approximately 10,900 NM above the Earth. The operational satellites are often referred to as the GPS constellation. The satellites are not geosynchronous but instead orbit the Earth in periods of approximately 12 hours. Each satellite is equipped with highly stable atomic clocks and transmits a unique code and navigation message. Transmitting in the UHF range means that the signals are virtually unaffected by weather although they are subject to line-of-sight limitations. The satellites must be above the horizon (as seen by the receiver's antenna) to be usable.

The GPS uses longitude and latitude as the basis to establish position every reading. These meridians and parallels are the basis of all navigation.

The GPS provides an accurate ground speed. This is the speed you are moving over the ground, and is valuable information not available directly from an aircraft instrument. It can be used for determining how strong the wind is blowing and from what direction while in flight. If you are flying directly into a 30 MPH headwind and your true airspeed is 30 MPH, you are standing still and the GPS would read 0 ground speed. If you are in a 30 MPH tailwind, and you are flying 30 MPH true airspeed, the GPS would read 60 MPH since you are traveling that speed over the ground.

Navigation with GPS can be as simple as selecting a "waypoint" or destination such as an airport, road intersection, town, remote location, position within a large town, or any location with maps or position with simple lat-long coordinates. You can usually select this on a map, find the location in the GPS database or input the longitude and latitude coordinates into the GPS. Before you take off, selecting this waypoint will provide you the distance directly to the waypoint. The upgraded map units will draw a direct line to follow to the waypoint.

Once en route, it will provide a direct and accurate reading of degrees to fly directly to the waypoint, degrees you are flying, distance to waypoint, and time to reach waypoint flying at the current airspeed and wind conditions.

2. What are the limitations of a GPS? (FAA-H-8083-25)

When using a sophisticated and highly capable aircraft instrument navigation system such as GPS, there is a strong temptation to rely almost exclusively on that unit, to the detriment of using other techniques of position keeping. The prudent pilot will never rely on only one aircraft instrument for navigation, when other common sense sources are available for cross-check and backup. If this is a portable device, batteries must be used; the prudent pilot will carry an extra set of batteries.

Aircraft with Ballistic Parachute Systems

Generally, powered parachutes do not use ballistic parachute systems so these questions are for airplanes and weight-shift control aircraft with these systems.

1. Why is a ballistic parachute system installed on a LSA?

A ballistic parachute system is installed for an added measure of safety. These have been installed on standard category aircraft also.

2. How does a ballistic parachute operate?

When actuated, a rocket pulls a parachute away from the aircraft to full line stretch quickly. The parachute bridle is attached to a secure location on the fuselage for a gentle ride to the ground.

3. How should the ballistic parachute be rigged?

These must be rigged by a professional for proper trajectory of the rocket and chute, and a clear path for the bridle to not become tangled in the airframe. The actuation handle must be rigged to be easily accessible by the pilot, and have minimum curvature in the actuation cable for an easy pull when needed.

4. What is the procedure regarding the engine before using the ballistic parachute?

Shut down the engine before the handle is pulled to minimize the possibility of the system becoming tangled in the propeller.

5. What is an added precaution about having a ballistic parachute system?

Extreme caution must be exercised on the ground and in the air to ensure the system is not accidentally deployed. "Remove before flight" safety pins, proper placement of the handle, and pilot/passenger operational procedures are checklist items to ensure proper operation of this system.

Instructor/Pilot-Rigged Ballistic Parachute Systems

These 3 questions are for instructors and/or pilots who rig their own ballistic parachute system.

1. What are the important elements in rigging the system?

Important rigging elements include handle operation with no sharp turns in the actuation cable, rocket clear firing path, and bridle attached to aircraft to account for descent attitude.

2. What are the possible actuation handle positions and the advantages and disadvantages of each location?

The actuation handle should be located in a way so it cannot be accidentally actuated. It should be located in a position where you can actuate it under high-G loading, and have enough pull to actuate it completely.

3. What are the attachment points for the BRS bridle system and the advantages and disadvantages of each?

If you attach the BRS bridle system near the center of gravity on top then you will come down on your wheels. If you attach it to another location you will descend in another nonlevel condition.

Aircraft with Communication Systems Installed

1. What are the two primary functions for communications in LSA?

Communications within the aircraft between the pilot and passenger, and communications between the pilot and anyone outside the aircraft. These two functions are many times combined into one integrated system.

2. Describe the communication system within the cockpit.

Communications within the aircraft is accomplished with two sets of headphones each with a microphone. The pilot and passenger can have conversations with each other. Sometimes the system will be voice actuated. Many times the system will be noise canceling so the pilot and passenger headphones eliminate much of the engine and air noise to reduce fatigue while flying to make it much more enjoyable to be in the air.

3. Describe the communication system used to broadcast outside the cockpit.

A radio is required for the pilot to communicate with anybody outside the aircraft. The radio can be built into the aircraft or a portable can easily be rigged up to the system. The radio is set to the UNICOM, CTAF, or ATC frequency. The pilot must use the "Push To Talk" (PTT) button to broadcast out on the selected radio frequency. The pilot and passenger will also hear anyone broadcasting on the same frequency.

4. Describe an integrated inside/outside communications system.

Many systems use a radio intercom box to plug all the components into. Some systems have optional CD/tape/video input/outputs and some have optional PTT buttons so both people can broadcast out.

Airplanes

1. **What are the four main control surfaces and what are their functions?** (FAA-H-8083-25)

    Elevators—The elevators control the movement of the airplane about its lateral axis. This motion is called pitch.

    Ailerons—The ailerons control the airplane's movement about its longitudinal axis. This motion is called roll.

    Rudder—The rudder controls movement of the airplane about its vertical axis. This motion is called yaw.

    Trim tabs—Trim tabs are small, adjustable hinged-surfaces on the aileron, rudder, or elevator control surfaces. They are labor-saving devices that enable the pilot to release manual pressure on the primary control.

2. **How are the various flight controls operated?** (AFM)

    The flight control surfaces are manually actuated through use of either a rod or cable system. A control wheel or stick actuates the ailerons and elevator, and rudder/brake pedals actuate the rudder. The trim tabs are set with a trim wheel or manually prior to flight.

3. **What are flaps and what is their function?** (FAA-H-8083-25)

    The wing flaps are movable panels on the inboard trailing edges of the wings. They are hinged so that they may be extended downward into the flow of air beneath the wings to increase both lift and drag. Their purpose is to permit a slower airspeed and a steeper angle of descent during a landing approach. In some cases, they may also be used to shorten the takeoff distance.

4. **How is steering accomplished on the ground?** (AFM)

    Light airplanes are generally provided with nose-wheel steering capabilities through a simple system of mechanical linkage connected to the rudder pedals. When a rudder pedal is depressed, a spring-loaded bungee (push-pull rod) connected to the pivotal portion of a nose-wheel strut will turn the nose-wheel.

5. **What color of dye is added to the following aircraft fuel grades?**
    80, 100, 100LL, Turbine (FAA-H-8083-25)

Grade	Color
80	Red
100	Green
100LL	Blue
Turbine	Colorless

6. **How does the aircraft cabin heat work?** (AFM)

    Fresh air, heated by an exhaust shroud, is directed to the cabin through a series of ducts. Other heating systems can be used for specific aircraft.

7. How does the pilot control temperature in the cabin? (AFM)

Temperature is controlled by mixing outside air (cabin air control) with heated air (cabin heat control) in a manifold near the cabin firewall. This air is then ducted to vents located on the cabin floor.

Weight-Shift Control (WSC)

1. How do you control the pitch, speed and angle of attack of the weight-shift control?

Push the bar out, nose up to create a higher angle of attack, pull the bar in, nose down to create a lower angle of attack.

2. How is the yaw controlled in a weight-shift control aircraft?

There is no yaw control in a weight-shift. It tracks straight with no yaw control needed because of the swept wings and wing twist design.

3. What is the primary roll control system in a weight-shift control aircraft?

When you shift your weight to one side, it loads up the wing where the weight is shifted and increases the twist on that side and decreases the twist on the opposite side. This slows down the less efficient wing with greater twist, and speeds up the more efficient wing with less twist. For example, if you shift your weight to the right, the right wing loads up creating greater washout or twist on the right side, reducing lift and dropping the right wing into a right turn.

A floating crossbar design is commonly used which aids and enhances the wing twisting capabilities and improves the roll control. The crossbar shifts side-to-side, 1–3 inches. This is the system that varies the twist of the wing.

4. How is the weight-shift control wing trimmed to fly different speeds?

There are a number of ways a weight-shift control wing can be trimmed. It is important to follow the manufacturer's recommendation for the specific trim used for each wing.

Many weight-shift control wings allow movement of the hang point forward and backward, typically about 4 inches. This is normally a ground adjustment for trim speed. Moving the hang point forward increases speed, backward decreases speed.

Another ground adjustment for trim is tightening and loosening the hail back cables for the cross-tube. Tightening the cable flattens the wing, decreasing the twist, allowing the wing to be more efficient because the tips produce more lift. In this configuration the wing angle of attack is more constant and therefore more efficient. This lowers the nose and increases the speed. With the wing tighter, the wing does not respond as easy to roll control and is stiffer. This can be an advantage for cross-country flight but the decreased maneuverability is not as desirable for takeoffs and landings. A stiffer wing with less twist (washout) is less forgiving in stall, but is used for high-performance wings.

A popular inflight trim adjustment is the raising and lowering of the luff lines (also called reflex lines). This is accomplished through a cable that runs from the top of the king post to a control on the down tube where the pilot can adjust the tension in flight. Tightening the tension, raises the trailing edge of the wing and slows the wing, less tension lowers the training edge and increases the speed.

5. **What systems on a flex wing create a nose-up force when the nose of the wing is at a zero angle of attack? (Such as from a severe dive, which could happen as a result of a whip stall, power-on stall, and/or severe turbulence.)**

Luff lines (reflex cables) hold the middle-of-wing trailing edge up when it is unloaded at zero or negative angles of attack, creating a reflex and a positive force to bring the nose up and increase the angle of attack back to normal loading and flying position.

Washout tubes maintain the twist/washout of the wing at negative angles of attack, creating a downward force at the tips in back of the center of gravity. This rotates the nose up, where it can obtain some positive angle of attack in order to pull the nose up to a normal flying attitude.

Both systems keep the trailing edge up, creating a positive stability in order to raise the nose in this situation.

Powered Parachute (PPC)

1. **How do you turn a PPC?**

The PPC turns by pulling down the back of the trailing edge to turn it in that direction by pulling down on the control line or pushing on the steering bar. This pulls down the trailing edge, creating more drag on that side, rolls/turn the wing in that direction.

2. **During flight, what will advancing the thrust do?**

Throttle controls vertical speed in a PPC. Advancing the throttle will produce decreased descent rates or increased climb rates. Speed in a PPC in normal flight is controlled by the weight and not the throttle.

3. **How is the torque effect of an engine that rotates clockwise in a powered parachute counteracted?**

A clockwise or right-turning propeller when viewed from the rear creates an opposite reaction to turn the undercarriage aircraft to the left. Therefore, a slight right-hand turn needs to be built into the aircraft to accommodate for this torque. Many designs are used by manufacturers to accomplish this. Decreasing the length of the right-hand riser will accomplish this by bringing the right hand side of the wing down slightly.

4. **Describe the steering bars.**

The steering bars are your main control to turning in flight. Pushing on the right-hand steering bar will pull the right-hand control line, lower the trailing edge of the right-hand wing, create more drag on the right-hand side and turn the aircraft to the right.

5. What is the purpose of the fan guard that surrounds the propeller?

To protect the parachute lines from hitting the prop.

6. What do cross-ports in the parachute ribs do?

Cross-ports in the wing ribs allow air to flow sideways from cell to cell, called cross flow in the wing. This results in the cells next to each other to transfer pressure inside the wing and cells to pressurize neighboring cells.

7. How is yaw controlled in a PPC?

There is no yaw control in a PPC. It is designed to track straight with no yaw control needed.

8. How is pitch controlled in a PPC?

There is no pitch control for a PPC. The angle of attack is set by the factory. Because of this, there is no significant speed control for the wing except for pulling both trailing edges down simultaneously—which is typically used only for landing.

9. What is the trim control system on a PPC?

There is not normally a trim system for a PPC. Some trim systems are available which can increase the angle of attack or decrease the angle of attack by changing the length of the lines proportionally front and back, but it is uncommon. Other PPC may have separate trim systems for each riser to trim out the torque.

• •

G. Aeromedical Factors

Tips

- You will be required to answer three of the nine items listed below, so you must be prepared to discuss any of them—read, study and understand how to answer these questions.

• •

Questions—Aeromedical Factors

1. **What are the effects of alcohol, drugs, and over-the-counter medications?** (FAA-H-8083-25)

   Any alcohol, drug, or over-the-counter medication will degrade pilot performance. Avoid flying with any of these. If you are sick, simply decide not to fly.

2. **What are the symptoms, causes, effects, and corrective actions of the following?** (FAA-H-8083-25)

   a. hypoxia

   b. hyperventilation

   c. middle ear and sinus problems

   d. spatial disorientation

   e. motion sickness

   f. carbon monoxide poisoning

   g. stress and fatigue

   h. dehydration

   i. hypothermia

   a. *Hypoxia*—Headache, drowsiness, dizziness, and euphoria are symptoms of oxygen deficiency that impairs functions of the brain during flight at higher altitudes than normally acclimated to. Correct by using oxygen or reducing altitude.

   b. *Hyperventilation*—Symptoms are rapid or extra deep breathing caused by a deficiency of carbon dioxide in the body. Caused by emotional tension, anxiety, or fear with unusual deep or rapid breathing. Correct by controlling/reducing rate and depth of breathing.

   c. *Middle ear and sinus problems*—The middle ear analyzes sound from the eardrum, and is sealed off from the outer ear by the eardrum. It is filled with air and connected to the throat through a tube that equalizes the pressure. Climbing more easily allows the pressure to equalize through the tube; but descending, the air does not escape and equalize as easily. Quick descents can cause pressure on the eardrum and result in pain. Yawning, chewing gum, or swallowing helps open the tubes to allow the pressure to equalize easier. Extreme measures are closing your mouth, holding your nose, and blowing to force the air up into the middle ear.

Continued

Sinus problems, throat infections, flu, or colds block the tube and make matters worse to the point of extreme pain with eardrum rupture possible. Flying with sinus problems should therefore be avoided.

d. *Spatial disorientation*—Symptoms include misleading information being sent to the brain about actual flight attitude from complex motions, forces and visual scenes by sensory organs. Keeping a visual horizon reference or using the appropriate instruments (if available) is the best way to correct and prevent, rather than relying on your feeling to determine flight attitude.

e. *Motion sickness*—Symptoms are nausea and lack of balance caused by the unnatural motion of continued bumps, spirals, turns, or basic vibration or jogging of the aircraft. The inner ear which controls the sense of balance causes this. Factors such as anxiety, unfamiliarity, and particularly looking down at something or reading, rather than looking out at the horizon are causes. Stuffy or claustrophobic conditions can also be contributors. Preventative and corrective actions are fresh air, reducing motion if possible, looking out at the horizon, loosening clothing, and avoiding unnecessary head movements. Landing as soon as possible is the best way to recover, since it is difficult to overcome during flight.

f. *Carbon monoxide poisoning*—Symptoms are headache, drowsiness, and dizziness. It is odorless, colorless, and a tasteless gas contained in exhaust fumes. Susceptibility increases with altitude. Causes loss of muscular power. Correct by reducing exhaust gasses by opening windows, shutting off heater, or breathing fresh air.

g. *Mental stress*—Mental upsets or general problems from work, finances, family, or friends can create anger, worry and anxiety. This can hinder good judgment, decisions, perception, and the ability to concentrate on the tasks necessary for safe aviation. Simply not flying is the best action for stress. However, the pilot's ability to turn off the world, and focus on flying exclusively can be a stress reliever *if* the pilot can accomplish this, otherwise flying can add to the stress and cause bad decisions, quicker panic, and catastrophic results. Healthy physical and mental life management is the best stress reliever.

Physical fatigue—Lack of sleep, unhealthy physical condition, and not eating properly are factors that contribute to fatigue before you leave the ground. Fatigue will grow over the flight especially with noise, physical discomfort, high altitude, eyestrain, workload and stress. Being in good physical and mental condition before flight and creating a comfortable environment while flying can reduce fatigue.

h. *Dehydration*—Symptoms are fatigue which progresses to dizziness, weakness, nausea, tingling of the hands and feet, abdominal cramps, and extreme thirst. It is a lack of water in the body. Caused by flying long periods in hot summer temperatures or at high altitudes and not drinking water. Can be prevented and corrected by drinking water.

i. *Hypothermia*— Cold temperatures for long periods reduce the inner body core temperature when the heat produced by the body is less than the amount of heat being lost to the body's surroundings. This loss of heat is highly accelerated in open cockpits with wind chill. The first symptom is being cold and continues with weakness, shivering, and lack of physical control, slurred speech followed by unconsciousness and death. Dressing warmly and/or aircraft heating systems to remain warm during flight avoid this problem. Carrying an appropriate survival kit prepares you against hypothermia if you are forced down in cold temperatures.

• •

H. Performance and Limitations

Tips

- Study the areas that apply to your aircraft
- Have the weight and balance information on your aircraft for the checkride, including any limitations such as:

  What is the maximum passenger weight you can carry with full fuel? _____

  What are the critical airspeeds of your aircraft? _____
- You need to be proficient in your own aircraft, and in the aircraft you will use for the test.

Checklist

- ☐ Performance data and limitations sheet
- ☐ Total weight within limits
- ☐ Balance within limits for complete flight
- ☐ Density altitude performance:
  - takeoff distance and clearance over objects on takeoff.
  - climb rate performance acceptable for flight situations.
- ☐ Takeoff, clearance over 50-foot obstacle takeoff and landing performance within limitations considering density altitude and condition of the runway.
- ☐ Performance within aircraft capabilities and operating limitations for complete flight including fuel burned with reserves, speed, altitude and climb rates required for complete flight with diversions.

Questions—Performance and Limitations

Not all the questions in this section are applicable to all pilots—they are broken down further into groups applicable to the different operations and the category of aircraft:

- All Sport Pilots
- Fixed Wing Airplanes (AIR) only
- Weight-Shift Control (WSC) only
- Powered Parachute (PPC) only

For All Sport Pilots

1. **Define the following:** (FAA-H-8083-25)

   Empty weight—The airframe, engine, and all items of operating equipment that have fixed locations and are permanently installed in the aircraft. Includes hydraulic fluid, unusable fuel, and undrainable oil.

   Gross weight—The maximum allowable weight of both the airplane and its contents.

   Useful load—The weight of the pilot, copilot, passengers, baggage, usable fuel and drainable oil.

   Center of gravity—The point about which an aircraft would balance if it were possible to suspend it at that point.

2. **What performance characteristics will be adversely affected when an aircraft has been highly loaded or overloaded?** (FAA-H-8083-1)

   a. Higher takeoff speed
   b. Longer takeoff run
   c. Reduced rate and angle of climb
   d. Lower maximum altitude
   e. Shorter range
   f. Reduced cruising speed
   g. Reduced maneuverability
   h. Higher stalling speed
   i. Higher landing speed
   j. Longer landing roll
   k. Excessive weight on the nose-wheel

3. What are the standard weights assumed for the following when calculating weight and balance problems? (FAA-H-8083-25)

Crew and passengers .... 170 lbs each
Gasoline .... 6 lbs/U.S. gal
Oil .... 7.5 lbs/U.S. gal
Water .... 8.35 lbs/U.S. gal

4. What are some of the main elements of aircraft performance? (FAA-H-8083-25)

a. Takeoff and landing distance

b. Rate of climb

c. Ceiling

d. Payload

e. Range

f. Speed

g. Fuel economy

5. What factors affect the performance of an aircraft during takeoffs and landings? (FAA-H-8083-25)

a. Air density (density altitude)

b. Surface wind

c. Runway surface

d. Upslope or downslope of runway

e. Weight

6. What effect does wind have on aircraft performance? (FAA-H-8083-25)

Takeoff—a headwind will increase the airplane performance by shortening the take-off distance and increasing the angle of climb. However, a tailwind will decrease performance by increasing the takeoff distance and reducing the angle of climb. The decrease in airplane performance must be carefully considered before a downwind takeoff is attempted.

Landing—a headwind will increase airplane performance by steepening the approach angle and reducing the landing distance. A tailwind will decrease performance by decreasing the approach angle and increasing the landing distance. Again, the pilot must take the wind into consideration prior to landing.

Cruise flight—winds aloft have somewhat an opposite effect on airplane performance. A headwind will decrease performance by reducing ground speed, which in turn increases the fuel requirement for the flight. A tailwind will increase performance by increasing the ground speed, which in turn reduces the fuel requirement for the flight.

7. How does weight affect takeoff performance? (FAA-H-8083-25)

Increased gross weight can have a significant effect on takeoff performance:

a. Higher liftoff speed;

b. Greater mass to accelerate (slow acceleration);

c. Increased retarding force (drag and ground friction); and

d. Longer takeoff distance.

8. How does weight affect landing performance? (FAA-H-8083-25)

The effect of gross weight on landing distance is that the airplane will require a greater speed to support the airplane at the landing angle of attack and lift coefficient resulting in an increased landing distance. The aircraft also has a higher descent rate for the same power setting.

9. How is rate of climb (ROC) calculated with added weight?

The rate of climb for an aircraft is directly proportional to the weight added.

Simply, $ROC^2 = ROC^1 (Total\ Weight^1 / Total\ Weight^2)$

10. What is "density altitude"? (FAA-H-8083-25)

Density altitude is pressure altitude corrected for nonstandard temperature. Under standard atmospheric condition, air at each level in the atmosphere has a specific density, and under standard conditions, pressure altitude and density altitude identify the same level. Therefore, density altitude is the vertical distance above sea level in the standard atmosphere at which a given density is found.

11. How does air density affect aircraft performance? (FAA-H-8083-25)

The density of the air has a direct effect on:

a. Lift produced by the wings;

b. Power output of the engine;

c. Propeller efficiency; and

d. Drag forces.

12. What factors affect air density? (FAA-P-8740-2)

Altitude—the higher the altitude, the less dense the air.

Temperature—the warmer the air, the less dense it is.

Humidity—more humid air is less dense.

13. How do temperature, altitude, and humidity affect density altitude? (FAA-P-8740-2)

Density altitude will increase (low air density) when one or more of the following occurs:

- High air temperature
- High altitude
- High humidity

Density altitude will decrease (high air density) when one or more of the following occurs:

- Low air temperature
- Low altitude
- Low humidity

14. What effect does an increase in density altitude have on takeoff and landing performance? (FAA-P-8740-2)

An increase in density altitude results in:

a. Increased takeoff distance (greater takeoff TAS required).

b. Reduced rate of climb (decreased thrust and reduced acceleration).

c. Increased true airspeed on approach and landing (same IAS).

d. Increased landing roll distance.

15. What important takeoff performance information is typically found in POH graphs/tables for specific aircraft under different weight and density altitude situations? (AFM)

- Normal takeoff ground-run in feet
- Obstacle clearance (50 feet) ground-run in feet

16. What important climb performance information is typically found in POH graphs/tables for specific aircraft under different weight and density altitude situations? (AFM)

- Rate of climb under various conditions
- Best climb airspeed under various conditions
- Cruise performance charts

17. What is "pressure altitude" and why is it important? (FAA-H-8083-25)

This is the altitude indicated when the altimeter setting window (barometric scale) is adjusted to 29.92. This is the altitude above the standard datum plane, a theoretical plane where air pressure (corrected to 15°C) equals 29.92 in. Hg. Pressure altitude is used to compute density altitude, true altitude, true airspeed, and other performance data.

18. **The following questions may be asked by the examiner and are designed to provide pilots with a general review of the basic information they should know about their specific aircraft before taking a flight check or review. (AFM)**

    What is the make and horsepower of the engine? _____   _____

    How many usable gallons of fuel can you carry? _____

    Where are the fuel tanks located, and what are their capacities? _____
    _____

    Where are the fuel vents for your aircraft? _____

    What is the octane rating of the fuel used by your aircraft? _____

    Where are the fuel sumps located on your aircraft? _____

    (4-stroke) What are the minimum and maximum oil capacities? _____
    _____

    (2-stroke premix) What is the mixing ratio? _____

    What oil is being used? _____

    (4-stroke) What is the maximum oil temperature and pressure? _____

    What is the nosewheel turning limitations for your aircraft? _____

    What is the maximum allowable crosswind component for the aircraft? _____

    What is the maximum allowable weight for the aircraft? _____

    What takeoff distance is required for standard conditions? _____

    What is your maximum allowable useful load? _____

19. **Airplane and weight-shift control basic information.**

    What is the normal climb-out speed? _____

    What is the best rate-of-climb speed? _____

    What is the best angle-of-climb speed? _____

    What is the stall speed in the normal landing configuration? _____

    What is the stall speed in the clean configuration? _____

    What is the normal approach-to-land speed? _____

    What is maneuvering speed? _____

    What is red-line speed? _____

    What engine-out glide speed will give you maximum range? _____

    (Airplane only) What is the maximum flap extension speed? _____

20. **Solve a weight and balance problem for the flight you plan to make with one passenger at 170 pounds.**

    Does your load fall within the weight envelope for the conditions? _____

    (Airplane only) Does your load fall within the balance envelope? _____

    What is the final gross weight? _____

    How much fuel can be carried? _____

    How much baggage can be carried with full fuel? _____

For Fixed Wing Airplanes

1. **Define the following:** (FAA-H-8083-25)

   Arm—The horizontal distance in inches from the reference datum line to the center of gravity of the item.

   Moment—The product of the weight of an item multiplied by its arm. Moments are expressed in pound-inches.

   Center of gravity—The point about which an aircraft would balance if it were possible to suspend it at that point. Expressed in inches from datum.

   Datum—An imaginary vertical plane or line from which all measurements of arm are taken. Established by the manufacturer.

2. **What basic equation is used in all weight and balance problems to find the center of gravity location of an airplane and/or its components?** (FAA-H-8083-25)

   Weight x Arm = Moment

   By rearrangement of this equation to the forms:

   Weight = Moment ÷ Arm

   $$\text{Arm (CG)} = \frac{\text{(Total) Moment}}{\text{(Total) Weight}}$$

   With any two known values, the third value can be found.

   Remember: **W A M** (Weight x Arm = Moment)

3. **What effect does a forward center of gravity have on an aircraft's flight characteristics?** (FAA-H-8083-25)

   Higher stall speed—stalling angle of attack is reached at a higher speed due to increased wing loading.

   Slower cruise speed—increased drag; greater angle of attack is required to maintain altitude.

   More stable—the center of gravity is farther forward from the center of pressure which increases longitudinal stability.

   Greater back elevator pressure required—longer takeoff roll; higher approach speeds and problems with landing flare.

4. **What effect does a rearward center of gravity have on an aircraft's flight characteristics?** (FAA-H-8083-25)

   Lower stall speed—less wing loading.

   Higher cruise speed—reduced drag; smaller angle of attack is required to maintain altitude.

   Less stable—stall and spin recovery more difficult; the center of gravity is closer to the center of pressure, causing longitudinal instability.

For Weight-Shift Control

1. What are the balance requirements for your aircraft?

The passenger seat is normally designed to be directly under the hang point of the wing. Therefore, no adjustments are normally required for flying alone or with two people or different passenger weights. The POH provides different hang points for different speeds and loadings. A forward hang point is a faster trim speed, an aft hang point is a slower trim speed. The POH specifies what loading can be used for what trim positions.

For Powered Parachute

1. What are the balance requirements for your aircraft?

The passenger seat is designed to be directly under the hang point of the wing. Therefore, no adjustments are normally required for flying alone or two people or different passenger weights. The POH provides different hang points for different front seat pilot weights. With less pilot weight up front, the hang point moves back. With more pilot/front seat weight, the hang point moves forward to keep the carriage level (nose not too high or too low).

· ·

I. Principles of Flight

This section covers basic aerodynamics.

Tips

- Study the areas that apply to your aircraft.
- You need to be proficient in your own aircraft, and in the aircraft you will use for the test.

Checklist

- ☐ Axis or rotation, forces of flight (lift, drag, weight, thrust)
- ☐ Stability
- ☐ Turns, loads and load factors
- ☐ Angle of attack, stalls and spin avoidance/recovery
- ☐ Ground effect
- ☐ Wake turbulence understanding and avoidance
- ☐ Torque effect
- ☐ Primary and secondary flight controls effects and technique

Questions—Principles of Flight

Not all the questions in this section are applicable to all pilots—they are broken down further into groups applicable to the different operations and the category of aircraft. Study only the questions that apply to you and your intended operations:

- All Sport Pilots
- Fixed Wing Airplanes (AIR) only
- Weight-Shift Control (WSC) only
- Powered Parachute (PPC) only

For All Sport Pilots

1. **What are the four dynamic forces that act on an airplane during all maneuvers?** (FAA-H-8083-25)

   Lift—the upward acting force

   Gravity—or weight, the downward acting force

   Thrust—the forward acting force

   Drag—the backward acting force

2. **What flight condition will result in the sum of the opposing forces being equal?** (FAA-H-8083-25)

   In steady-state, straight-and-level, unaccelerated flight, the sum of the opposing forces is equal to zero. There can be no unbalanced forces in steady, straight flight (Newton's Third Law). This is true whether flying level or when climbing or descending. This simply means that the opposing forces are equal to, and thereby cancel the effects of each other.

3. **What is an airfoil? State some examples.** (FAA-H-8083-25)

   An airfoil is a device that gets a useful reaction from air moving over its surface, namely *lift*. Wings, horizontal tail surfaces, vertical tail surfaces, and propellers are examples of airfoils.

4. **What is the "angle of incidence"?** (FAA-H-8083-25)

   The angle of incidence is the angle formed by the longitudinal axis of the airplane and the chord of the wing. It is measured by the angle at which the wing is attached to the fuselage. The angle of incidence is fixed and cannot be changed by the pilot for airplanes and powered parachutes, but it is typically changed for pitch control by the weight-shift pilot.

5. **What is a "relative wind"?** (FAA-H-8083-25)

   The relative wind is the direction of the airflow with respect to the wing. When a wing is moving forward and downward the relative wind moves backward and upward. The flight path and relative wind are always parallel but travel in opposite directions.

6. **What is the "angle of attack"?** (FAA-H-8083-25)

    The angle of attack is the angle between the wing chordline and the direction of the relative wind.

7. **What is "Bernoulli's Principle"?** (FAA-H-8083-25)

    The pressure of a fluid (liquid or gas) decreases at points where the speed of the fluid increases. In the case of airflow, high speed flow is associated with low pressure and low speed flow with high pressure. The airfoil of an aircraft is designed to increase the velocity of the airflow above its surface, thereby decreasing pressure above the airfoil. Simultaneously, the impact of the air on the lower surface of the airfoil increases the pressure below. This combination of pressure decrease above and increase below produces lift.

8. **What are several factors that will affect both lift and drag?**

    Wing area—Lift and drag acting on a wing are roughly proportional to the wing area. A pilot can change wing area by using certain types of flaps (i.e., Fowler flaps, in airplanes).

    Shape of the airfoil—As the upper curvature of an airfoil is increased (up to a certain point) the lift produced increases. Lowering an aileron or flap device can accomplish this. Also, ice or frost on a wing can disturb normal airflow, changing its camber, and disrupting its lifting capability.

    Angle of attack—As angle of attack is increased, both lift and drag are increased, up to a certain point.

    Velocity of the air—An increase in velocity of air passing over the wing increases lift and drag.

    Air density—Lift and drag vary directly with the density of the air. As air density increases, lift and drag increase. As air density decreases, lift and drag decrease. Air density is affected by these factors: pressure, temperature, and humidity.

9. **What is "torque effect"?** (FAA-H-8083-25)

    Torque effect involves Newton's Third Law of Physics—for every action, there is an equal and opposite reaction. Applied to the aircraft, this means that as the internal engine parts and the propeller are revolving in one direction, an equal force is trying to rotate the aircraft in the opposite direction. It is greatest when at low airspeeds with high power settings and a high angle of attack.

10. **What effect does torque reaction have on an aircraft on the ground and in flight?** (FAA-H-8083-25)

    In flight—torque reaction is acting around the longitudinal axis, tending to make the aircraft roll. To compensate, some of the older airplanes are rigged in a manner to create more lift on the wing that is being forced downward. The more modern aircraft are designed with the engine offset to counteract this effect of torque. Some of the powered parachutes lower the right wing slightly to account for torque. Each LSA manufacturer uses a different approach to account for torque, if it is built into the design.

On the ground—during the takeoff roll, an additional turning moment around the vertical axis is induced by torque reaction. As the left side of the aircraft is being forced down by torque reaction, more weight is being placed on the left main landing gear. This results in more ground friction on the left tire than on the right, causing a left turning moment.

11. What are the factors that contribute to torque effect? (FAA-H-8083-25)

Torque reaction of the engine and propeller. For every action there is an equal and opposite reaction. The rotation of the propeller (from the cockpit) to the right tends to roll or bank the aircraft to the left.

Gyroscopic effect of the propeller. Gyroscopic precession applies here—the resultant action or deflection of a spinning object when a force is applied to the outer rim of its rotational mass. If the axis of a propeller is tilted, the resulting force will be exerted 90° ahead in the direction of rotation and in the same direction as the applied force. It is most noticeable on takeoffs in taildraggers when the tail is raised.

Airplanes only. Corkscrewing effect of the propeller slipstream. High-speed rotation of an airplane propeller results in a corkscrewing rotation to the slipstream as it moves rearward. At high propeller speeds and low forward speeds (as in a takeoff), the slipstream strikes the vertical tail surface on the left side pushing the tail to the right and yawing the airplane to the left.

Asymmetrical loading of the propeller (P-Factor). When an airplane is flying with a high angle of attack, the bite of the downward moving propeller blade is greater than the bite of the upward moving blade. This is due to the downward moving blade meeting the oncoming relative wind at a greater angle of attack than the upward moving blade. Consequently there is greater thrust on the downward moving blade on the right side, and this forces the aircraft to yaw to the left.

12. What is "centrifugal force"? (FAA-H-8083-25)

Centrifugal force is the "equal and opposite reaction" of the airplane to the change in direction, and it acts "equal and opposite" to the horizontal component of lift.

13. What is "load factor"? (FAA-H-8083-25)

Load factor is the ratio of the total load supported by the airplane's wing to the actual weight of the airplane and its contents. In other words, it is the actual load supported by the wings divided by the total weight of the airplane. It can also be expressed as the ratio of a given load to the pull of gravity; i.e., to refer to a load factor of three as "3 Gs." In this case the weight of the airplane is equal to 1 G, and if a load of three times the actual weight of the airplane were imposed upon the wing due to curved flight, the load factor would be equal to 3 Gs.

14. For what two reasons is load factor important to pilots? (FAA-H-8083-25)

    a. The dangerous overload that is possible for a pilot to impose on the aircraft structure.

    b. An increased load factor increases the stalling speed and makes stalls possible at seemingly safe flight speeds.

15. What situations may result in load factors reaching the maximum or being exceeded? (FAA-H-8083-25)

Level turns—The load factor increases at a terrific rate after a bank has reached 45° or 50°. The load factor in a 60°-bank turn is 2 Gs. The load factor in an 80°-bank turn is 5.76 Gs. The wing must produce lift equal to these load factors if altitude is to be maintained.

Turbulence—Severe vertical gusts cause a sudden increase in angle of attack, resulting in large loads which are resisted by the inertia of the aircraft.

Speed—The amount of excess load that can be imposed upon the wing depends on how fast the airplane is flying. At speeds below maneuvering speed, the airplane will stall before the load factor can become excessive. At speeds above maneuvering speed, the limit load factor for which an airplane is stressed can be exceeded by abrupt or excessive application of the controls or by strong turbulence.

16. What effect does an increase in load factor have on stalling speed? (FAA-H-8083-25)

As load factor increases, stalling speed increases. Any aircraft wing can be stalled at any airspeed within the limits of its structure and the strength of the pilot. At a given airspeed the load factor increases as angle of attack increases, and the wing stalls because the angle of attack has been increased to a certain angle. Therefore, there is a direct relationship between the load factor imposed upon the wing and its stalling characteristics. A rule for determining the speed at which a wing will stall is that the stalling speed increases in proportion to the square root of the load factor.

17. Define the term "maneuvering speed." (FAA-H-8083-3)

Maneuvering speed is the maximum speed at which abrupt control movement can be applied or at which the airplane could be flown in turbulence without exceeding design load factor limits. When operating below this speed, a damaging positive flight load should not be produced because the aircraft should stall before the load becomes excessive.

18. Discuss the effect on maneuvering speed of an increase or decrease in weight. (FAA-H-8083-25)

Maneuvering speed increases with an increase in weight and decreases with a decrease in weight. An aircraft operating at a reduced weight is more vulnerable to rapid accelerations encountered during flight through turbulence or gusts. Design limit load factors could be exceeded if a reduction in maneuvering speed is not accomplished. An aircraft operating at or near gross weight in turbulent air is much less likely to exceed design limit load factors and may be operated at the published maneuvering speed for gross weight if necessary.

19. What causes an aircraft wing to stall? (FAA-H-8083-25)

A wing stalls when the critical angle of attack has been exceeded. When the angle of attack increases to approximately 18° to 20°, the air can no longer flow smoothly over the top wing surface. Because the airflow cannot make such a great change in direction so quickly, it becomes impossible for the air to follow the contour of the wing. This is the stalling or critical angle of attack. This can occur at any airspeed, in any attitude, with any power setting.

20. What is "ground effect"? (FAA-H-8083-3)

Ground effect is a condition of improved performance an aircraft experiences when it is operating near the ground. A change occurs in the three-dimensional flow pattern around the wing because the airflow around the wing is restricted by the ground surface. This reduces the wing's upwash, downwash, and wingtip vortices. In order for ground effect to be of a significant magnitude, the wing must be quite close to the ground.

This has little effect for PPC because the wing is so high off the ground. This has some effect for WSC since the wing is lower but still relatively high in relation to its wingspan. It has the largest effect for airplanes, especially low-wing designs.

21. What major problems can be caused by ground effect, especially for low-wing airplanes? (FAA-H-8083-3)

During landing, at a height of approximately one-tenth of a wingspan above the surface, drag may be 40 percent less than when the airplane is operating out of ground effect. Therefore, any excess speed during the landing phase may result in a significant float distance. In such cases, if the pilot does not exercise care, he/she may run out of runway and options at the same time.

During takeoff, due to the reduced drag in ground effect, the aircraft is capable of takeoff well below the recommended speed. However, as the airplane rises out of ground effect with a deficiency of speed, the greater induced drag may result in very marginal climb performance, or the inability of the airplane to fly at all. In extreme conditions, such as high temperature, high gross weight, and high density altitude, the airplane may become airborne initially with a deficiency of speed and then settle back to the runway.

For Fixed Wing Airplanes

1. What is a "spin"? (FAA-H-8083-25)

A spin in a small airplane or glider is a controlled (recoverable) or uncontrolled (possibly unrecoverable) maneuver in which the airplane or glider descends in a helical path while flying at an angle of attack greater than the critical angle of attack. Spins result from aggravated stalls in either a slip or a skid. If a stall does not occur, a spin cannot occur.

2. What causes a spin? (FAA-H-8083-25)

The primary cause of an inadvertent spin is exceeding the critical angle of attack while applying excessive or insufficient rudder, and to a lesser extent, aileron.

3. When are spins most likely to occur? (FAA-H-8083-25)

A stall/spin situation can occur in any phase of flight but is most likely to occur in the following situations:

a. Engine failure on takeoff during climb-out—pilot tries to stretch glide to landing area by increasing back pressure or makes an uncoordinated turn back to departure runway at a relatively low airspeed.

b. Crossed-control turn from base to final (slipping or skidding turn)—pilot overshoots final (possibly due to a crosswind) and makes uncoordinated turn at a low airspeed.

c. Engine failure on approach to landing—pilot tries to stretch glide to runway by increasing back pressure.

d. Go-around with full nose-up trim—pilot applies power with full flaps and nose-up trim combined with uncoordinated use of rudder.

e. Go-around with improper flap retraction—pilot applies power and retracts flaps rapidly resulting in a rapid sink rate followed by an instinctive increase in back pressure.

4. What procedure should be used to recover from an inadvertent spin? (FAA-H-8083-25)

- Close the throttle (if not already accomplished).
- Neutralize the ailerons.
- Apply full opposite rudder.
- Briskly move the elevator control forward to approximately the neutral position. (Some aircraft require merely a relaxation of back pressure; others require full forward elevator pressure).
- Once the stall is broken the spinning will stop. Neutralize the rudder when the spinning stops.
- When the rudder is neutralized, gradually apply enough aft elevator pressure to stop the descent and return to level flight.

5. What causes "adverse yaw"? (FAA-H-8083-25)

When turning an airplane to the left for example, the downward deflected aileron on the right produces more lift on the right wing. Since the downward deflected right aileron produces more lift, it also produces more drag, while the opposite left aileron has less lift and less drag. This added drag attempts to pull or veer the airplane's nose in the direction of the raised wing (right); that is, it tries to turn the airplane in the direction opposite to that desired. This undesired veering is referred to as adverse yaw.

6. What situations could lead to an unintentional stall?

- Engine failure at high angle of attack on takeoff
- Slow approach speeds during landing
- Wind shear and/or turbulence

For Weight-Shift Control

1. **What are the forces on the wing and undercarriage at high angles of attack?**

   Undercarriage is forward of the center of gravity and therefore causes the aircraft nose to rotate down to a lower angle of attack. The root portion of the wing is partially stalled, creating less lift forward of the center of gravity, wanting to rotate the nose down to a lower angle of attack. Both of these factors provide excellent stability at high angles of attack.

2. **What are the forces on the wing and undercarriage when the wing is at a low angle of attack in a dive?**

   Undercarriage is aft of the center of gravity and therefore causes the nose to rotate up to a higher angle of attack. The tips of the wing are not producing much lift, if any, with the nose producing most of the lift wanting to rotate the nose up to a higher angle of attack. Both of these factors provide excellent stability at low angles of attack.

3. **Where is the wing root of the weight-shift control aircraft?**

   The root of the wing is the lateral center of the wing, right above the pilot, an equal distance between each wing tip.

4. **Explain the twist of a weight-shift aircraft and the angle of attack as it changes from the root to the tips.**

   The fundamental design of the flex wing is for the wing to twist from a high angle of attack at the nose, to a lower angle of attack at the tips.

5. **Explain how the wing stalls as the nose is raised past the critical angle of attack.**

   As the nose is raised, the root of the wing starts to stall. As the nose is raised further, the stall moves from the root out towards the tips. In an almost full stall most of the wing is stalled, but the tips keep flying.

6. **Explain the flight characteristics when the weight-shift control aircraft is flying at minimum controllable airspeed (slow flight).**

   The bar pressure wants to speed the wing up and return it to its natural trim speed. The wing is hard to control, mushy, and difficult to maintain straight flight.

7. **What is trim speed?**

   The natural speed of the wing when there is no pitch pressure on the bar.

8. **Explain the flight characteristics when the weight-shift control is flying at a speeds above trim.**

   The bar pressure wants to slow the aircraft to trim. The aircraft is generally more responsive to control inputs.

9. **How does the wing design feature "washout" affect the production of lift?**

   The washout/twist in the wing, starts with a high angle of attack at the root/nose, and decreases the angle of attack as you approach each tip. This washout and also called wing twist. The wing twist, sweep (nose angle), and airfoil shape are all designed as a system to make the nose lose lift first, while the tips keep flying at high angles of attack.

10. **What is the difference between a small wing and a large wing on the speed of the aircraft and its takeoff and landing characteristics?**

    Small wings are generally faster and stall at a higher speed; they take a longer takeoff roll and sometimes require a bigger engine to handle the faster speed. Large wings fly slower and are used for shorter and slower takeoffs and landings.

Weight-Shift Control — Instructor

1. **What wing components are under compression during flight?**

   Control bar uprights and wing cross-tube.

2. **Explain the static stability characteristics of the weight shift pitch control.**

   The wing is statically stable when the control bar is moved from trim. Slowed from trim, the control bar moves toward the trim speed. Faster than trim, the control bar wants to return to trim.

3. **Explain the dynamic stability characteristics of the weight shift pitch control.**

   The wing is dynamically stable when the control bar is moved from trim. Slower or faster than trim, releasing the control bar would create dampening pitch oscillations and return the aircraft to trim over time.

4. **How do you match engine sizes to wing sizes?**
   - Faster and smaller wing requires more power.
   - Slower and larger wing can use smaller engines.
   - Larger wings can use larger engines for quick takeoffs and greater climb rates and angles.
   - Smaller engine does not typically go on a small, fast wing.

For Powered Parachute

1. **What is the pendulum effect for a PPC, and what are its effects during flight?**

   Since the undercarriage hangs so far below the wing it is like a pendulum on a string. This is where the term "pendulum effect" was born. The pendulum effect tends to stabilize the undercarriage below the wing during unaccelerated flight. If you are in a turn, the pendulum is swinging and has momentum. This momentum must be accounted for before reversing direction by gradually coming out of the turn. It is similar to slinging a weight around on a string. It will keep rotating and must be slowed down in a controlled manner.

2. **Will a PPC wing stall?**

   Yes, any wing will stall when the critical angle of attack is exceeded.

3. **What situations would put you in a situation where the PPC wing will stall?**

   a. A bad wing that has been improperly rigged, not inspected. *Example:* If the front lines are highly loaded and have stretched out past their acceptable tolerance, this could create a higher angle of attack and lead to a stall.

   b. The pilot could induce a stall through over-performance such as high climb rates, spirals, pumping the wing by simultaneously pushing on the control bars plus pulling the control lines to swing the undercarriage far out in front, stalling the wing.

   c. Wind shear or flying in heavy turbulence.

4. **How can you avoid getting into a situation where the PPC wing would stall?**

   a. Proper assembly, inspection, preflight.

   b. Flying in good weather and avoiding turbulence and wind shear.

   c. Flying within the pilot and PPC wing capabilities and limitations.

5. **What aerodynamically causes a chute to partially or completely collapse?**

   Lack of pressure being rammed into the front opening and/or filling a section of the wing internally through cross-ports.

6. **What situations would cause all or part of the canopy to collapse?**

   Flying in wind shear or turbulence. *Example:* You are flying on a very unstable day in a big thermal where all the air is going up. You fly to the edge of the thermal and one side of the wing flies into the downdraft of the thermal. The side of the wing in the downdraft collapses.

7. **What procedure should you perform if part of your wing collapses?**

   Simply wait for it to re-inflate; this is what it is designed to do.

8. **What do cross-ports in the parachute ribs do?**

   Cross-ports in the wing ribs allow air to flow sideways from cell to cell, called crossflow, in the wing. This results in the cells next to each other transferring pressure inside the wing and cells pressurizing neighboring cells.

9. **Is splicing severed suspension lines okay?**

   Splicing lines is dangerous because you can change the airfoil, or the lines could come loose and go through the prop.

10. **What would tying a severed suspension line do?**

    This would shorten it and create a discontinuity in the wing shape, which could lead to problems.

II. PREFLIGHT PROCEDURES

Tips

- Follow the POH for your specific aircraft.
- Use checklists for preflight inspection, systems, cockpit management, engine starting, taxi, and before-takeoff check.

A. Preflight Inspection

Preflight Checklist For All

The following is provided as an example of a light-sport aircraft routine preflight inspection checklist. Use POH for specific aircraft.

Cockpit and Controls

- ☐ Ignition switch off
- ☐ Seats adjusted for pilot and passenger controls, systems, and panel use
- ☐ Seatbelt security and placement
- ☐ Instruments intact and usable
- ☐ Airplane flight controls—hand controls smooth movement fore/aft, right/left, plus all 4 corners travel. If just assembled, verify that flight controls move all three control surfaces in correct direction.
- ☐ WSC flight controls—full movement fore and aft, side to side, no binding at hang point.
- ☐ PPC flight controls, the steering bars function, pulleys operational.
- ☐ Engine controls operate and lock properly (throttle and mixture starting controls).
- ☐ Brakes have proper throw and pressures (right and left if both).
- ☐ Steering wheel smooth operation. Verify direction.
- ☐ Eye protection clean with clear view (that is, the canopy for a closed cockpit, or the face shield/glasses in open cockpit fit well and are secured).

Landing Gear

- ☐ Check suspension general function and operation.
- ☐ Brake fluid, for hydraulics or mechanical actuation control, check general condition and that it is functional.
- ☐ Tires have proper air pressure (main and nose/tail wheels).
- ☐ Nose- or tailwheel operates smoothly and in the correct direction.

Continued

Wing

- [ ] All structural wing attachment points general condition and fastener security.
- [ ] Leading edge and forward airfoil shape good (PPC fabric and baffles in good condition).
- [ ] Wing material or surface condition good, upper and lower.
- [ ] For airplane, aileron travel is smooth, full travel, skin is in good condition and secured. Flap operation is smooth, full travel, skin is in good condition and secured. Flaps lock in proper positions.
- [ ] Airspeed indicator and static port (if equipped), cover is removed and free of debris.

Powerplant (Propulsion System)

- [ ] Check engine mounts from the engine to the airframe, general condition and fastener security.
- [ ] Propeller and reduction system security and general condition, should be secure from propeller to airframe.
- [ ] Propeller blade general condition good. Rotate propeller in same direction that it turns (make sure both ignition systems are off) to inspect all blades.
- [ ] Check exhaust system—springs with safety wire, vibration mount condition, free of cracks, general condition good.
- [ ] Ignition system, spark plug caps secured, and the general condition of wires.
- [ ] Fuel system—fuel tank security, fuel pickup, low point water check, condition of lines, fuel filter, security of all lines to fittings, verify fuel vent open, verify fuel quantity for flight.
- [ ] Induction system—air inlet filter condition good and secured with safety, carburetor secure and in good condition, air/fuel mixture inlets and lines secure and operational.
- [ ] Fluid levels—oil and coolant levels are checked. Make sure all caps are secured after checking fluids.

Control Cables and Control Rods

- [ ] Turnbuckles safetied with wire, routing and all attachments general condition.
- [ ] Cables and rods general condition, attachments, and tautness good over complete routing.

Airplane Only—Tail

- [ ] General condition of fabric or covering top, bottom and sides.
- [ ] Elevator and rudder full-travel, smooth operation.
- [ ] Structural wires or struts general condition, fasteners, and operation.
- [ ] Trim tab operation/condition (if applicable). Ground tabs secure.

Overall: Verify the aircraft is in a safe condition to fly!

Weight-Shift Control Checklists

Airplane and PPC, skip these WSC checklists.

WSC Assembly Checklist

Find a suitable area to set up the wing, preferably grass, cement, or pavement, trying to keep out of the wind; then:

- ☐ Align the wing perpendicular to the wind if there is any (presently or expected).
- ☐ Rotate the wing bag so the zipper is facing up.
- ☐ Unzip the bag and assemble the control frame without attaching the wires to the nose.
- ☐ Rotate the wing up onto its control frame, remove and roll up the cover bag.
- ☐ Undo the straps that hold the wing, and spread the wings slightly.
- ☐ Roll the pads and the tie straps up into the cover bag so they do not blow away.
- ☐ If the king post is loose, insert it onto the keel to stand upright—spread the wings as necessary to keep the king post straight up.
- ☐ Spread the wings out carefully and evenly.

Separate the battens right and left, and separate out the straight battens (if you have them for a double-surface wing)—set them to the side. Lay the battens out longest to shortest, from the root to the tip, next to the pocket they go into, both sides; then:

- ☐ Insert the battens from the root to the tip each side about 3/4 spanwise on each side. Most batten attachments are double pull. Leave the tip battens for later.
- ☐ Check to make sure all the wires are straight, not wrapped around, and clear to tension wing.
- ☐ Tension the wing by pulling back on the haulback cable, pulling the crossbar back into position.
- ☐ Secure the haul back cable on the back of the keel.

Go around front and secure the control bar cables to the underside nose attachment; then:

- ☐ Insert the tip battens on each side. Insert the washout tube into the leading edge to provide the tips with a twist minimum. Ensure the last tip batten is secure and in place.
- ☐ Insert the bottom battens, if you have a double-surface.
- ☐ Lift up on the back of the keel and put the wing on its nose.
- ☐ Lower the undercarriage mast and line up the undercarriage in back of the wing exactly in the middle.
- ☐ Move the undercarriage forward and attach the mast to the proper location on the wing keel. Attach the back up cable at this time also.
- ☐ Lift up the nose and let the undercarriage roll backwards until the wing is level.
- ☐ Put on the brakes, chock the back of the undercarriage wheels.
- ☐ Lift the wing up into position and lock the undercarriage mast. Install the front undercarriage bar (stall bar) into position.
- ☐ Secure the control bar to the stall bar with a bungee.
- ☐ Attach any fairing as required.

WSC Tuning Checklist

Important note: Any wing adjustment can change the handling and stability characteristics of the wing. It is very important to first follow the POH, and then contact a factory representative before making any adjustments not specified in the POH.

Tuning the wing to fly straight:

☐ Look for any asymmetric right and left tendencies by standing in back of the wing as a starting point and check for symmetry in the twist angle.

☐ Research the history of the wing to find out what might have happened that would cause the asymmetric tendencies (i.e., cause it to not fly straight).

☐ Inspect the leading edge for any discontinuities, bumps, or crunched Mylar.

☐ Make sure the zippered pockets on double-surface wings are zippered and symmetrical on both sides.

☐ Check the battens to make sure the right and left are the same and symmetrical. Check to ensure the battens match the manufacturer's batten pattern.

If these checks and corrections do not cause the wing to fly straight, then you must adjust the tension of the sail or the twist in the wing per the manufacturer's instructions. More twist on one side will slow that side down. Some wings have an adjustment at the tip where you can rotate the wing tip around the leading edge. Specific instructions are in the wing operations manual from the manufacturer.

Another method is to add more tension on a side, which will flatten that side and speed that side up. You may have to use the techniques described in the next section for one side of the wing to adjust it to fly straight, by speeding a side up or slowing a side down.

Tuning the wing to fly slower or faster:

Also, adding tension can also be used to tune the wing to fly straight:

☐ Tightening the baton tension with the baton strings will speed the wing up but reduce the handling, because it is a tighter wing.

☐ Tightening the baton tension on one side will speed that side up. Reducing the tension on one side will slow that side down.

☐ Pulling the leading-edge tension from the tip tighter will speed up the wing, but reduce the handling because it will be a tighter wing.

☐ Tightening the leading-edge tension on one side will speed that side up. Reducing the tension on one side will slow that side down.

Tuning the wing to fly slower or faster (typical adjustments):

☐ Some wings have the ability to move the hang point attachment forward to go faster, and back to slow the trim down.

☐ Tighten the tension in the wing to flatten it out and speed it up, but pull back more on the cross-tube haul-back cables. This speeds up the wing, but causes it to be less stable, stiffer handling—yet provide better glide performance.

Raising and lowering the luff lines will also change the speed of the wing. Lower luff lines speed the wing up and make it less stable, raising the luff lines slow the wing and make it more stable. Some manufacturers make this an adjustable setting that can be varied during flight; with other manufacturers, this adjustment must be made on the ground. Other manufacturers do not recommend that a customer perform this adjustment at all, because it can lower the certified stability of the wing.

Powered Parachute Only — Canopy Layout

- ☐ Position aircraft for best takeoff direction.
- ☐ Remove canopy bag from undercarriage without twisting risers/lines.
- ☐ Remove canopy from bag into appropriate layout position.
- ☐ Remove riser/lines cover.
- ☐ Check lines for proper inflation.
- ☐ Ensure lines are not tangled or twisted, and positioned so they will not be sucked into the propeller during inflation.

B. Cockpit Management

Checklists
Exhibit knowledge

- ☐ All necessary certificates and documents required to fly are on board.
- ☐ Airspace sectionals, maps, and A/FD needed for takeoff, destination, and diversion airports on board.
- ☐ All required *checklists* on board.
- ☐ Ballistic parachutes actuation handles are usable, but not in a position for accidental deployment.

Organize

- ☐ Maps, checklists, and operational procedures are usable during flight and arranged neatly for easy access and use.
- ☐ For open cockpits or wind in cockpit, use kneeboards as necessary.
- ☐ Wires, routing, plug-ins and all cockpit systems will not interfere with controls operation, visibility, and safety for all systems.
- ☐ All items secured so they're not tossed about in turbulence, or picked up by wind at operational airspeeds during flight.

Continued

Brief occupant

- ☐ Seatbelts fasten and unfasten procedures.
- ☐ Positive exchange of controls.
- ☐ Door latching, window securing, cockpit entrance and exit procedures are understood for all planned flight situations. This includes emergency exit.
- ☐ Look for other air traffic for collision avoidance.
- ☐ Ballistic parachute operation procedures.
- ☐ Engine-out situation and procedures for planned flight with diversions.
- ☐ Fire extinguisher operation.
- ☐ Hand signals in case electric loads must be shut off or internal aircraft communications not functioning.
- ☐ Water landings with engine-out situation, if planned flight is over water.
- ☐ All safety systems as required.
- ☐ Brief passenger on all necessary items of flight and emergency procedures.
- ☐ Brief passenger on what they can hold onto, and what not to touch.
- ☐ In open cockpits, make sure nothing can fall out of pockets in flight. This is especially important for weight-shift control, PPC and airplanes with the propeller in back.

C. Engine Starting

Checklists

Ready aircraft to enter cockpit

- ☐ Untie aircraft, secure tie down ropes in aircraft or coil neatly if they stay at airport.
- ☐ Remove ground chocks and secure in aircraft.
- ☐ Locate a suitable area with minimum dust, free of dirt that could be picked up, preferably a paved clear area, away from people and objects.
- ☐ Position aircraft so prop blast is clear, verify brakes on, throttle is closed and propeller area is cleared.
- ☐ Position into wind if possible for best warm up and cooling.

Cockpit entry for flight

- ☐ Seats adjusted for full operation of all controls.
- ☐ Seats locked into position.
- ☐ Put on seatbelts (lap first than shoulder) and adjust so all controls and systems can be fully operated.
- ☐ Check all control systems for proper operation.
- ☐ Check all systems operations.
- ☐ Remove safety pin for ballistic chute operation.
- ☐ Install helmet and headphones, check intercom and radio communication systems.
- ☐ Install eye protection for open cockpits (safety glasses, helmet shields).

Starting engine

☐ Key in, ignition on, master power on.

☐ Check gages for operation and fuel level.

☐ Fuel pump on.

☐ System switches on. (Some POHs list this step after engine startup.)

☐ Ignition systems switches left and right on.

☐ Choke/enrichener on (or pump primer as appropriate).

☐ Throttle down/closed with brakes on.

☐ Look at propeller area and make sure area is cleared, then yell out the window "Clear prop."

☐ Start engine.

☐ Make sure the airplane does not move, hands on ignition switches for quick shutdown if necessary.

☐ Adjust choke or enrichener to keep engine running smoothly.

☐ Continue to monitor area and shut down the engine if any person or animal approaches.

☐ Check gages for proper ranges (oil pressure, RPM, charging voltage, engine temperatures within ranges).

D. Taxiing

Checklists

☐ Plan taxi path to runway to avoid paths that would put your light-sport aircraft behind propwash or jet blast. Closely observe other aircraft that could start up when you are taxiing in back of them, and taxi in front of them if practical.

☐ Release brake—parking brake (if applicable) or toe brakes.

☐ When first rolling, immediately check brakes, steering, and shut down if either is not functioning properly.

☐ Observe proper right-of-way while taxiing:

- Landing aircraft has right-of-way to taxiing aircraft.
- Two aircraft approaching head-on will turn right (similar to what you would do in a car).
- Two aircraft traveling in same direction, the forward aircraft has right-of-way because it cannot normally see the aircraft in back.
- With two airplanes converging, the pilot who sees the aircraft on the right must avoid that aircraft. The aircraft on the right has the right-of-way.

☐ Maintain appropriate speed for taxi. A GPS provides this speed since the airspeed indicator is not effective at these slower speeds. A rule of thumb is normally 5 MPH or brisk walking speed, or 10 MPH for long unobstructed areas.

Powered Parachute Only

☐ Normally, taxi to takeoff locations with canopy packed in bag, especially in any wind.

☐ If you need to taxi, advance throttle to inflate canopy, get straight above, and reduce/adjust throttle to keep canopy above head.

☐ Do not taxi with canopy in crosswinds or head/tailwinds above capabilities.

Airplane Only (position controls properly for wind conditions)

☐ **Strong tailwind**—pitch control pushed forward to keep the wind from lifting the tail, ailerons neutral.

☐ **Strong headwind**—pitch control neutral or back to hold tail down, ailerons neutral.

☐ **Strong quartering tailwind**— elevator neutral or down (control column forward/nose down), aileron down on the side from which the wind is blowing (stick or wheel turned away from wind) so the air flowing over it will force the wing down.

☐ **Strong quartering headwind**—the elevator in neutral position (taildragger elevator up/stick back), and the upwind aileron should be up (stick or wheel turned into wind) to keep wing from lifting.

Weight-Shift Control Only (position controls properly for wind conditions)

☐ **Strong tailwind**—pitch control normal or slight nose up with wings level.

☐ **Strong headwind**—pitch control nose down wings level.

☐ **Strong quartering tailwind**—nose normal with upwind wing slightly down so wind cannot catch it, but not to low to cause excess stress on undercarriage mast.

☐ **Strong quartering headwind**—nose down with upwind wing slightly down so wind cannot catch it, but not too low to cause excess stress on undercarriage mast.

Runway Incursions (observe all taxiway and runway markings)

Runway incursions taxi special safety note—Runway incursion avoidance procedures are most important and must be adhered to for your safety, and the general public's safety. *You must taxi slowly and observe the basic airport markings/signs.* When taxiing across any runway or entering a runway to takeoff, you must get clearance to proceed. There could be large aircraft that are not able to respond to the quick movements of LSAs. A most important runway marker is the "hold short line." You always stop before this line and get clearance before you cross it.

- At a towered airport, obtain a clearance from the tower. Always read back clearance before proceeding.

- At a nontowered airport, the procedure checklist is as listed below.

  ☐ Listen and monitor all air traffic on the CTAF radio frequency taxiing and in the pattern.

  ☐ Observe all air traffic taxiing and in the pattern. A 360-degree turn is typically done to see in all directions.

  ☐ When all air traffic is clear from observations and radio communications, and you are holding short before the line, announce you are entering the runway. This is your clearance at a self-announce UNICOM or MULTICOM airport.

E. Before-Takeoff Check

This check is usually made after taxi near the takeoff area, to make sure engine has had time to warm up.

Checklists

☐ Position clear of other aircraft so propeller will not pick up dirt or debris that could damage the propeller or any part of the aircraft, especially the tail.

☐ Make sure the propeller blast will not cause a hazard to anything in back of the aircraft.

☐ Roll slightly forward so the nosewheel is pointed straight.

Follow the POH for the specific aircraft (run-up example shown here)

☐ Trim set to proper speed for takeoff

☐ Brakes set

☐ Ignition check—always divide attention inside and out of the cockpit in case the brakes cannot hold the aircraft still at the higher power settings (some ignition checks are done at idle, see POH for your engine specifics). If the brakes start to slip and the aircraft starts moving, decrease power immediately and reevaluate how to run up and keep the aircraft stationary during run-up.

   • Run up engine to consistent RPM higher than idle.

   • Switch from both ignition systems to one and watch for a slight drop in RPM. Do the same for the other ignition system.

   • Verify engine temperatures (EGT, CHT, oil and/or water) and oil pressure are within the ranges they should be.

☐ Verify engine temperatures are within takeoff specifications before takeoff (warm up engine completely).

III. Airport Operations

A. Radio Communications and ATC Light Signals

Tips

- If you are taking the test in an aircraft with a radio, you will have to transmit and operate it during the test.
- If you are taking a test in an aircraft without a radio, these procedures are covered verbally before the flight portion.

Checklists

Basic communications tips

- ☐ Listen before you transmit so as not to interrupt active communications.
- ☐ Think about what you are going to say before transmitting.
- ☐ Speak clearly at a moderate rate.
- ☐ If you are significantly slow, below 45 MPH in the pattern, and communicating with a nontowered airport, state your speed during your initial transmissions so other aircraft know your speed.
- ☐ If you are slow and doing a smaller pattern, announce "tight pattern" (or "inside pattern") so other aircraft will know you are flying a smaller pattern close to the runway.
- ☐ If you are seeking an endorsement to fly in Class B, C, or D airspace, use the procedures outlined in AIM Chapter 4, Section 2.

Nontowered airports checklist using CTAF UNICOM or MULTICOM

Taxi/takeoff

- ☐ Check internal communications and push-to-talk broadcast functionality.
- ☐ Transmit using recommended phraseology per AIM (examples follow below).

Taxiing

- ☐ Who you are calling *(Carson UNICOM)*
- ☐ What and who you are—use specific terminology per AIM Chapter 4 *(Light-sport aircraft Six Three Zero Papa Hotel)*
- ☐ Where you are and what you are doing *(Taxiing North to South midfield across runway two seven)*
- ☐ What your intentions are *(Will taxi to runway two seven for takeoff)*

Continued

Getting ready to enter runway for takeoff

- ☐ Who you are calling *(Carson UNICOM)*
- ☐ What and who you are *(Light-sport aircraft Six Three Zero Papa Hotel)*
- ☐ Where you are *(Holding short for runway 27)*
- ☐ What your intentions are *(Will enter main runway 27 once aircraft on final approach lands and clears runway)*

In pattern (may abbreviate if you are broadcasting continuously)

- ☐ Who you are calling *(Carson this is light-sport aircraft Papa Hotel midfield downwind for a touch and go)*

Approaching airport

- ☐ Minimum 10 miles from airport broadcast your position and intentions.
- ☐ Who you are calling *(Carson UNICOM)*
- ☐ What and who you are *(Light-sport aircraft Six Three Zero Papa Hotel)*
- ☐ Approaching an airport it may be appropriate to state your speed if you think you are going slower than the other aircraft *(flying 55 knots)*
- ☐ Where you are *(15 miles west of Carson Airport at nine thousand feet)*
- ☐ What your intentions are *(approaching and will be landing at airport)*
- ☐ Ask for any airport advisories if you like *(any airport advisories?)*—This is where you can find out the active pattern depending on wind conditions. If you were in the pattern and heard this question, you could provide this information to incoming aircraft as a courtesy, such as, "Active left hand pattern using runway two seven. Light winds."

Entering pattern

- ☐ Who you are calling *(Carson Traffic)*
- ☐ What and who you are *(Light-sport aircraft Six Three Zero Papa Hotel)*
- ☐ Where you are *(five miles southwest, will be entering downwind at forty-five degrees in five minutes)*
- ☐ What your intentions are *(for runway 27 full stop)*

Airport Traffic Area Light Signal Communications

Light	On Ground	In Air
Steady Green	Cleared for Takeoff	Cleared to Land
Flashing Green	Cleared to Taxi	Return for Landing
Steady Red	Stop	Yield, Continue Circling
Flashing Red	Taxi Clear of Runway	Unsafe, Do Not Land
Flashing White	Return to Start	Not Used
Alternate Red/Green	Exercise Extreme Caution	Exercise Extreme Caution

Towered airports (for pilots seeking operations in Class B, C or D airspace)

Always provide your full aircraft ID and always transmit back (read back) tower instructions to make sure there is no misunderstanding of the instructions provided. Use AIM Chapter 4 Section 2 *Phraseology* and *Aircraft Call Signs*. All E-LSA must include "experimental" in their aircraft ID to the tower.

General procedure

☐ Pilot calls up with ID and position

☐ Tower replies acknowledging aircraft

☐ Pilot's message of intentions

☐ Tower replies with instructions

Taxi and takeoff

Must have clearance to enter the taxiway, runway and takeoff.

☐ Check internal communications

☐ Listen to ATIS for recorded airport advisories, listen for update Alpha, Bravo, Charlie etc., if airport has ATIS

☐ Switch to ground control (if available)

Continued

☐ Transmit using recommended phraseology

- Start with ATIS "update Bravo" so the tower knows you listened to most recent ATIS broadcast.
- Who you are calling *(Tahoe ground control)*
- What and who you are *(Light-sport aircraft make/model, Six Three Zero Papa Hotel)*
- Where you are *(west apron)*
- What your intentions are *(request taxi to takeoff)*
- Read back tower instructions and follow tower directions exactly through takeoff and exiting airport until tower states "frequency change approved." This is when you can change to different frequency. Normally this is ten miles from airport.

Approaching Active Towered Airport

Five minutes from the 10-mile radius of airport, broadcast your position and intentions

- Who you are calling *(Tahoe tower)*
- What and who you are *(Light-sport aircraft make/model, Six Three Zero Papa Hotel)*
- Where you are *(ten miles north, nine thousand feet)*
- What your intentions are *(Approach and landing instructions, OVER)*
- Follow all tower instructions and repeat back so there is no confusion.

B. Traffic Patterns

Tips

- Research the patterns of your airport or any other airport patterns you may be using during your Practical; study the A/FD to become familiar with the services available and local procedures (noise abatement, traffic patterns, communications, etc.).

Checklists

General pattern checklist

☐ Communicate as required to know where all aircraft are operating in the airport area, and they all know where you are.

☐ Divide attention in and out of the cockpit. Visually scan the area for other aircraft throughout pattern.

☐ Patterns are turns to the left unless specified otherwise in the A/FD, segmented circle, or wind variations.

☐ At towered airports follow directions of control tower. Read back instructions so there is no confusion.

☐ Maintain pattern altitude ±100 feet.

☐ Airplane and weight-shift control maintain speed ±10 knots.

Takeoff and closed pattern

Closed pattern means staying in the pattern, not exiting or entering.

Before takeoff, determine proper airport pattern from A/FD for departure airport, planned airport and airports with diversions —

☐ Left hand

☐ Right hand

☐ Noise abatement if necessary

☐ Prescribed path

☐ Altitudes

Takeoff, departure, upwind leg

☐ After takeoff, climb to 500 feet AGL straight upwind before exiting pattern or turning onto crosswind leg.

☐ Climb at proper airspeeds as specified in the POH.

☐ Use POH for flap retraction, airspeeds, and engine temperatures and operating limitations. This is a critical time for monitoring proper engine temperatures. Takeoff and initial climb is when the probability of engine problems are the greatest.

☐ Divide attention inside and out of the cockpit.

☐ Locate suitable engine-out emergency landing areas throughout the climb.

☐ Radio broadcast position and intentions using appropriate terminology before first turn.

Crosswind leg (first 90-degree turn flying perpendicular to runway)

☐ Climb to pattern altitude, maintain ±100 feet.

Downwind leg (second 90-degree turn flying parallel to runway opposite direction to takeoff)

☐ Establish ground track parallel to runway at pattern altitude.

☐ Radio broadcast position "midfield downwind tight pattern" location example with appropriate terminology.

☐ Start preparing for landing with POH landing checklist.

☐ Start descending towards end of downwind leg if appropriate for your aircraft and specific airport pattern.

Base leg (third 90-degree turn headed back towards final approach track perpendicular to runway)

☐ Prepare aircraft configuration for landing.

☐ Reduce speed as necessary.

☐ Descend from pattern altitude.

☐ Scan the final approach area before turning onto final approach for faster aircraft that are on final approach.

☐ Radio broadcast position and intentions before turning onto final approach.

Final approach (fourth 90-degree turn headed directory towards the runway)

☐ Line up in the middle of the runway exactly on the centerline and maintain this centerline approach accounting for wind.

☐ Maintain approach speed.

☐ Be prepared to do a go-around if needed.

Entering pattern

☐ Determine proper pattern entry location and altitude for specific airport from A/FD.

☐ Determine active direction of pattern from other aircraft if possible by requesting airport advisory before entering area.

☐ If no aircraft are using pattern, determine appropriate pattern from wind direction and segmented circle.

☐ Descend to pattern altitude and than enter downwind leg at 45 degrees in the middle of the downwind leg headed directly at the middle of the runway. Turn into the downwind leg and finish pattern similar to closed pattern description above.

Exiting pattern

☐ Exiting the pattern is usually straight out from the departure leg or turning 45 degrees in the direction of the pattern to exit the area.

C. Airport Runway Markings and Lighting

Tips

• Use the Sport Pilot Test Prep or AIM Chapter 2 to familiarize yourself with the color airport marking signs, along with this checklist.

Checklists

Runway numbers and letters

☐ Determined from the approach direction.

☐ Number is the magnetic heading of the runway rounded to the nearest 10°.

Closed runways

☐ Marked by an "X."

Visual Approach Slope Indicator (VASI) two bars, near and far

☐ Provide visual glide path.

☐ Both bars as red, the aircraft is below the glide path.

☐ Close bar is white, while the far bar remains red, on glide path.

☐ Both bars white is above glide path.

At dusk or during low visibility

☐ Land airports have a rotating beacon green or green/white.

☐ White runway edge and blue taxiway edge lights can be turned on by keying the mike while on the UNICOM frequency: 3 times for low light, 5 times for medium light, and 7 times for maximum intensity light.

Looking at Figure 72 in the FAA Sport Pilot Computer Testing Supplement:

A is a surface painted runway marking.

B is a stop bar/ILS hold.

C is vehicle lanes.

D is hold marking for land and hold short operations.

E is taxiway/taxiway hold marking.

F is taxiway edge marking (do not cross).

Looking at Figure 71 in the FAA Sport Pilot Computer Testing Supplement:

A is a taxiway/runway hold position sign.

B is a runway approach hold position sign.

C is an ILS critical area hold position sign.

D is a no entry sign.

E is a taxiway location sign.

F is a runway location sign.

G is a runway safety area/obstacle free zone boundary.

H is an ILS critical area boundary.

I is an inbound destination sign.

J is an outbound destination sign.

K is a taxiway direction sign.

L is a runway distance remaining (in 1,000-foot increments).

M is a runway/runway hold position sign.

N is a taxiway ending marker.

IV. TAKEOFFS, LANDINGS, AND GO-AROUNDS

The specific procedures in your POH should be used for all flight operations and maneuvers for your aircraft, with the following checklist provided as a general guideline. All takeoffs and landings, especially for short and rough field, must evaluate the wind conditions to land and takeoff into the wind when possible to provide the best (slowest) possible groundspeed. Airspeeds are always increased in turbulent conditions to avoid stalls when flying near the ground.

Tips

- Study the areas that apply to your own aircraft, and the aircraft in which you will take the test.

A. Normal and Crosswind Takeoff and Climb

Checklists

Airplane and WSC normal takeoff

- ☐ Advance the throttle to takeoff power and keep the nose pointed straight down the runway.
- ☐ Takeoff roll (ground roll)—aircraft accelerates to sufficient airspeed to become airborne.
- ☐ Lift-off (rotation)—rotate the nose up to increase angle of attack to provide the lifting force to leave the ground.
- ☐ Initial climb—Do not jump into the air, lift off and gain speed by initially climbing slowly. Lifting off immediately out of ground effect can stall the aircraft and should be avoided.
- ☐ Accelerate to appropriate airspeed (usually best climb speed for normal takeoffs).
- ☐ Maintain climb speed +10/-5 knots.
- ☐ Maintain climb over centerline of runway to a safe maneuvering altitude or enroute climb.

Powered parachute takeoff (no crosswind required)

- ☐ Advance the throttle to raise canopy.
- ☐ Adjust throttle to maintain canopy above head, wait for all cells to fill, check to make sure all lines are clear and straight.
- ☐ Divide attention between steering the cart and proper canopy inflation.
- ☐ Wait for the canopy to stabilize directly above.
- ☐ Advance throttle to takeoff power.
- ☐ After liftoff, maintain climb over centerline of runway to a safe maneuvering altitude or enroute climb.

Airplane strong crosswind takeoff

Same as normal takeoff, but additionally—

- ☐ Stick to the windward side, aileron up to keep windward wing from lifting off.
- ☐ Obtain additional airspeed before liftoff.

Weight-shift control strong crosswind takeoff

Same as normal takeoff, but additionally—

- ☐ Obtain additional speed before rotating off.

B. Normal and Crosswind Approach and Landing

Checklists

Airplane and WSC normal approach and landing

- ☐ Survey the area for proper touchdown point, considering wind, terrain, and runway options.
- ☐ After turning from base to final approach, confirm altitude for normal approach.
- ☐ Align the aircraft directly on the centerline of the runway and maintain this throughout approach.
- ☐ Aircraft—Adjust flaps to landing setting as specified in POH.
- ☐ Maintain attitude and approach speed (normally 1.3 V_{SO} accounting for wind gust factor, or as specified in POH).
- ☐ Reduce engine power as necessary to achieve appropriate descent rate and glide angle (use POH settings for particular aircraft).
- ☐ Aircraft—Retrim to minimize control pressures at approach speed.
  - Trimming the aircraft is a personal preference and done in various ways.
  - Some trim to approach speed and pull back on the controls to minimum controlled airspeed (slow flight) to land.
  - Others trim to slower airspeeds and ease back the pressure for landing.
- ☐ Maintain the proper glide angle and flare appropriately in order to touch down softly at or within 400 feet of intended point. Use minimum throttle to establish a safe glide to the intended touchdown point.
- ☐ Airplane—Push the stick forward to keep the aircraft on the runway without popping off.
- ☐ Weight-shift control—Pull the nose down to keep the aircraft on the runway without popping off.

Powered parachute approach and landing

☐ After turning from base to final approach, confirm altitude for normal approach.

☐ Align the aircraft course/direction directly on the centerline of the runway and maintain this throughout approach.

☐ Reduce engine power as necessary, typically to idle (use POH settings for aircraft).

☐ Maintain the proper approach glide angle to land in the first third of the runway. Use minimum throttle to establish a safe glide to the intended touchdown point.

☐ With tension in the control lines, start flare at what appears to be 20 feet high slowly and steadily slowing the PPC until touchdown. Descent rate determines amount of flare required for soft touchdown.

☐ Maintain power as required to keep canopy inflated and taxi to appropriate location.

☐ When reaching your area to stop, shut down engine first and pull both control lines to deflate the canopy to fall behind you.

Airplane only—crosswind approach and landing

☐ Use same technique as normal landings, always lining up directly on the runway centerline with the following differences for crosswind. The main objective at touchdown is to have the aircraft flying straight and not landing sideways, imposing excessive side loads on the landing gear.

☐ Normal wing low side-slip method—

- Start in a crabbed position after turning from base to final lined up in center of runway.
- Line up aircraft straight with runway by applying rudder.
- Immediately lower upwind wing to account for drift.
- Maintain directional control directly down runway with rudder and maintain position in center of runway by varying how much the upwind wing is lowered.
- Maintain side slip (upwind wing low/ aircraft pointed straight down runway centerline) until touchdown.

☐ Crab method—

- Crab method is easier to maintain position in the center of the runway by simply crabbing into the wind.
- Requires exact timing with rudder to straighten aircraft and aileron just before touchdown to not impose side loads on the landing gear.

Weight-shift control only—power-on and crosswind approach and landing

Use same technique as normal landings, always lining up directly on the runway centerline and touchdown techniques, but add the following checklists:

Power-on approach and landing

- ☐ Use power to reduce glide angle.
- ☐ Increase speed to be above normal approach speed.
- ☐ Reduce throttle on touchdown.

Crosswind approach and landing

- ☐ Keep nosewheel pointed straight or slightly down the runway since the back wheels touch first and rotate the aircraft straight before the nose wheel touches. Generally, in any type of landing, it is best not to force the nose wheel, since most designs are self-cambering; you just need to keep it headed in the right direction without much force.

C. Airplane Only—Soft-Field Takeoff and Climb

Soft field/rough field takeoff and climb

Objective is to transfer the weight from the wheels to the wings as soon as possible.

- ☐ Taxi out with sufficient speed that you do not get bogged down.
- ☐ Raise the nose as soon as possible to get the nosewheel off the ground.
- ☐ Apply more back pressure raising the nose more than a normal takeoff to transfer the weight from the wheels to the wings.
- ☐ Maintain back pressure to lift off into the ground effect as soon as possible.
- ☐ Once you lift off, lower the nose slightly to keep the wheels off the ground while accelerating in the ground effect.
- ☐ Once you have reached a sufficient speed, climb out of the ground effect.
- ☐ Maintain selected airspeed +10/-5 knots.

D. Airplane Only—Soft-Field Approach and Landing

Soft field/rough field approach and landing

Objective is to touch down smoothly at the slowest possible speed.

- ☐ Plan the landing so you are near the best area when you slow down and do not have to taxi in soft or rough terrain.
- ☐ Approach normally and make sure you are at the highest possible nose up and slowest at touchdown.
- ☐ Nose wheel airplanes maintain back pressure on stick to keep nose wheel off ground as long as possible.
- ☐ Brakes are not normally needed with the extra friction of the ground, braking can create extra forces on the nose wheel not wanted.
- ☐ Maintain sufficient speed so that you do not get bogged down.

E. Airplane Only—Short-Field (confined area) Takeoff and Maximum Performance Climb

Short field takeoff and maximum performance (V_X highest angle) climb

The objective is for the shortest ground roll and steepest climb.

- ☐ Aircraft POH usually have specific flap settings, airspeeds, and takeoff distances plus distances over 50 foot objects and should be used. The following is a generic procedure for reference.
- ☐ Evaluate wind direction and calculate best takeoff direction.
- ☐ Get to the greatest possible takeoff distance end of the runway or takeoff area to provide maximum ground roll.
- ☐ Account for wind in takeoff area and wind shear possibilities.
- ☐ Hold brakes, run throttle up, release brakes.
- ☐ Perform normal takeoff but establish best angle of climb airspeed to make it over obstacle.

F. Airplane Only—Short-Field (confined area) Approach and Landing

Short or restricted field approach and landing

Objective is to land in a restricted area or over obstacles into a short field requiring flight at slower than normal airspeeds close to the ground.

- ☐ Survey the landing area for best touchdown point.
- ☐ Establish glide with minimum power, flaps down, and approach speed 500 feet above the intended touchdown point.
- ☐ Touch down smoothly at minimum controlled airspeed, at or within 200 feet beyond the specified touchdown point.
- ☐ After landing, maintain control column back to brake the aircraft with maximum drag.
- ☐ Once the nose drops through, apply wheel brakes to slow the aircraft as necessary, maintaining control.

G. Airplane Only—Forward Slip to a Landing

Forward slip to landing

Objective: a forward slip can be used to increase the descent rate and assist in losing altitude for rapid descents and short field approach and landing.

- ☐ Survey the landing area and establish best touchdown point.
- ☐ Airplane is banked and opposite rudder is applied to fly the airplane sideways, increasing drag and the sink rate of the airplane. Maintain appropriate airspeed.
- ☐ Correct from slip for smooth and soft landing, at or within 400 feet beyond the specified touchdown point.

H. Weight-Shift Control Only—Steep Approach to Landing

The objective here is that you need to know what to do if you are on final approach and are too high and must increase your glide angle to land in the appropriate place. Consider three possible scenarios: slightly higher, significant altitude, and very high over.

- ☐ Reduce throttle to idle.
- ☐ Survey the landing area for the appropriate direction to land.
- ☐ Survey the altitude, glide angle, and best touchdown points to determine technique to use.
- ☐ Slightly higher than needed, minor steep approach needed to land on spot—speed up past the best Lift over Drag (L/D) of wing to reduce glide angle. Greater speed means less glide angle. Reduce speed to approach speed 50 feet above ground.

☐ Significant altitude must be lost to make landing area. Extra speed technique above is not steep enough. Do turns from right to left across centerline of runway as required to reduce altitude. Straighten out to be at approach speed lined up ready to start roundout a minimum of 50 feet over the ground.

☐ If the angle is extremely steep with a minimum of 500 feet above the ground, a 360-degree turn is an option for a steep approach. Maintain altitude as required with the throttle to come out of the 360 a minimum of 100 feet above the ground. Establish runway centerline 50 feet above ground.

☐ From 50 feet AGL, perform normal landing at or within 400 feet beyond the specified touchdown point.

If any of these techniques will be unsafe, then simply do a go-around.

I. Go-Around/Rejected Landing (for all)

Go-arounds and rejected landings are normal and are not emergency maneuvers and should be used if there is any question as to the success of a good landing.

Go-arounds are usually done from a bad approach but can also be due to:

- Unexpected appearance of hazards on the runway
- Overtaking another airplane
- Wind shear
- Wake turbulence
- Mechanical failure

Decide to perform a go-around sooner rather than later. The closer you are to the ground, the more challenging the go-around will be.

Go-around procedure

☐ Full power applied immediately, smoothly and without hesitation.

☐ Airplane and WSC—Gain airspeed if necessary. Typically the nose must be lowered after full power is applied to obtain the best speed to start climbing. If the nose is raised to gain altitude without the proper airspeed, the aircraft can stall close to the ground with serious consequences.

☐ Airplane only—As specified in the POH, clean up the configuration by reducing flaps as appropriate to establish best climb speed.

V. Performance Maneuvers

Tips

- Determine cruise throttle settings, and performance throttle settings for aircraft to remain level before performing maneuver.
- Pick a road to have a solid reference.
- Ease out of your turn so you have better control over your final heading. This is a tight tolerance.

Checklists

Airplane and weight-shift control only steep turns

- ☐ Determine solid reference line before starting maneuver (straight road, long fence, river, anything that is easy to orient yourself to).
- ☐ Clearing turn—look for other aircraft before performing maneuver. If you do not clear a turn before you perform the maneuver, you will fail this task.
- ☐ Increase and establish appropriate airspeed before maneuver, to account for increase in stall speed for 45-degree bank.
- ☐ Roll into 45-degree bank and bump throttle up as required to maintain altitude.
- ☐ Maintain bank angle ±10 degrees.
- ☐ Make 360° turn, maintain focus on altitude with throttle, bank angle, and outside the cockpit for other aircraft. Collision avoidance is very important to examiner's and your safety.
- ☐ Maintain altitude ±100 feet, airspeed ±10 knots.
- ☐ Roll out at the entry heading, ±10 degrees.

Weight-shift control only—energy management

This is your ability to vary airspeed and foot throttle simultaneously to manage your energy. This will typically be done low over a runway so it is easy to judge the altitude and ability to stay on the centerline.

- ☐ Set hand throttle and maintain direction down runway centerline.
- ☐ Establish speed to be at trim or above (minimum 1.3 V_S calm conditions, 1.5 V_S for bumpy or crosswinds).
- ☐ Maintain altitude and straight course directly down centerline though variations in throttle and speed changes/bar movement.

Powered parachute only—constant altitude turns

- ☐ Plan the maneuver no lower than 300 feet AGL.
- ☐ Roll into a constant bank turn as specified by examiner.
- ☐ Apply the amount of throttle needed to maintain altitude.
- ☐ Roll out of the 360-degree turn and reduce throttle to maintain altitude.

VI. GROUND REFERENCE MANEUVERS

Tips

- Determine cruise throttle settings, and performance throttle settings before performing maneuvers.
- Pick landmarks that are easily recognizable.
- Ease out of your turns so you have better control over your final heading.

Wind considerations

In turns—

1. Ground speed will be the same when the airplane has the same headwind component.
2. Ground speed will be the same when the airplane has the same tailwind component.
3. Steepest angle of bank is required at the points where the airplane is flying downwind.
4. Shallowest angle of bank is at the points when flying upwind.

For crab angles—

1. Airplane will have to be crabbed into the wind the greatest amount where it is flying crosswind.
2. There is no crab angle when the airplane is flying directly upwind or downwind.

To double-check proper ground track—

(This is especially helpful for turns around a point.)

1. As you enter the maneuver, determine the checkpoints you will need to fly over during the maneuver.
2. Monitor checkpoints throughout maneuvers and adjust bank angles to stay on track.

A. Rectangular Course

Objectives

- Time the start of a turn so it will be fully established at a definite point over the ground.

- Time the recovery from the turn so a definite ground track is established.

- The estimation of a ground track and the determination of the appropriate "crab" angle:

  — For best results when planning a rectangular course, the flight path should be positioned outside the field boundaries just far enough that they may be easily observed from either pilot seat by looking out the side of the airplane. The closer the track of the airplane is to the field boundaries, the steeper the bank necessary at the turning points.

  — Rectangular course is the foundation for flying airport patterns.

Checklist

☐ Have a solid reference area before starting maneuver.

☐ Establish the altitude above the ground at which you want to start the maneuver (minimum feet AGL given for the maneuver in the PTS, plus 100 feet)—

Minimums to start maneuver
- airplanes 700 feet AGL
- weight-shift control 500 feet AGL
- powered parachutes 300 feet AGL

☐ Clear all turns. Look for other aircraft before performing maneuver. Simply, if you would not clear a turn before you begin the maneuver, you will fail this task and the flight test.

☐ Bump throttle up as required to maintain altitude during turns.

☐ Make turn, maintain focus on altitude with throttle, bank angle, and outside the cockpit for other aircraft. Collision avoidance is very important to examiners and your safety.

☐ Roll out at the appropriate headings.

☐ Make turn, roll out, establish ground track, etc.

☐ Maintain altitude ±100 feet.

☐ Airplanes and weight-shift control maintain speed ±10 knots.

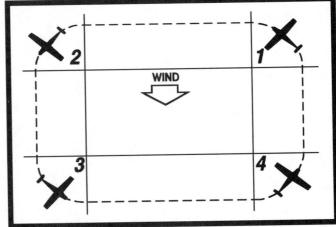

Rectangular Course.

B. S-Turns

Objectives

- Build from rectangular course objectives, with the addition of constant turning in alternate directions.
- Compensate for wind drift during turns.
- Orient the flight path with ground references.
- Follow an assigned ground track of two semicircles.
- Arrive at specified points on assigned headings.

Checklist

- ☐ Have solid reference line before starting maneuver.
- ☐ Establish the altitude above the ground at which you want to start the maneuver (minimum feet AGL given for the maneuver in the PTS, plus 100 feet)—

  Minimums to start maneuver
  - airplanes 700 feet AGL
  - weight-shift control 500 feet AGL
  - powered parachutes 300 feet AGL

- ☐ Clear all turns. Look for other aircraft before performing maneuver. If you do not clear a turn before you begin the maneuver, you will fail this task and the flight test.
- ☐ Bump throttle up as required to maintain altitude during turns.
- ☐ Make turn, maintain focus on altitude with throttle, bank angle, and outside the cockpit for other aircraft. Collision avoidance is very important to examiners and your safety.
- ☐ Maintain altitude ±100 feet and airspeed ±10 knots.
- ☐ Roll out at the appropriate headings.
- ☐ Always cross the line perpendicular with wings level.

S-turns in wind (in addition to above checklist)

- ☐ Orient the wind so it is perpendicular to the reference line (roads, powerline, fence, railroad).
- ☐ Enter the S-turn from downwind.
- ☐ In the first half of an S-turn, the bank should begin shallow and increase in steepness as the aircraft turns crosswind.
- ☐ The second semicircle requires a slower bank angle increase to go upwind, and quicker rollout to finish the maneuver.

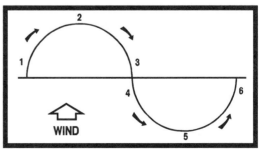

S-Turn Diagram.

C. Turns Around a Point

Objectives

- Build off S-turns objectives, but in a continuous turn.
- Further perfect your turning technique.
- Understand the radius of the turn is a distance affected by the degree of bank used in turning, with relation to a definite object.
- Develop a keen perception of altitude.
- Perfect the ability to correct for wind drift during turns.
- Understand the closer to the object the greater the bank angle.

Checklist

- ☐ Have solid reference point before starting maneuver.
- ☐ Establish the altitude above the ground at which you want to start the maneuver (minimum feet AGL given for the maneuver in the PTS, plus 100 feet)—

  Minimums to start maneuver
  - airplanes 700 feet AGL
  - weight-shift control 500 feet AGL
  - powered parachutes 300 feet AGL

- ☐ Clear turn. Look for other aircraft before performing maneuver. If you do not clear a turn before you begin it, you will fail this task and the test.
- ☐ Increase airspeed before maneuver, to account for increase in stall speed.
- ☐ Roll into turn and bump throttle up as required to maintain altitude.
- ☐ Make turn, maintain focus on altitude with throttle, bank angle, and outside the cockpit for other aircraft. Collision avoidance is very important to examiners and your safety.
- ☐ Maintain altitude ±100 feet and airspeed ±10 knots.
- ☐ Roll out at the appropriate heading.

Turns around a point in wind (in addition to above checklist)

- Heading—the wings will be in alignment with the pylon only during the time the airplane is flying directly upwind or directly downwind. At all other points, a wind correction angle (crab angle) will keep the wings from pointing directly at the pylon.
- Bank angle—Generally do not exceed a 45°-bank in a turn around a point maneuver. The best place to start is the point where the bank angle will be steepest, which is when flying downwind where the remainder of the maneuver, the bank will be shallowing out.

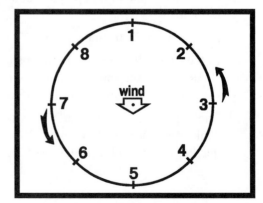

Ground Track Diagram.

VII. Navigation

Tips

- Use a sectional on a kneeboard.
- Use a global positioning system (GPS) with fresh batteries and/or power from aircraft electrical system. A good reliable GPS with a map capability is most helpful.
- It is recommended that for navigation, your main system is pilotage, and GPS is only used as a secondary system.
- If you own, or your practical will be taken in an old vintage aircraft with VOR navigation, you will need to study the private pilot navigation techniques which are not covered here.

A. Pilotage and Dead Reckoning

Pilotage is navigation by reference to landmarks and checkpoints.

Checklist

☐ Identify areas with prominent features that can be identified on the map and visually from the air, such as:

- Roads
- Lakes
- Rivers
- Power lines
- Mountains
- Water towers/tanks

☐ Fill out and use the navigation log from the cross-country planning.

☐ Fly using known landmarks during your flight. Flying for lengthy periods over desolate areas with no landmarks is not recommended.

☐ Fly the planned path using known landmarks, correcting for the wind with a GPS or dead reckoning computations.

☐ Maintain altitude ±200 feet and headings ±15 degrees.

B. Diversion

Diverting to another airport using a suitable route from —

- Changing weather that could create bad visibility.
- Increased turbulence continuing in the direction you intend to fly.
- Increased headwind and fuel required significantly more than predicted.
- System malfunction.
- Poor preflight planning.
- Make the decision to divert as soon as possible and not wait too long.

Checklist
Once you decide to divert—

- ☐ Maintain control of the aircraft,
- ☐ Choose a suitable airport within range,
- ☐ Start the diversion with a known landmark for future reference from a known point,
- ☐ Set the new waypoint in the GPS, and select "go to."
- ☐ Track and closely monitor your distance and direction.
- ☐ Maintain altitude ±200 feet, heading ±15 degrees.

C. Lost Procedures

If you are off course where landmarks cannot be recognized, you have several courses of action you can use:

- ☐ Climb to see more and increase radio reception.
- ☐ Look for names on water towers if near a town.
- ☐ Use GPS to locate another airport or find a landmark. GPS units with maps have roads, cities, lakes, and other prominent landmarks.
- ☐ Use nearby frequencies on the sectional chart/map to talk and reach an air traffic controller. They can sometimes direct you to the nearest airport.
- ☐ If things become critical switch to emergency frequency 121.5 —
    - Communicate — 121.5 is guarded by FSS's, control towers, military towers, approach control facilities, and Air Route Traffic Control Centers.
    - Confess — Once communications are established, let them know your problem.
    - Comply — Follow instructions.
- ☐ Set the transponder to 7700.

Checklist

It is most likely that diversion and lost procedure tasks will be covered verbally with "scenarios." The following checklists can be used for these example scenario conditions:

What actions should be taken if you become disoriented or lost on a cross-country flight?

Condition A: plenty of fuel and weather conditions good and you have a GPS with map capability.

☐ Straighten up and fly right. Fly a specific heading in a direction you believe to be correct (or circle, if unsure); don't wander aimlessly.

☐ Set a waypoint for a known airport or location and fly to it.

Condition B: plenty of fuel and weather conditions good but no GPS or your GPS has failed.

☐ Straighten up and fly right. Fly a specific heading in a direction you believe to be correct (or circle, if unsure); don't wander aimlessly.

☐ If you have been flying a steady heading and keeping a relatively accurate navigation log, it's not likely you will have a problem locating your position.

☐ Use knowledge of your last known position, elapsed time, approximate wind direction and ground speed, to establish how far you may have traveled since your last checkpoint.

☐ Use this distance as a radius and draw a semicircle ahead of your last known position on chart. For example, you estimate your ground speed at 60 knots. If you have been flying 20 minutes since your last checkpoint, then the no-wind radius of your semi-circle is 20 miles projected along the direction of your estimated track.

☐ If still unsure of your position, climb, loosen up the eyeballs and start some first-class pilotage. Look for something big. Don't concern yourself with the minute or trivial at this point. Often, there will be linear features such as rivers, mountain ranges, or prominent highways and railroads that are easy to identify. You can use them simply as references for orientation purposes and thus find them of great value in fixing your approximate position.

Condition C: low on fuel; weather deteriorating; inadequate experience; darkness imminent; and/or equipment malfunctioning. Now you have a problem that needs to be solved. You have made a number of mistakes by this time. Your decision now could be your last decision if it is the wrong one.

☐ Get it on the ground! Most accidents are the product of mistakes which have multiplied over a period of time and getting lost is no exception; don't push your luck. It may well be that in doing so, you have added the final mistake which will add another figure to the accident statistics. If terrain or other conditions make landing impossible at the moment, don't waste time, for it is of the essence: don't search for the perfect field—anything usable will do. Remember, most people on the ground know where they are; and you do not.

VIII. SLOW FLIGHT AND STALLS

This section is for airplane and weight-shift control only (no powered parachute checklists).

Tips

- Be familiar with the aircraft.
- Practice in the aircraft before the test. Study the areas that apply to your aircraft.
- **You must clear the area before any of these maneuvers are performed or you will fail the checkride.**

A. Maneuvering During Slow Flight

Checklist

☐ Select an altitude so that the maneuver can be completed no lower than 1,000 AGL; typically 1,500 AGL is used.

☐ Perform clearing turns to make sure the area is clear of other aircraft.

☐ Establish and maintain airspeed where any further increase in angle of attack would cause a stall. Maintain PTS tolerances for:

- straight and level flight
- turns
- climbs
- descents

☐ Perform with different situations as required in the PTS.

B. Power-Off Stalls

Checklist

☐ Get the aircraft to appropriate altitude above ground where the maneuver can be completed no lower than 1,000 feet AGL; minimum 1,500 feet AGL is typically used.

☐ Configure the aircraft for landing.

☐ Perform clearing turns to make sure the area is clear of other aircraft.

☐ Establish approach speed, power setting, and glide simulating approach to landing.

☐ Raise nose smoothly to an angle that will induce a stall.

☐ Reduce pitch angle/nose attitude/angle of attack immediately.

☐ Apply maximum allowable power to minimize the altitude lost if required. *Important note:* Some aircraft have a nose-up tendency when full power is applied. Follow the POH procedures for throttle use for each particular aircraft.

☐ Establish proper speed.

☐ Maintain PTS tolerances for straight and turning stalls.

☐ Airplanes only—retract flaps after proper speed is established.

☐ Airplanes only—any side rotation should simultaneously be stopped with the rudder. Use of the ailerons to lift a fallen wing can further stall the wing and cause the aircraft to spin. Initially it is best to leave the ailerons neutral and stop any rotation with the rudder—**not** with the ailerons.

C. Airplane Only—Power-On Stalls

Checklist

☐ Get the aircraft to appropriate altitude above ground where the maneuver can be completed no lower than 1,000 feet AGL; minimum 1,500 feet AGL is typically used.

☐ Configure the aircraft typically used on takeoff.

☐ Perform clearing turns to make sure the area is clear of other aircraft.

☐ Establish takeoff climb speed simulating climbout with no less than 65% power.

☐ Raise nose smoothly to an angle that will induce a stall.

☐ Reduce pitch angle/nose attitude/angle of attack immediately.

☐ Apply maximum allowable power to minimize altitude lost if required. *Important Note:* some aircraft have a nose-up tendency when full power is applied. Follow the POH procedures for throttle use for each particular aircraft.

☐ Establish proper speed.

☐ Maintain PTS tolerances for straight and turning stalls.

☐ Retract flaps after proper speed is established.

D. Airplane Only—Spin Awareness

Checklist

The sport pilot practical test for spin awareness is oral only with no actual spins performed, covering:

Aerodynamic factors that cause spins.

☐ Airplane must be stalled to spin.

☐ A yawing moment must be introduced to progress from a stall to a spin.

☐ Aft CG provides a better opportunity for an airplane to spin and a more difficult spin recovery.

Flight situations where spins might occur:

• Approach to landing with crossed controls

• Takeoff with crossed controls

• Trying to recover from a stall rotation with the ailerons

Spin avoidance:

☐ Maintain proper airspeed and coordinated flight to avoid stalls.

☐ Proper stall recovery, especially using rudder rather than ailerons for directional control.

Spin recovery procedures (POH procedures must be used for particular aircraft):

- ☐ Reduce power to idle.
- ☐ Position the ailerons to neutral.
- ☐ Apply full positive and brisk opposite rudder against rotation.
- ☐ Apply a positive and brisk forward movement of the elevator control forward of neutral to break stall.
- ☐ After spin rotation stops neutralize rudder.
- ☐ Slowly apply back elevator pressure to raise the nose to level flight.

E. Weight-Shift Control Only—Whip Stall and Tumble Awareness

A whip stall is when the nose gets so high that the wing is completely stalled. With the large area of the wing now in back of the CG, the nose whips down and a fast rotation of the wing can keep it rotating into a tumble. Whip stall and tumble awareness are covered verbally in the test.

Flight situations where unintentional whip stalls and tumbles may occur:

- Extreme turbulence.
- Pilot-induced, by performing maneuvers where the nose angle exceeds 45 degrees above the horizon.

Techniques used to avoid whip stalls and tumbles:

- ☐ Fly within the limitations of the wing and pilot.
- ☐ Avoid situations where the nose gets above 30 degrees to the horizon.
- ☐ Proper training.
- ☐ Flying in no more than moderate turbulence.

The likely results of exciting a whip stall and tumble are:

- A whip stall alone could break the control bar or damage the ribs or chest of the pilot as the whip stall starts to rotate the nose down.
- A tumble would more likely break some structure on the aircraft.

IX. Emergency Operations

Tips

- Study the areas that apply to your aircraft.
- It is easiest to show as you explain, than to just explain verbally.
- You need to be proficient in your own aircraft, and the aircraft in which you will take the test.

General plan for all emergency procedures, ABCs:

A predetermined plan for each situation.

Be ready to make good decisions when each situation occurs—review and practice.

Control—first and foremost maintain control of aircraft.

A. Emergency Approach and Landing (Simulated)

Partial or complete power loss

Important safety note: One of the most important safety procedures is to simulate engine-out situations and develop the capability to glide and land on a predetermined spot. This is an important exercise to practice with your instructor, once you solo, and throughout your flying career. The higher you fly, the longer the time you have to evaluate the situation and the more landing options you have. Throughout your flights, you should always be thinking "if the engine goes quiet right now, I would…." Have a predetermined plan running in the back of your mind. Plan your flight and be at an altitude where you feel confident that if the engine quits or loses power, you have a plan. Fly from suitable landing area to suitable landing area.

Checklists

First and foremost, fly the aircraft and maintain control.
For decisions on determining a suitable landing area consider—

- ☐ Wind—Upwind/headwind landings are easier and safer than downwind landings, especially if it could be a hard landing, slower impact speeds are better.
- ☐ Obstacles—Good obstacles are those that can slow you down nicely as energy absorbers, such as tall grass, wheat, corn or other uniform crops. Bad obstacles are those that slow you down too fast, hazards such as big trees, buildings, large rocks, or other large solid objects.
- ☐ Terrain—Uphill landings slow you down better than downhill landings. Rocky and uneven terrain surfaces can create more problems than smooth more predictable terrain.

Partial or complete power loss soon after takeoff—determination of best suitable landing area:

☐ Lower nose and establish best glide-ratio speed.

☐ Maintain control of the aircraft.

☐ Assess altitude to determine whether you turn back 180 degrees to runway or land straight out considering wind/obstacles/terrain.

- Significant altitude is lost in a 180-degree turn back to the runway with a resultant downwind landing. Expect little time to react with fast landing speeds. A steep turn close to the ground can be deadly.
- Landings straight ahead are preferred if possible since they are upwind. It is generally suggested turning maximum of 60 degrees. Use slight turns to avoid objects.

Partial or complete power loss during flight enroute—determination of best suitable landing area:

☐ Lower nose and establish best glide-ratio speed.

☐ Maintain control of the aircraft.

☐ Look for a suitable landing area considering wind/obstacles/terrain.

☐ Only after the aircraft is under control and a suitable landing area is established should you try to restart the engine if you have enough altitude and time. Again, always maintain control of the aircraft.

☐ Determine best approach considering wind/obstacles/terrain.

Partial or complete power loss emergency landing:

☐ Lower the flaps per POH once the intended landing area is easily within reach, considering wind and reduced glide ratio with flaps.

☐ Shut off the electrical and fuel supply to reduce the chance of a spark and fire.

☐ Undo cockpit exits so they are not jammed during hard landing, for quick exit of aircraft if necessary to avoid fire.

☐ Slow down the aircraft as much as possible before touching anything.

☐ Use terrain or obstacles to slow down—

- Soft, uniform objects, such as tall grass, crops, etc.
- Steer the fuselage clear of solid large obstacles; if necessary, let the wings strike large solid obstacles to slow the aircraft down. Continue to steer the fuselage clear of large solid objects.

Emergency Descent

In the case of an uncontrollable fire or any other emergency situation requiring an immediate landing, descend as rapidly as possible to a lower altitude. Consult the POH for the best procedure that will ensure positive control of the aircraft is maintained and the structural limitations of the aircraft are not exceeded. This is a very important maneuver to practice in order for it to become standard procedure that must be carried out when the situation is truly an emergency. This should be learned with a **qualified instructor** familiar with the aircraft, and practiced as a routine procedure in your aircraft.

☐ Reduce throttle to idle.

☐ Airplanes with flaps only—determine in POH what is optimum procedure for quickest descent before flight.

- Extend flaps and operate at maximum flap extension speed V_{FE}. Slipping the airplane can increase the descent rate if allowed in the POH at higher airspeeds.
- No flaps, and operate in the yellow range as high as possible lowering airspeed in turbulent conditions as appropriate. Slipping the airplane can increase the descent rate if allowed in the POH at higher airspeeds.

☐ Establish a suitable landing area if needed and plan the descent to the landing area.

- Fly towards the intended landing area, then descend over that location.
- If you must lose altitude immediately, descend to a lower altitude first, then fly over to landing area.

☐ Establish a circular path so you can visually see and avoid air traffic from all directions during the descent.

☐ Maintain a 30- to 45-degree bank angle, for positive G forces on the airplane.

☐ Monitor aeromedical factors, due to higher G-loading factors and spatial disorientation.

☐ Recover from descent with adequate altitude to set up for appropriate landing.

B. Systems and Equipment Malfunctions

Engine roughness because of engine malfunction or propeller imbalance:

☐ Reduce throttle.

☐ Locate a suitable landing area.

☐ Check to make sure choke or enrichener system has not been accidentally turned to rich.

☐ Monitor engine instruments for signs of the problem.

☐ If continued power is necessary to reach suitable landing area, try different throttle settings for smoothest operation. Roughness may vary with different settings.

☐ If vibration or roughness is severe, land as soon as practical.

Engine instruments malfunction:

☐ Higher temperatures should be dealt with immediately by reducing throttle, before evaluating the integrity of the reading. High temperatures usually mean higher temperatures.

☐ If erroneous readings show on your engine instruments, decide whether or not it is an error in the instrument.

☐ When CHT, EGT, water, and oil temperature thermocouple probes fail, they depict a reduction in temperature, not a higher value. Bad grounds will also produce lower readings.

☐ Compare to other gages and running characteristics of the engine (sound, feel).

Engine overheat:

☐ Reduce throttle.

☐ Increase airspeed for more ram air cooling of air, water and oil engine cooling systems.

☐ Locate a suitable landing area.

☐ Use minimum throttle required to make it to the suitable landing area.

Carburetor or induction icing (symptom—slow loss in RPM/power):

☐ Awareness and avoidance—

- Be aware of the carburetor system icing conditions when the temperature is between 20°F and 70°F, and the relative humidity is high.
- Use a carb heater if you are going to fly in conditions favorable for icing.
- Most four-stroke float/butterfly carburetors should use carb heat to avoid ice.

☐ Apply carb heat if available initially before reducing power to keep the carb heated air hot. Expect slight loss in power initially as a result of the hot air into the engine, but expect an increase in RPM as the ice clears and opens the throttle gradually to full capacity.

☐ Locate a suitable landing area if no carb heat is available or the power keeps decreasing.

☐ Keep the throttle open to obtain maximum power.

☐ Move the throttle back and forth gently to free ice from the air valve if nothing else works. Forcing it could damage the air valve creating other problems.

☐ Use available power to land at a suitable landing area.

Four-stroke engines only—Loss of oil pressure:

☐ Reduce power.

☐ Search for a suitable landing area since engine may not last very long.

☐ Observe engine temperatures for condition of engine.

☐ Land as soon as practical.

tarvation (symptom—slow loss in power, rough engine running):

starvation can be hard to detect as the specific problem while flying, since a reduction ower could be the result of many other factors.

☐ Locate a suitable landing area.

☐ Make sure the fuel shut-off valve has not been accidentally closed or vibrated shut.

Electrical malfunction:

☐ Switch off main electrical (not ignition) and nonessential loads to save battery.

☐ Switch on selected loads needed to isolate problem.

☐ Many times electrical malfunction is the generator, inverter, or other downstream systems, if the ignition system is supplying a spark to the plugs and the engine stays running. (Vintage aircraft with separate generator systems producing power could also fail, creating a malfunction.)

☐ LSA can fly safely with no power and no immediate emergency landing is required.

☐ Fly normally to destination unless alternate airport is necessary.

Vintage aircraft only—vacuum/pressure and associated flight instruments malfunction:

Typically, only vintage aircraft use vacuum/pressure instruments for more advanced instruments and are not a factor for sport pilot visual flight reference.

Pitot/static malfunction:

If basic airspeed, rate of climb, and/or altimeter instrument systems appear to be functioning improperly, the aircraft is still safe to fly.

☐ Use common sense and visual reference to safely fly to the airport.

☐ Pitot is used for airspeed (along with a static port for faster aircraft)—
  • A plugged or leaky pitot tube would normally indicate slower airspeeds than normal.
  • Fly the aircraft at an airspeed fast enough to ensure you do not stall.
  • Use the feel and sound of the wind to determine airspeed.
  • Maintain adequate airspeed for landings. More airspeed is better than less. Just float above the runway normally until the aircraft settles on the wheels.
  • Use GPS to assess airspeed, corrected for wind if necessary.

☐ Static ports—
  • Many slower aircraft do not use static ports, they measure the static at the instrument itself; but totally enclosed-cabin or faster aircraft use static ports.
  • Static ports are used for altitude and rate-of-climb plus airspeed on faster aircraft.
  • Climbing—plugged static ports would indicate lower climb rates, lower altitudes and higher airspeeds.
  • Descending—plugged static ports would indicate lower descent rates, higher altitudes and lower airspeeds.
  • Use GPS for altitude and vertical speed estimation as a reference, if needed.

Airplane Only

Flap malfunction—both sides uniform, flaps up:

☐ Plan on extra approach and landing speeds during landings.

☐ Plan on extra runway length needed for landings.

Flap malfunction—both sides uniform, flaps down:

☐ Maintain airspeeds within POH operational limits.

☐ Land at suitable airport considering slower speeds and greater fuel usage.

Flap malfunction—one side only causing strong bank and adverse yaw:

☐ Counteract bank and adverse yaw with ailerons and rudder.

☐ Maintain adequate airspeed.

☐ Move flap actuation control to other position to equalize flaps.

Inoperative trim:

☐ Plan on extra control forces throughout flight adding fatigue over time.

☐ Must always hold stick/wheel to keep control of aircraft.

Door or window opening inadvertently:

Most aircraft are designed so this is not a big problem and not considered a serious emergency.

☐ Reduce speed to minimize noise and flapping.

☐ Only attempt to latch it if you can maintain control of the aircraft while doing so.

☐ If on passenger's side, instruct passenger to close it just as they were briefed on the ground.

☐ If severe flapping is encountered that could fatigue attachment and loosen door/window, then land as soon as practical and secure.

Smoke in the cabin:

☐ Turn off heater.

☐ Shut off all electric loads except ignition.

☐ Open different windows/doors to get best results (if smoke increases, shut windows/doors).

☐ Descend and land as soon as possible.

☐ Orient the aircraft in different positions to see if smoke can be minimized during descent. (Example: yawing nose to right might clear smoke for pilot, high or low angles of attack might create different airflows within cabin.)

☐ Breathe oxygen if available and necessary.

Fuel fire

Symptoms: fuel is hot and less easy to detect. High heat and less detectable smoke.

☐ If a fuel fire and a suitable landing area is within reach, shut off fuel and land.

☐ Dive the aircraft to blow out fire during emergency descent.

Cabin fire:

☐ Switch off all electric loads except ignition system.

☐ Instruct passenger to operate fire extinguisher as discussed during preflight briefing.

☐ If no passenger, operate fire extinguisher while maintaining control of aircraft.

☐ Locate a suitable landing area and land if needed.

Flight control malfunction:

☐ Use trim to fly aircraft.

☐ Many times this failure is in one direction only.

☐ Figure a way to fly aircraft with remaining (functional) controls.

Ballistic recovery system malfunction/deployment, if applicable:

☐ Prepare to come down under canopy.

☐ If windy, after landing you can get dragged by the chute, prepare to exit the aircraft as soon as possible.

Any other emergency appropriate to the airplane:

☐ List any other systems that may be unique to your aircraft and checklists to follow in an emergency/failure.

C. Emergency Equipment and Survival Gear

Emergency equipment

Fire extinguisher:

☐ Charged

☐ Location for passenger and/or pilot

☐ Operational procedures for pilot and passenger with and without verbal communications.

Ballistic parachute:

Important note: Determine if ballistic parachute is best option for the following emergency conditions. "**Aircraft becomes uncontrollable**" is the main reason for emergency parachute deployment. An emergency parachute deployment can be worse than simply flying the aircraft to the ground. It should be used in a "low probability high consequence event" such as:

☐ Mid-air collision where your aircraft is uncontrollable.

☐ Structural failure where the aircraft becomes uncontrollable.

☐ Near-miss with large aircraft close to the ground where aircraft becomes uncontrollable.

☐ Loss of control from control system malfunction.

☐ Pilot incapacitation including heart attack, stroke, temporarily blinded medically, a bird strike in an open cockpit causing loss of sight, vertigo, spatial disorientation, or simply freezing up in a stressful situation.

☐ Bad pilot decision—

  • Engine failure over hostile terrain or tall trees with no viable landing area.

  • Overshoot or undershoot for emergency landing.

  • Water landings.

Actuation procedure—

☐ Shut off engine.

☐ Allow a minimum altitude of 300 feet AGL.

☐ Orient aircraft for best clear shot of ballistic parachute.

☐ Control the aircraft directly over the area where you want to come down. You will drift with the wind when the parachute is deployed.

☐ Pull hard on the handle to actuate parachute under variable G loading conditions.

☐ Plan for hard water, rough terrain, or tree landing by keeping limbs in and face covered.

☐ Large space blanket doubling as tarp/blanket and signaling device.

☐ Food

☐ Clothing for area you will be flying over and possible cold weather conditions: hats, gloves, jackets and boots.

☐ Basic tools for utilizing aircraft for survival, such as crescent wrench and screwdrivers.

☐ Valid credit card, cash

Additional items specific to unique terrain and climate zone:

Mountain terrain—

☐ Saw

☐ Shovel

☐ Water or water purifier

Large bodies of water—

☐ Floatation device

☐ Drinking water if over ocean, water purifier if over large lakes.

Desert conditions—

☐ Water

☐ Hats for shade

Extreme temperature changes—

☐ Sun shade hat

☐ Layered clothing

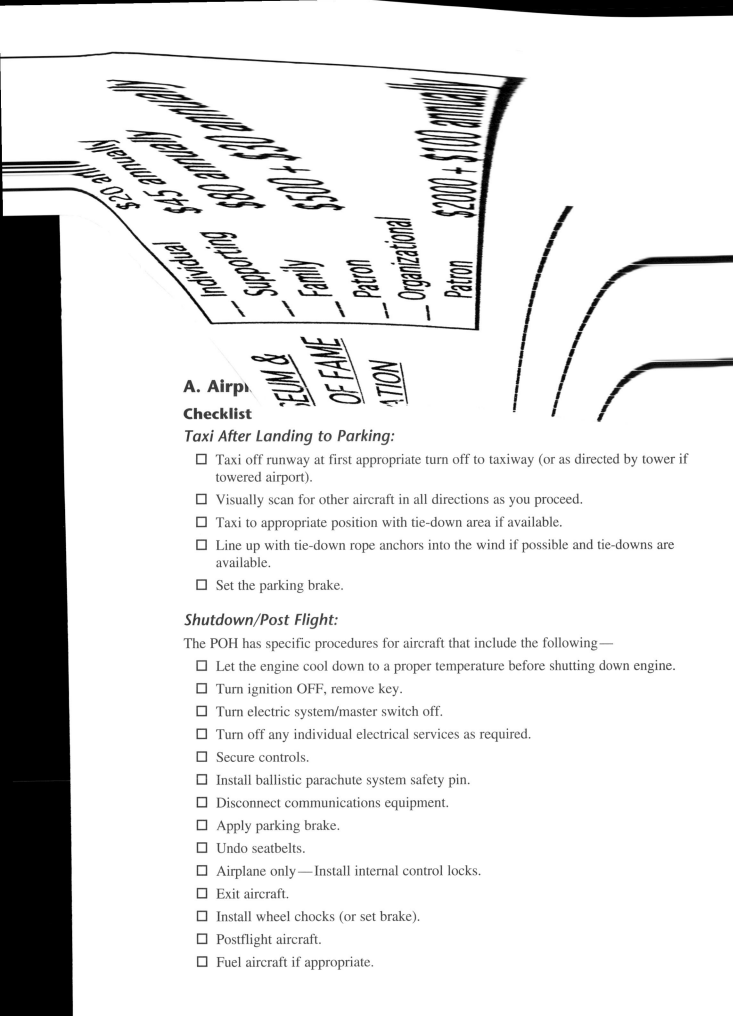

A. Airp...

Checklist

Taxi After Landing to Parking:

☐ Taxi off runway at first appropriate turn off to taxiway (or as directed by tower if towered airport).

☐ Visually scan for other aircraft in all directions as you proceed.

☐ Taxi to appropriate position with tie-down area if available.

☐ Line up with tie-down rope anchors into the wind if possible and tie-downs are available.

☐ Set the parking brake.

Shutdown/Post Flight:

The POH has specific procedures for aircraft that include the following—

☐ Let the engine cool down to a proper temperature before shutting down engine.

☐ Turn ignition OFF, remove key.

☐ Turn electric system/master switch off.

☐ Turn off any individual electrical services as required.

☐ Secure controls.

☐ Install ballistic parachute system safety pin.

☐ Disconnect communications equipment.

☐ Apply parking brake.

☐ Undo seatbelts.

☐ Airplane only—Install internal control locks.

☐ Exit aircraft.

☐ Install wheel chocks (or set brake).

☐ Postflight aircraft.

☐ Fuel aircraft if appropriate.

Secure aircraft:

☐ Airplane only—Close and secure canopy doors.

☐ Weight-shift control only—Secure control bar to front tube and tie wings to tie-downs; or, for more secure overnight tie-down, drop wing so the control bar is on the ground and wings level. Tie down wings at leading edge/crossbar junction.

☐ Tie down both wings at specific tie-down points specified in POH, tail if appropriate.

☐ Install any pitot tube covers and plug any open areas from dust and water.

☐ Airplane only—Install any external control locks.

☐ Install sun shades or other covering that would protect the cockpit, canopy, fuselage and wing from rain, dust and the sun.

☐ If it is to be stored for a longer period, plug intake and exhaust holes to protect against corrosion.

Postflight documentation:

☐ Record the engine time and fill in pilot logbook.

☐ Report any defects or squawks from postflight inspection.

B. Powered Parachute

Checklist

Taxi After Landing to Parking:

☐ Taxi off runway at first appropriate turn off to taxiway (or as directed by tower if towered airport).

☐ Visually scan for other aircraft in all directions as you proceed.

☐ Taxi to appropriate position where you can drop canopy and pack into bag.

☐ Shut down the engine and drop canopy.

☐ Pack canopy into bag.

☐ Restart and taxi to appropriate parking position.

☐ Set the parking brake (if appropriate).

- ☐ Turn electric system/master switch off.
- ☐ Turn off any individual electrical services as required.
- ☐ Disconnect communications equipment.
- ☐ Undo seatbelts.
- ☐ Exit aircraft.
- ☐ Install wheel chocks (or set brake).
- ☐ Postflight aircraft.
- ☐ Fuel aircraft if appropriate.

Secure aircraft:

- ☐ Install any pitot tube covers and plug any open areas from dust and water.
- ☐ Install sun shades or other covering that would protect the cockpit, canopy, fuselage and wing from rain, dust and the sun.
- ☐ If it is to be stored for a longer period, plug intake and exhaust holes to protect against corrosion.

Post flight documentation:

- ☐ Record the engine time and fill in pilot logbook.
- ☐ Report any defects or squawks from post flight inspection.

Part 3 **Instructor Checkride Guide**

Introduction

This last part of the *Sport Pilot Checkride* is for flight instructors only. The tables at the end of the PTS flight instructor section specify the additional tasks required—besides those for sport pilot—for the flight instructor initial checkride and proficiency checks. An instructor candidate can be tested by the examiner on all the sport pilot material in Part 2 of this book.

Covered in Part 3 is additional information for the instructor practical test that does not fit into the previous sport pilot areas of operation. It contains the questions most commonly asked by examiners for flight instructor candidates. During the instructor practical, all the sport pilot questions can be asked by the examiner but in their answers, instructor candidates should have a higher level of correlation knowledge plus the additional capabilities to:

- Demonstrate knowledge
- Discuss common errors
- Demonstrate and explain
- Analyze and correct mistakes

Part 3 is specifically for instructors and should be disregarded by the sport pilot applicant.

The reference book used throughout this section is the FAA *Aviation Instructor's Handbook* (FAA-H-8083-9). This is the only additional reference you will need to study and utilize throughout your career as an instructor.

The Flight Instructor PTS covers the three areas of operation:

1. Fundamentals of Instruction
2. Technical Subject Areas
3. Preflight Lesson on a Maneuver to be Performed in Flight

A. The Learning Process

1. Briefly define "learning." (FAA-H-8083-9)

Learning can be defined as a change in behavior as a result of experience.

2. What are the basic characteristics of learning? (FAA-H-8083-9)

Learning is purposeful—Each student sees a learning situation from a different viewpoint, and each has specific instentions and goals. Students learn from any activity that tends to further their goals.

Learning is a result of experience—Learning is an individual process from individual experience. Knowledge cannot be poured into the student's head.

Learning is multifaceted—It may involve verbal, conceptual, perceptual, or emotional elements, and elements of problem solving all taking place at once.

Learning is an active process—For students to learn, they must react and respond.

3. What are the principles (laws) of learning? (FAA-H-8083-9)

They are rules and principles that apply generally to the learning process. The first three are the basic laws; the last three are the result of experimental studies.

R eadiness
E xercise
E ffect
P rimacy
I ntensity
R ecency

4. What is the principle of readiness? (FAA-H-8083-9)

Individuals learn best when they are ready to learn, and they do not learn if they see no reason for it or lack motivation. If students have a strong purpose, a clear objective, and a well-fixed reason for learning something, they make more progress.

5. What is the principle of exercise? (FAA-H-8083-9)

Those things most often repeated are best remembered. It is the basis of practice and drill.

6. What is the principle of effect? (FAA-H-8083-9)

It states that learning is strengthened when accompanied by a pleasant or satisfying feeling, but weakened when associated with an unpleasant feeling.

7. What is the principle of primacy? (FAA-H-8083-9)

Primacy, the state of being first, often creates a strong, almost unshakable, impression; therefore what is taught must be right the first time.

8. What is the principle of intensity? (FAA-H-8083-9)

A vivid, dramatic, or exciting learning experience teaches more than a routine or boring experience.

9. What is the principle of recency? (FAA-H-8083-9)

The things most recently learned are best remembered.

10. What is the basis of all learning? (FAA-H-8083-9)

All learning comes from perceptions that are directed to the brain by one or more of the five senses (sight, hearing, touch, smell, and taste).

11. How do people learn? (FAA-H-8083-9)

All learning involves the following:

Perception—Initially all learning comes from perceptions directed to the brain by one or more of the five senses (sight, hearing, touch, smell and taste).

Insight—The grouping of perceptions into a meaningful whole.

Motivation—The most dominant force governing the student's progress and ability to learn.

12. What are the four basic levels of learning? (FAA-H-8083-9)

Rote learning—The ability to repeat back something one has been taught, without understanding or being able to apply what has been learned.

Understanding—Perceiving and learning what has been taught.

Application—Achieving the skill to apply what has been learned and to perform correctly.

Correlation—Associating what has been learned with other things previously learned or encountered.

13. State several principles used in learning a skill. (FAA-H-8083-9)

a. Physical skills involve more than muscles: Perceptions change as the physical skill becomes easier.

b. Desire to learn: Shorter initial learning time and more rapid progress takes place when a desire to learn exists.

c. Patterns to follow: The best way to prepare a student is to provide a clear step-by-step example.

d. Perform the skill: The student needs coordination between muscles and visual and tactile senses.

e. Knowledge of results: It is important for students to be aware of their progress.

g. Duration and organization of the lesson: In planning for student performance, the length of time devoted to practice is very important.

h. Evaluation versus critique: In the initial stages, practical suggestions are more valuable than a grade.

i. Application of skill: Students must use what has been learned—they must learn the skill so well that it becomes easy to perform.

14. Why do individuals forget what has been learned? (FAA-H-8083-9)

Disuse—A person forgets things that are not used.

Interference—A certain experience has overshadowed it, or the learning of something similar has interfered.

Repression—The submersion of ideas into the unconscious mind; they may unintentionally repress unpleasant material, or that which produces anxiety.

15. What actions can the instructor take to help individuals remember what they have learned? (FAA-H-8083-9)

a. Praise stimulates remembering.

b. Recall is prompted by association.

c. Favorable attitudes aid retention—people learn and remember only what they wish to know.

d. Learning with all our senses is most effective—the best perception results from all senses working together.

e. Meaningful repetition aids recall.

16. What kind of learning occurs when a student learns a maneuver through learning a different maneuver? (FAA-H-8083-9)

This is positive transfer of learning.

B. Human Behavior and Effective Communication

1. **Control of human behavior involves understanding human needs. Name the five basic needs.** (FAA-H-8083-9)

   a. Physical

   b. Safety

   c. Social

   d. Egoistic

   e. Self-fulfillment

2. **What are defense mechanisms?** (FAA-H-8083-9)

   Certain behavior patterns are called defense mechanisms because they are subconscious defenses against the realities of unpleasant situations.

3. **What are eight common defense mechanisms?** (FAA-H-8083-9)

   Compensation—Students often attempt to disguise the presence of a weak or undesirable quality by emphasizing a more positive one.

   Projection—Students relegate the blame for their own shortcomings and mistakes to others, or attribute their motives, desires, and characteristics to others.

   Rationalization—Justifying actions that otherwise would be unacceptable; substitution of excuses for reasons.

   Denial of Reality—Students may ignore or refuse to acknowledge disagreeable realities.

   Reaction Formation—Developing a who-cares-how-other-people-feel attitude to cover up feelings of loneliness and a hunger for acceptance.

   Flight—Escaping from frustrating situations by taking flight, physically or mentally; examples are faked illness or daydreaming.

   Aggression—Students may ask irrelevant questions, refuse to participate, etc., when they cannot deal directly with the cause of their frustration.

   Resignation—Students may become so frustrated that they lose interest and give up.

4. **What are the three basic elements of communication?** (FAA-H-8083-9)

   The source—sender, speaker, transmitter, or instructor.

   The symbols—words or signs.

   The receiver—listener, reader, or student.

b. Confusion between the symbol and the symbolized object

c. Overuse of abstractions

d. Interference

6. **Why is it important that an instructor be a good listener?** (FAA-H-8083-9)

Instructors must know something about their students in order to communicate effectively, and must determine the abilities of the students and understand the students to properly communicate. One way to become better acquainted with students is to be a good listener.

7. **How can an instructor teach his students to be good listeners?**
(FAA-H-8083-9)

Teach them to apply the following steps for effective listening:

a. Take notes.

b. Listen for main ideas.

c. Guard against daydreaming.

d. Be emotionally calm.

e. Listen to understand, not refute.

f. Be responsible for listening.

g. Be ready to listen.

8. **Why is good questioning by the instructor an important tool for determining if effective communication has taken place?** (FAA-H-8083-9)

Good questioning can determine how well the student understands. It also shows the student that the instructor is paying attention, and that the instructor is interested in the student's response.

C. The Teaching Process

1. **What are the four basic steps involved in the teaching process?** (FAA-H-8083-9)

   a. Preparation

   b. Presentation

   c. Application

   d. Review and evaluation

2. **What responsibilities does the flight instructor have in the "preparation" stage of a lesson?** (FAA-H-8083-9)

   For each lesson or instructional period, the instructor must prepare a lesson plan. This plan includes:

   a. A statement of lesson objectives.

   b. The procedures and facilities to be used during the lesson.

   c. The specific goals to be attained.

   d. The means to be used for review and evaluation.

   The lesson plan should also include home study or other special preparation to be done by the student. The instructor should make certain that all necessary supplies, materials, and equipment needed for the lesson are readily available and that the equipment is operating properly.

3. **What are the elements of performance-based objectives?** (FAA-H-8083-9)

   Performance-based objectives consist of three parts:

   a. Description of the skill or behavior—Desired outcome of training stated in concrete terms that can be measured.

   b. Conditions—The framework under which the skill or behavior will be demonstrated.

   c. Criteria—The standard which will be used to measure the accomplishment of the objective.

4. **What are the three most common methods of presentation?** (FAA-H-8083-9)

   a. Lecture method

   b. Demonstration/performance method

   c. Guided discussion

particular lesson? (FAA-H-8083-9)

   a. Introduction

   b. Development

   c. Conclusion

2. **What are the basic elements of the introduction step?** (FAA-H-8083-9)

Attention—Gain the student's attention and focus it on the subject involved.

Motivation—Should appeal to each student personally and accentuate their desire to learn.

Overview—Tell the student what is to be covered; give a clear presentation of the objectives and key ideas; provide a road map of the route to be followed.

3. **Discuss the development step of a presentation.** (FAA-H-8083-9)

This is the main part of the lesson. The instructor develops the subject matter in a manner that helps the student achieve desired objectives, and logically organizes the material to show the relationships of the main points.

4. **Discuss the conclusion step of a presentation.** (FAA-H-8083-9)

An effective conclusion retraces the important elements of the lesson and relates them to the objective. This review and wrap-up of ideas reinforces the student's learning and improves the retention of what has been learned.

5. **What are the five most common teaching methods?** (FAA-H-8083-9)

   a. Lecture method

   b. Guided discussion method

   c. Demonstration/performance method

   d. Cooperative or group learning

   e. Computer-based training

6. **Discuss the lecture method of teaching.** (FAA-H-8083-9)

The lecture is used primarily to introduce students to a new subject, but it is also a valuable method for summarizing ideas, showing relationships between theory and practice, and re-emphasizing main points.

7. **Describe the cooperative or group learning method of teaching.** (FAA-H-8083-9)

It is an instructional strategy that organizes students into small groups that work together to maximize their own and each other's learning. The most significant characteristic of group learning is that it continually requires active participation of the student.

8. **What is the guided discussion method of teaching?** (FAA-H-8083-9)

   This method relies on the students to provide ideas, experiences, opinions, and information. Through the skillful use of "lead-off" type questions, the instructor "draws out" what the student knows, rather than spending the entire class period telling them.

9. **What are the different types of questions that may be used in a guided discussion?** (FAA-H-8083-9)

   Overhead—Directed at entire group; used to stimulate thought and response; good lead-off question.

   Rhetorical—Used to stimulate thought; usually asked and answered by the instructor.

   Direct—Used to get a response from a specific individual.

   Reverse—Instructor redirects student's question in an effort to let the student provide the answer.

   Relay—Instructor redirects student's question to the group for an answer instead of to the individual.

10. **What is the demonstration/performance method of teaching?** (FAA-H-8083-9)

    This method of teaching is based on the simple yet sound principle that we learn by doing.

11. **What are the five essential phases of the demonstration/performance method of teaching?** (FAA-H-8083-9)

    a. Explanation

    b. Demonstration

    c. Student performance

    d. Instructor supervision

    e. Evaluation

12. **Discuss the computer-based training method of teaching.** (FAA-H-8083-9)

    Computer-based training (CBT) is the use of the personal computer as a training device (sometimes called computer-based instruction, CBI). One of the major advantages of CBT is that students can progress at a rate that is comfortable for them, and are often able to access the CBT at their own convenience rather than that of the instructor.

should not rely exclusively on a CBT program on traffic patterns and landings to do the ground instruction for a student pilot, then expect the student to demonstrate patterns and landings in the aircraft.

Computer-based training should not be used by the instructor as stand-alone training any more than a textbook or video. Like a video or a textbook, CBT is an aid to the instructor. The instructor must be actively involved with the students when using instructional aids. This involvement should include close supervision, questions, examinations, quizzes, or guided discussions on the subject matter.

E. Critique and Evaluation

1. What is the basic purpose of a critique? (FAA-H-8083-9)

A critique should improve students' performance and provide them with something constructive with which to work and upon which they can build.

2. What are the characteristics of an effective critique? (FAA-H-8083-9)

A critique should be:

a. *Objective*—Focused on student performance; should not reflect the personal opinions of the instructor.

b. *Flexible*—Fit in tone, technique, and content to the occasion and to the student.

c. *Acceptable*—Students must first accept the instructor. Effective critiques are presented with authority, conviction, sincerity, and from a position of recognizable competence.

d. *Comprehensive*—Cover a few major points or a few minor points as well as the student's overall strengths and weaknesses.

e. *Constructive*—Provide positive guidance for correcting the faults and strengthening the weaknesses.

f. *Well-organized*—Follow some pattern of organization.

g. *Thoughtful*—Geared toward the student's need for self-esteem, recognition, and approval from others.

h. *Specific*—Comments and recommendations should not be so general that the student can find nothing to hold on to.

3. Name several useful methods for critique of a student's performance. (FAA-H-8083-9)

a. *Instructor/Student critique*—instructor leads a group discussion in which members of the class are invited to offer criticism of a performance.

b. *Student-led critique*—instructor asks a student to lead the critique.

c. *Small group critique*—a class is divided into small groups and each group is assigned a specific area to analyze.

d. *Individual student critique by another student*—another student presents the entire critique.

e. *Self-critique*—student is required to critique personal performance.

f. *Written critique*—several advantages; the instructor can devote more time and thought to it than to an oral critique in the classroom; students can keep written critiques and refer to them whenever they wish; when the instructor requires all the students to write a critique of a performance, the student/performer has the permanent record of the suggestions, recommendations, and opinions of all the other students.

4. What are the "ground rules" for critiquing? (FAA-H-8083-9)

a. Except in rare and unusual instances, do not extend the critique beyond its scheduled time and into the time allotted for other activities. A point of diminishing returns can be reached quickly.

b. Avoid trying to cover too much. A few well-made points will usually be more beneficial than a large number of points that are not developed adequately.

c. Allow time for a summary of the critique to reemphasize the most important things a student should remember.

d. Avoid dogmatic or absolute statements, remembering that most rules have exceptions.

e. Avoid controversies with the class, and do not get into the delicate position of taking sides with group factions.

f. Never allow yourself to be maneuvered into the unpleasant position of defending criticism. If the criticism is honest, objective, constructive, and comprehensive, no defense should be necessary.

g. If part of the critique is written, make certain that it is consistent with the oral portion.

5. What types of oral questions should the instructor avoid? (FAA-H-8083-9)

a. "Puzzle" type questions with many parts and subparts.

b. "Oversize" questions that are too general, covering a wide area.

c. "Toss-up" questions where there is more than one correct answer.

d. "Bewilderment" questions that are not clear as to their content.

e. "Trick" questions that cause students to think they are engaged in a battle of wits.

f. "Irrelevant" questions that are unrelated to what is being discussed.

You should indicate to the student you don't know the answer, but will help the student find the correct answer.

7. **What are the five characteristics of a good written test?** (FAA-H-8083-9)

   Reliability—it yields consistent results.

   Validity—it measures what should be measured.

   Usability—it is easy to understand and grade.

   Comprehensiveness—it must sample whatever is being measured.

   Discrimination—it will detect small differences.

8. **Where can a flight instructor find the performance standards for evaluation of a particular maneuver?** (FAA-H-8083-9)

   The Practical Test Standards which establish the minimum standards for the certification of pilots. They are available from ASA and online.

F. Flight Instructor Characteristics

1. **What are the four main responsibilities for aviation instructors?** (FAA-H-8083-9)

   a. Helping students learn

   b. Providing adequate instruction

   c. Demanding adequate standards

   d. Emphasizing the positive

2. **How can an instructor provide a more positive and efficient learning experience?** (FAA-H-8083-9)

   a. Devise a plan of action.

   b. Create a positive student-instructor relationship.

   c. Present information and guidance effectively.

   d. Transfer responsibility to the student as learning occurs.

   e. Evaluate student learning and thereby measure teaching effectiveness.

3. **Faulty performance of a maneuver due to student overconfidence should be corrected in which way?** (FAA-H-8083-9)

   Students who are fast learners may develop overconfidence that could result in faulty performance. For such students, the instructor should constantly raise the standard of performance for each lesson, demanding greater effort.

4. **Why is it important for an instructor to continuously evaluate standards of performance?** (FAA-H-8083-9)

Instructors fail to provide competent instruction when they permit their students to get by with a substandard performance, or without learning thoroughly an item of knowledge pertinent to safe piloting. More importantly, such deficiencies may in themselves allow hazardous inadequacies in student performance later on.

5. **Discuss the significance of always emphasizing the positive when providing flight instruction.** (FAA-H-8083-9)

Aviation instructors have a tremendous influence on their students' perception of aviation. The way instructors conduct themselves, the attitudes they display, and the way they develop their instruction all contribute to either positive or negative impressions by their students. Much of the success of the instructor depends on the ability to present instruction so that students develop a positive image of aviation.

6. **What are several examples of additional responsibilities that all flight instructors have?** (FAA-H-8083-9)

    a. Evaluation of student piloting ability

    b. Pilot supervision

    c. Practical Test recommendations

    d. Flight instructor endorsements

    e. Additional training and endorsements

    f. Pilot proficiency

7. **What are important personal characteristics that a flight instructor should possess?** (FAA-H-8083-9)

    a. *Sincerity*—should be straightforward and honest.

    b. *Acceptance of the student*—should accept students as they are including all their faults and problems.

    c. *Personal appearance and habits*—should be neat, clean and appropriately dressed.

    d. *Demeanor*—should be calm, thoughtful, and disciplined.

    e. *Safety practices and accident prevention*—practices emphasized by instructors have a lasting effect on students.

    f. *Proper language*—should speak normally, without inhibitions, and develop the ability to speak positively and descriptively without excesses of language.

    g. *Self-improvement*—should be constantly alert for ways to improve their qualifications, effectiveness, and the services they provide to students.

b. Keep students informed.

c. Approach students as individuals.

d. Give credit when due.

e. Criticize constructively.

f. Be consistent.

g. Admit errors.

G. Planning Instructional Activity

1. Define the following terms. (FAA-H-8083-9)

Curriculum—a set of courses in an area of specialization offered by an educational institution. A curriculum for a pilot school usually includes courses for the various pilot certificates and ratings.

Training syllabus—a summary or outline of a course of study; a syllabus defines the unit of training, states what the student is expected to accomplish during the unit, shows an organized plan for instruction, and dictates the evaluation process.

Training course outline—within a curriculum, may be described as the content of a particular course. It normally includes statements of objectives, descriptions of teaching aids, definitions of evaluating criteria, and indications of desired outcome.

2. How are the objectives and standards developed for a course of training? (FAA-H-8083-9)

The overall objectives of an aviation training course are usually well established, and the general standards are included in various rules and related publications. Eligibility, knowledge, proficiency, and experience requirements for pilots and maintenance students are stipulated in the regulations, and the standards are published in the applicable PTS.

3. Why is it so important to develop and assemble learning blocks in their proper relationship? (FAA-H-8083-9)

Training for any such complicated and involved task as piloting or maintaining an aircraft requires the development and assembly of many segments or blocks of learning in their proper relationships, because a student can master the segments or blocks individually and can progressively combine these with other related segments. The result is such that the student meets the overall training objectives.

4. What should each lesson of a training syllabus include? (FAA-H-8083-9)

a. The objective.

b. The content.

c. The completion standards.

5. Would it be acceptable for an instructor to depart from the order specified in the training syllabus? (FAA-H-8083-9)

The syllabus must be flexible and used primarily as a guide. When necessary, the order of training can and should be altered to suit the progress of the student and the demands of special circumstances (such as weather variations, aircraft availability, etc). For example, previous experience or different rates of learning often will require some alteration or repetition to fit individual students.

6. What is a lesson plan? (FAA-H-8083-9)

A lesson plan is an organized outline for a single instructional period. It is a necessary guide for the instructor in that it tells what to do, in what order to do it, and what procedure to use in teaching the material of a lesson.

7. What is the purpose of lesson plans? (FAA-H-8083-9)

They are designed to ensure each student receives the best possible instruction under the existing conditions. An adequate lesson plan:

a. Ensures a wise selection of material and the elimination of unimportant details.

b. Makes certain that due consideration is given to each part of the lesson.

c. Aids the instructor in presenting a suitable sequence for efficient learning.

d. Provides an outline of the teaching procedure to be used.

e. Serves as a means of relating the lesson to the objectives of the course of training.

f. Gives the inexperienced instructor confidence.

g. Promotes uniformity of instruction regardless of the instructor or the date on which the lesson is given.

8. What are characteristics of a good lesson plan? (FAA-H-8083-9)

a. *Unity*—Each lesson should be a unified segment of instruction.

b. *Content*—Each lesson should contain new material as well as a short review of earlier lessons.

c. *Scope*—Each lesson should be reasonable in scope.

d. *Practicality*—Each lesson should be planned in terms of the conditions under which the training is to be conducted.

e. *Flexibility*—Although the lesson plan provides an outline and training sequence, it should allow some flexibility.

f. *Relation to Course of Training*—Each lesson should be planned and taught so that its relation to the course objectives are clear to each student.

g. *Instructional Steps*—Each lesson, when adequately developed, falls logically into the four steps of the teaching process: preparation, presentation, application, and review and evaluation.

...y is it important that the instructor and student understand the "positive exchange of flight controls" concept as it relates to flight training? (FAA-H-8083-9)

During flight training, there must always be a clear understanding between students and flight instructors of who has control of the aircraft. The preflight briefing should includes the procedure for the exchange of flight controls. A positive three-step process in the exchange of flight controls between pilots is a proven procedure, and is strongly recommended.

2. **Describe the three-step process used for the positive exchange of flight controls.** (FAA-H-8083-9)

   a. When the flight instructor wants the student to take control of the aircraft, the instructor says to the student: "You have the flight controls."

   b. The student acknowledges immediately by saying: "I have the flight controls."

   c. The flight instructor again says: "You have the flight controls."

   Note: During this procedure, a visual check is recommended to see that the other person actually has the flight controls. When returning the controls to the instructor, the student should follow the same procedure the instructor used.

3. **What is the purpose of using distractions during flight training?** (FAA-H-8083-9)

   To determine that the student possesses the skills required to cope with distractions while maintaining the degree of aircraft control required for safe flight. Pilots at all skill levels should be aware of the increased risk of entering into an inadvertent stall or spin while performing tasks that are secondary to controlling the aircraft.

4. **How should the instructor incorporate the use of distractions into his or her flight instruction?** (FAA-H-8083-9)

   The instructor should tell the student to divide his/her attention between the distracting task and maintaining control of the aircraft. The following are examples of distractions that can be used for this training:

   a. Drop a pencil. Ask the student to pick it up.

   b. Ask the student to determine a heading to an airport using a chart.

   c. Ask the student to get something from the back seat.

   d. Ask the student what the current ground speed is.

   e. Ask the student to identify terrain or objects on the ground.

   f. Ask the student to identify a field suitable for a forced landing.

5. **Define the term "aeronautical decision making." (FAA-H-8083-9)**

   Aeronautical decision making is the systematic approach to the mental process used by aircraft pilots to consistently determine the best course of action in response to a given set of circumstances.

6. **During flight, decisions must be made regarding events that involve interactions between the four risk elements. What are they? (FAA-H-8083-9)**

   Pilot-in-command—the aircraft—the environment—the operation.

7. **The DECIDE model for decision making involves which elements? (FAA-H-8083-9)**

   D etect a change needing attention.

   E stimate the need to counter or react to change.

   C hoose the most desirable outcome for the flight.

   I dentify actions to successfully control the change.

   D o something to adapt to the change.

   E valuate the effect of the action countering the change.

8. **Name the five hazardous attitudes and their antidotes that negatively impact a pilot's judgment and ability to make competent decisions. (FAA-H-8083-9)**

Attitude	Antidote
Anti-authority	Follow the rules, they are usually right.
Impulsivity	Think first—not so fast.
Invulnerability	It could happen to me.
Macho	Taking chances is foolish.
Resignation	I can make a difference, I am not helpless.

9. **What does crew resource management (CRM) refer to? (FAA-H-8083-9)**

   It is the application of team management concepts in the flight deck environment. Initially, it was "cockpit resource management," but as CRM programs evolved to include cabin crews, maintenance personnel, and others, the phrase "crew resource management" was adopted. This includes single pilots, as in most general aviation and light-sport aircraft. Pilots of small aircraft, as well as crews of larger aircraft, must make effective use of all available resources: human resources, hardware, and information.

10. **Which groups routinely working with the cockpit crew may also be viewed as effective components of CRM and the decision-making process in the cockpit? (FAA-H-8083-9)**

    They include, but are not limited to pilots, dispatchers, cabin crewmembers, maintenance personnel and air traffic controllers.

four fundamental risk elements affecting safety before, during, and after the flight.

12. **Situational awareness takes into consideration which four elements?** (FAA-H-8083-9)

The four elements to be taken into consideration with situational awareness are: Pilot—Aircraft—Environment—Type of Operation—and their interaction with each other.

13. **Why are pilots encouraged to use checklists?** (FAA-H-8083-9)

Checklists provide a logical and standardized method to operate a particular make and model airplane. Following a checklist reinforces the use of proper procedures throughout all major phases of flight operations.

14. **What are the two primary methods of checklist usage?** (FAA-H-8083-9)

a. *Read and Do*—The pilot picks up a checklist, refers to an item, and sets the condition. The items for any particular phase of flight would all be accomplished before the checklist is set aside.

b. *Do and Verify*—In this method, the condition of the items for a particular phase of operation are set from memory or flow pattern. Then, the checklist is read to verify that the appropriate condition for each item in that phase has been set. It is not wise for a pilot to become so reliant upon a flow pattern that he or she fails to verify with a checklist. Checking important items solely from memory is not an acceptable substitute for checklists.

A. Aeromedical Factors

1. When should a student pilot obtain a medical certificate if they are not going to use a driver's license as medical eligibility or they are going to obtain a private pilot certificate? (FAA-H-8083-25)

Prior to beginning flight training, a flight instructor should interview the prospective student about any health conditions and determine his or her ultimate goal as a pilot, and should advise the student to obtain the class of medical certificate required. Finding out first whether the student is medically qualified could save time and money.

2. Why is it important for students to obtain a medical certificate as soon as possible if they are not going to use a driver's license as medical eligibility or they are going to obtain a private pilot certificate? (AIM 8-1-1)

Student pilots should visit an Aviation Medical Examiner as soon as possible in their flight training in order to avoid unnecessary training expenses should they not meet the medical standards.

3. How can an individual obtain a medical certificate in the event of a possible medical deficiency? (14 CFR 67.409)

Any person who is denied a medical certificate by an aviation medical examiner may, within 30 days after the date of denial, apply in writing and in duplicate to the Federal Air Surgeon for reconsideration of that denial. Aviation Medical Examiners (AME) can issue a medical certificate with certain limitations on flying activities due to medical conditions that exist.

4. State several medical conditions that might prevent the issuance of a medical certificate. (14 CFR Part 67)

a. Clinical diabetes

b. Coronary heart disease/heart attack

c. Epilepsy

d. Disturbance of consciousness

e. Alcoholism

f. Drug dependence

g. Psychosis

5. What should students know about flight operations conducted while suffering from a medical deficiency? (14 CFR 61.53)

No person may act as pilot-in-command, or in any other capacity as a required flight crewmember, while having a known medical deficiency that would make him/her unable to meet the requirements for his/her current medical certificate.

Refer to sport pilot Aeromedical section for the causes, symptoms, effects and corrective action for medical factors and for the effects of alcohol and drugs with the relationship to flight safety.

B. Visual Scanning and Collision Avoidance

1. What is the relationship between a pilot's physical or mental condition and vision? (AIM 8-1-1)

The two are closely related. Even a minor illness suffered in day-to-day living can seriously degrade performance of many piloting tasks including the pilot's ability to effectively use his/her vision. Use the IMSAFE checklist: I'm physically and mentally safe to fly, not being impaired by: **I**llness, **M**edication, **S**tress, **A**lcohol, **F**atigue, **E**motion.

2. Name several factors that can degrade a pilot's vision. (AIM 8-1-6, 8-1-8)

a. *Visibility conditions*—smoke, haze, dust, rain, and flying towards the sun can greatly reduce the ability to detect targets.

b. *Windshield conditions*—dirty or bug-smeared windshields can greatly reduce the ability to see other aircraft.

c. *Bright illumination*—reflected off clouds, water, snow, and desert terrain that produces glare resulting in eyestrain and the inability to see effectively.

d. *Dim illumination*—small print and colors on aeronautical charts and aircraft instruments become unreadable.

e. *Dark adaptation*—eyes must have at least 20 to 30 minutes to adjust to the reduced light conditions.

3. Describe some of the various optical illusions a pilot can experience in flight. (AIM 8-1-5)

The "leans"—An abrupt correction of a banked attitude, which has been entered too slowly to stimulate the motion sensing system in the inner ear, can create the illusion of banking in the opposite direction. Examples include: Coriolis illusion, graveyard spin, graveyard spiral, somatogravic illusion, inversion illusion, elevator illusion, false horizon and autokinesis.

Runway width illusion—A narrower-than-usual runway can create the illusion that the aircraft is at a higher altitude than it actually is. Unrecognized, the pilot may fly a lower approach, with the risk of striking objects along the approach path or landing

Runway and terrain slope illusion—An upsloping runway, upsloping terrain or both, can create the illusion that the aircraft is at a higher altitude than it actually is. Unrecognized, the pilot may fly a lower approach. A downsloping runway, downsloping approach terrain, or both, can have the opposite effect.

Featureless terrain illusion—An absence of ground features, as when landing over water, darkened areas, and terrain made featureless by snow, can create the illusion that the aircraft is at a higher altitude than it actually is. Unrecognized, the pilot may fly a lower approach.

4. Explain the "see and avoid" concept. (14 CFR 91.113)

When weather conditions permit, regardless of whether the flight is conducted under instrument flight rules or visual flight rules, vigilance shall be maintained by each person operating an aircraft so as to see and avoid other aircraft.

5. Explain the practice of time-sharing your attention inside and outside the cockpit. (AIM 8-1-6)

Studies show that the time a pilot spends on visual tasks inside the cabin should represent no more than 1/4 to 1/3 of the scan time outside, or no more than 4 to 5 seconds on the instrument panel for every 16 seconds outside.

6. What is a good visual scanning technique? (AIM 8-1-6)

Effective scanning is accomplished with a series of short, regularly spaced eye movements that bring successive areas of the sky into the central visual field. Each movement should not exceed 10 degrees, and each area should be observed for at least 1 second to enable detection. Although horizontal back and forth eye movements seem preferred, each pilot should develop a scanning pattern that is most comfortable and then adhere to it to ensure optimum scanning.

C. Federal Aviation Regulations and Publications

1. What is 14 CFR Part 61? (14 CFR 61.1)

Part 61 prescribes the requirements for issuing pilot, flight instructor, and ground instructor certificates and ratings, the conditions under which those certificates and ratings are necessary, and their associated privileges and limitations.

2. What are the various certificates issued under Part 61? (14 CFR 61.5)

Pilot certificates—student pilot, sport pilot, recreational pilot, private pilot, commercial pilot, and airline transport pilot (ATP);

Flight instructor certificates; and

Ground instructor certificates.

3. **What are the various ratings that may be placed on a sport pilot instructor certificate?** (14 CFR 61.5)

"Sport Pilot" is the rating on the flight instructor certificate that must be accompanied by a sport pilot certificate. Instructor Category/Class/Make/Model are logbook endorsements.

4. **A temporary pilot certificate will remain effective for what length of time?** (14 CFR 61.17)

120 days.

5. **What is the duration of a flight instructor certificate?** (14 CFR 61.19)

A flight instructor certificate is effective only while the holder has a current pilot certificate, and it expires 24 calendar months from the month in which it was issued or renewed.

6. **What are the medical requirements certificates for sport pilot certificates?** (14 CFR 61.303)

Valid driver's license or at least a third class medical for sport pilot and sport pilot instructor.

7. **In the event an airman certificate, medical certificate, or knowledge test report is lost or destroyed, what procedure should be followed?** (14 CFR 61.29)

An application for the replacement of a lost or destroyed certificate or report is made by letter to the Department of Transportation, FAA;

A person who has lost a certificate or report may obtain a facsimile from the FAA confirming that it was issued. The facsimile may be carried as a certificate for a period not to exceed 60 days pending receipt of a duplicate certificate.

8. **To be eligible to take an FAA knowledge test, what must an applicant accomplish?** (14 CFR 61.35)

An applicant must have received an endorsement from an authorized instructor certifying that the applicant accomplished a required ground-training or a home-study course for the certificate or rating sought, and is prepared for the knowledge test; and must have proper identification at the time of application that contains the applicant's photograph, signature, date of birth (which shows the applicant meets or will meet the age requirements of this part for the certificate sought before the expiration date of the airman knowledge test report), and actual residential address (if different from the applicant's mailing address).

A letter from an ultralight organization is acceptable in lieu of an endorsement, for pilots registered before September 1, 2004.

- A certificate of graduation from a pilot training course by an FAA-certificated pilot school.
- An endorsement from an appropriately rated FAA-certificated ground or flight instructor.
- A certificate of graduation or statement of accomplishment from a ground school course (high school, college, adult education program, etc.).
- A certificate of graduation from an industry-provided aviation home study course.
- An endorsement from an appropriately rated FAA-certificated ground or flight instructor for completion of an individually developed home study course.
- An endorsement letter from the national ultralight organizations.

10. **What must an applicant do to be eligible for a sport pilot practical test for a certificate or rating?** (14 CFR 61.39)

- Pass the required knowledge test within the 24-calendar-month period preceding the month the applicant completes the practical test, if a knowledge test is required;
- Present the knowledge test report at the time of application for the practical test, if a knowledge test is required;
- Have the required training and obtained the aeronautical experience prescribed for the certificate or rating sought;
- Hold at least a current third-class medical certificate, or a valid U.S. driver's license;
- Meet the prescribed age requirement for the issuance of the certificate or rating sought;
- Have a logbook or training record endorsement, if required by the regulations, signed by an authorized instructor who certifies that the applicant: has received and logged 3 hours training time within 60 days preceding the date of application in preparation for the practical test; is prepared for the required practical test; and has demonstrated satisfactory knowledge of subject areas in which the applicant was deficient on the knowledge test; have a completed and signed 8710-11 application form.

11. **Other than the Practical Test Standards, what general guidelines will an examiner follow when judging the ability of an applicant for a pilot certificate or rating?** (14 CFR 61.43)

The examiner will judge based on that applicant's ability to safely:

a. Perform the tasks specified in the areas of operation in the Practical Test Standards for the certificate or rating sought;

b. Demonstrate mastery of the aircraft with the successful outcome of each task performed never seriously in doubt;

c. Demonstrate satisfactory proficiency and competency within approved standards;

d. Demonstrate sound judgment; and

e. Demonstrate single-pilot competence if the aircraft is type certificated for single-pilot operations.

12. **How can an applicant reapply for a knowledge or practical test they previously failed?** (14 CFR 61.49)

An applicant who fails may reapply for the test only after the applicant has received:

a. The necessary training from an authorized instructor, who has determined that the applicant is proficient to pass the test; and

b. An endorsement from an authorized instructor who gave the applicant the additional training.

D. Logbook Entries and Certificate Endorsements

1. **When entering time in a logbook, what time is considered as "training time"?** (14 CFR 61.51)

A person may log training time when that person receives training from an authorized instructor in an aircraft, flight simulator, or flight training device. The training time must be logged in a logbook and must be endorsed in a legible manner by the authorized instructor; and include a description of the training given, the length of the training lesson, and the instructor's signature, certificate number, and certificate expiration date.

2. **What logbook entries should be made by the flight instructor if a pilot demonstrates unsatisfactory performance during a Flight Review?** (AC 61-98A)

The instructor should sign the logbook to record the instruction given, and then recommend additional training in the areas of the review that were unsatisfactory. The instructor should not make record of an unsatisfactory review in the logbook.

before the month in which they act as pilot-in-command:

a. A pilot proficiency check conducted by the FAA, an approved pilot check airman, or U.S. Armed Forces, for a pilot certificate, rating, or operating privilege.

b. Completed one or more phases of an FAA-sponsored pilot proficiency award program (known as the "Wings" program).

c. A flight instructor who holds a current flight instructor certificate and has satisfactorily completed renewal of a flight instructor certificate need not accomplish the 1 hour of ground instruction.

Note: The flight review may be accomplished in combination with the requirements of §61.57 and other applicable recency-of-experience requirements at the discretion of the instructor.

4. What must be done if someone wants to add a category and/or a class to their sport pilot privileges (such as airplane land to weight-shift land)? (14 CFR 61.321)

Two CFIs are required:

CFI 1—Receive a logbook endorsement from an authorized instructor for training on aeronautical knowledge and skill per §61.309 and §61.311 for the additional light-sport aircraft privilege. Provide a recommendation on the FAA Form 8710-11 and fill it out this form for a proficiency check.

CFI 2*—The applicant must successfully complete a proficiency check from an authorized instructor, other than the instructor who trained and provided the recommendation on the for the proficiency check for the additional light-sport aircraft privilege.

CFI 2*—The instructor who conducted the proficiency check for the additional category/class also provides a logbook endorsement. This instructor will fill out the proficiency check area on the 8710-11 and send the form to the FAA.

* Be sure to check current regulations because the FAA may change the CFI 2 requirement to a DPE, in the near future.

5. If someone wants to operate an aircraft in the same category and class, but add an additional set of aircraft to an existing category/class, (such as airplane land below 87 knots to airplane land above 87 knots, or tricycle gear to tailwheel, or weight shift land to weight shift sea), what is the procedure? (14 CFR 61.323)

One CFI is required:

a. Receive and log ground and flight training from an authorized instructor in a make and model of light-sport aircraft that is within the same set of aircraft as the make and model of aircraft intended to operate;

b. Receive a logbook endorsement from this authorized instructor certifying they are proficient to operate the specific make and model of light-sport aircraft.

6. **What is the difference between a proficiency check and a logbook endorsement?** (14 CFR 61.321 and 61.323)

   A proficiency check is to add another category/class, requires an 8710-11 form, and requires an additional instructor (CFI 2*) to perform the proficiency check per Practical Test Standards (PTS).

   A logbook endorsement can be accomplished by a single instructor to fly an additional set of aircraft within the same category/class.

   Logbook endorsements are also used for FAA knowledge exam authorizations, numerous solo privileges, and recommendations for practical and proficiency checks.

7. **Someone currently authorized to fly a LSA airplane land wants to fly a LSA airplane with floats on water. Can this be done with a single instructor logbook endorsement?** (14 CFR 61.321)

   No. This is the same category but different class and therefore requires a proficiency check, training with one instructor, then the checkride with a separate instructor (CFI 2*).

8. **If you currently have authorization to fly a powered parachute land square wing, are you authorized to fly a powered parachute elliptical wing with a logbook endorsement with a single instructor?**

   Yes. This is the same category class, but a different set.

9. **How can you fly an additional class of aircraft not endorsed in your logbook?** (14 CFR 61.321)

   I must receive training from a CFI in the new class of aircraft, receive an endorsement for a proficiency check from the instructor who provided this training, and take a proficiency check with a different CFI than the one who provided me the training in the new class of aircraft (CFI 2*). This proficiency check results in an 8710-11 form and a logbook endorsement for the make/model aircraft, allowing me to fly aircraft within this new set.

---

* *Be sure to check current regulations because the FAA may change the CFI 2 requirement to a DPE, in the near future.*

(14 CFR 61.83)

An applicant must:

a. Be at least 16 years of age for other than the operation of a glider or balloon.

b. Be at least 14 years of age for the operation of a glider or balloon.

c. Be able to read, speak, write, and understand the English language.

11. How can a person obtain a student pilot certificate? (14 CFR 61.85)

An application for a student pilot certificate is made on an 8710-11 form and is submitted to:

a. A designated aviation medical examiner if applying for an FAA medical certificate under 14 CFR Part 67;

b. A Designated Pilot Examiner (DPE) for a student pilot certificate; or

c. A Flight Standards District Office for a student pilot certificate.

12. What minimum aeronautical knowledge must be demonstrated by a student pilot before solo privileges are permitted? (14 CFR 61.87)

A student pilot must demonstrate satisfactory aeronautical knowledge on a knowledge test.

The test must address the student pilot's knowledge of:

- Applicable sections of 14 CFR Parts 61 and 91;
- Airspace rules and procedures for the airport where the solo flight will be performed; and
- Flight characteristics and operational limitations for the make and model of aircraft to be flown.

The student's authorized instructor must:

- Administer the test; and
- At the conclusion of the test, review all incorrect answers with the student before authorizing that student to conduct a solo flight.

13. What minimum flight training must a student pilot receive before solo privileges are permitted? (14 CFR 61.87)

Prior to conducting a solo flight, a student pilot must have:

a. Received and logged flight training for the Part 61 maneuvers and procedures appropriate to the make and model of aircraft to be flown; and

b. Demonstrated satisfactory proficiency and safety, as judged by an authorized instructor, on the Part 61 maneuvers and procedures in the specific make and model of aircraft.

c. Received and logged flight training for the specific maneuvers specified for the category sought per 61.87.

14. **What endorsements are required for a student pilot to solo an aircraft?** (14 CFR 61.87)

    A student pilot may not operate an aircraft in solo flight unless they receive:

    a. An endorsement from an authorized instructor on his or her student pilot certificate for the specific make and model aircraft to be flown; and

    b. An endorsement in the student's logbook for the specific make and model aircraft to be flown by an authorized instructor, who gave the training within the 90 days preceding the date of the flight.

15. **What limitations are imposed upon flight instructors authorizing student pilot solo flights?** (14 CFR 61.87)

    No instructor may authorize a student pilot to perform a solo flight unless that instructor has:

    a. Given that student pilot training in the make and model of aircraft or a similar make and model of aircraft in which the solo flight is to be flown;

    b. Determined the student pilot is proficient in the Part 61 prescribed maneuvers and procedures;

    c. Determined the student pilot is proficient in the make and model of aircraft to be flown;

    d. Ensured that the student pilot's certificate has been endorsed by an instructor authorized to provide flight training for the specific make and model aircraft to be flown; and

    e. Endorsed the student pilot's logbook for the specific make and model aircraft to be flown, and that endorsement remains current for solo flight privileges, provided an authorized instructor updates the student's logbook every 90 days thereafter.

    The required flight training must be given by an instructor authorized, appropriately rated, and current to provide flight training.

16. **State the general limitations that apply to all student pilots.** (14 CFR 61.89)

    A student pilot may not act as pilot-in-command of an aircraft:

    a. Carrying a passenger;

    b. Carrying property for compensation or hire;

    c. For compensation or hire;

    d. In furtherance of a business;

    e. On an international flight; (with exceptions—see §61.89)

    f. With a flight or surface visibility of less than 3 statute miles during daylight hours;

    g. When the flight cannot be made with visual reference to the surface;

    h. In a manner contrary to any limitations placed in the pilot's logbook by an authorized instructor;

k. In Class B, C, and D airspace, at an airport located in Class B, C, or D airspace, and to, from, through, or on an airport having an operational control tower without having received the ground and flight training specified in §61.94 and an endorsement from an authorized instructor.

17. Before solo cross-country privileges are permitted, what minimum cross-country flight training requirements must a student pilot satisfy? (14 CFR 61.93)

The student pilot must receive and log flight training in the following maneuvers and procedures:

a. Aeronautical charts for VFR navigation using pilotage and dead reckoning with aid of a magnetic compass or a GPS;

b. Use of aircraft performance charts for cross-country flight;

c. Procurement and analysis of aeronautical weather reports and forecasts, recognizing critical weather situations and estimating visibility while in flight;

d. Emergency procedures;

e. Traffic pattern procedures that include area departure, area arrival, entry into the traffic pattern, and approach;

f. Collision avoidance, wake turbulence precautions, and windshear avoidance;

g. Recognition, avoidance, and operational restrictions of hazardous terrain features in the geographical area where the cross-country flight will be flown;

h. Proper operation of the instruments and equipment installed in the aircraft to be flown;

i. Use of radios for VFR navigation and two-way communications if installed and required;

j. Takeoff, approach, and landing procedures.

See specific category details in 14 CFR 61.93 (e) through (m).

18. Before a flight instructor can authorize a student pilot to conduct a solo cross-country flight, what requirements must be met? (14 CFR 61.93)

The instructor must have determined that:

a. The student's cross-country planning is correct for the flight;

b. Upon review, the current and forecast weather conditions show that the flight can be completed under VFR;

c. The student is proficient to conduct the flight safely; and

d. The student has the appropriate and current solo cross-country endorsement for the make and model of aircraft to be flown;

e. The student's solo flight endorsement is current for the make and model aircraft to be flown.

19. **Before a student pilot is permitted solo cross-country privileges, they must have received several endorsements. What are they?** (14 CFR 61.93)

Student pilot certificate endorsement: A student pilot must have a solo cross-country endorsement from the authorized instructor who conducted the training, and that endorsement must be placed on that person's student pilot certificate for the specific category of aircraft to be flown.

Logbook endorsement: A student pilot must have a solo cross-country endorsement from an authorized instructor placed in the student pilot's logbook for the specific make and model of aircraft to be flown.

For each cross-country flight, the authorized instructor who reviews the cross-country planning must make an endorsement in the person's logbook after reviewing that person's cross-country planning, as specified in §61.93(d). The endorsement must:

- specify the make and model of aircraft to be flown
- state that the student's preflight planning and preparation is correct
- state that the student is prepared to make the flight safely under the known conditions, and
- state that any limitations required by the student's instructor are met.

20. **What requirements must be met before a flight instructor can allow a student pilot to make repeated specific solo cross-country flights without each flight being logbook endorsed?** (14 CFR 61.93)

Repeated specific solo cross-country flights may be made to another airport within 50 NM of the airport from which the flight originated, provided:

a. The authorized instructor has given the student flight training in both directions over the route, including entering and exiting the traffic patterns, takeoffs, and landings at the airports to be used;

b. The authorized instructor who gave the training has endorsed the student's logbook certifying the student is proficient to make such flights;

c. The student has current solo flight endorsements in accordance with §61.87; and

d. The student has current solo cross-country flight endorsements in accordance with §61.87(c); however, for repeated solo cross-country flights to another airport within 50 NM from which the flight originated, separate endorsements are not required to be made for each flight.

21. **What actions must a flight instructor take to allow a student sport pilot to operate within class B, C or D airspace or an airport within class B, C, or D airspace, or any airport with a control tower?** (14 CFR 61.94)

A student pilot may not operate an aircraft on a solo flight in Class B, C or D airspace unless:

a. The student pilot has received both ground and flight training from an authorized instructor on the use of radios, communications, navigation systems and radar facilities.

b. Operations at airports with an operating control tower, must include three takeoffs and landings to a full stop, with each landing involving a flight in the traffic pattern, at an airport with an operating control tower.

d. The student receives ground and flight training for the specific Class B, C, or D airspace for which the solo flight is authorized, if applicable, within the 90-day period preceding the date of the flight in that airspace. The flight training must be received in the specific airspace area for which solo flight is authorized.

e. The authorized instructor who provides the training specified in 61.94(a) must provide a logbook endorsement that certifies the student has received that training and is proficient to conduct solo flight in that specific airspace or at that specific airport and in those aeronautical knowledge areas and areas of operation specified.

Flight Instructor Certificates

22. In what areas of aeronautical knowledge must an applicant for a sport pilot instructor certificate have received instruction? (14 CFR 61.407)

a. The fundamentals of instructing

b. Technical subject areas

c. Aeronautical knowledge and skill areas for a sport certificate applicable to the aircraft category for which flight instructor privileges are sought

23. What do the fundamentals of instruction include? (14 CFR 61.407)

a. The learning process.

b. Elements of effective teaching.

c. Student evaluation and testing.

d. Course development.

e. Lesson planning.

f. Classroom training techniques.

24. What are the technical subject areas? (Sport Pilot Practical Test Standards)

a. Aeromedical factors

b. Visual scanning and collision avoidance

c. Federal aviation regulations and publications

d. Logbook entries and certificate endorsements

25. Do flight instructors without a sport pilot rating (14 CFR Part 61, Subpart H) operate differently than instructors with a sport pilot rating? (14 CFR 61.181)

Yes, instructors without a sport pilot rating operate under Subpart H (61.181 to 61.199), where sport pilot instructors have new procedures in Subpart K (61.401 to 61.431) specifically for—

a. Eligibility and aeronautical knowledge.

b. Flight proficiency and endorsements.

c. Privileges and limits.

d. Transition provisions for registered ultralight flight instructors.

e. Logging of flight time, testing and recordkeeping.

26. What are the privileges of a flight instructor certificate with a sport pilot rating? (14 CFR 61.413)

If I hold a flight instructor certificate with a sport pilot rating, I am authorized, within the limits of my certificate and rating, to provide training and logbook endorsements for—

a. A student pilot seeking a sport pilot certificate;

b. A sport pilot certificate;

c. A flight instructor certificate with a sport pilot rating;

d. A powered parachute or weight-shift-control aircraft rating;

e. Sport pilot privileges;

f. A flight review or operating privilege for a sport pilot;

g. A practical test for a sport pilot certificate, or a flight instructor certificate with a sport pilot rating;

h. A knowledge test for a sport pilot certificate, or a flight instructor certificate with a sport pilot rating; and

i. A proficiency check for an additional category, class, or make and model privilege for a sport pilot certificate or a flight instructor certificate with a sport pilot rating.

As a flight instructor with a sport pilot rating I must:

a. Sign the logbook of each person to whom I have given flight training or ground training.

b. Keep a record of the name, date, and type of endorsement for:

- Each person whose logbook or student pilot certificate I have endorsed for solo flight privileges.

- Each person for whom I have provided an endorsement for a knowledge test, practical test, or proficiency check, and the record must indicate the kind of test or check, and the results.

- Each person whose logbook I have endorsed as proficient to operate —

  – An additional category or class of light-sport aircraft;

  – An additional make and model of light-sport aircraft;

  – In Class B, C, and D airspace; at an airport located in Class B, C, or D airspace; and to, from, through, or at an airport having an operational control tower; and

  – A light-sport aircraft with a V_H greater than 87 knots CAS.

- Each person whose logbook I have endorsed as proficient to provide flight training in an additional —

  – Category or class of light-sport aircraft; and

  – Make and model of light-sport aircraft.

Within 10 days after providing an endorsement for a person to operate or provide training in an additional category and class of light-sport aircraft I must —

a. Complete, sign, and submit to the FAA the 8710-11 form presented to me to obtain those privileges; and

b. Retain a copy of the 8710-11 form.

I must keep the records listed above for 3 years. I may keep these records in a logbook or a separate document.

28. How do you renew a flight instructor certificate? (14 CFR 61.197 and 61.425)

A person who holds a current flight instructor certificate may renew that certificate for an additional 24 calendar months if the holder:

a. Has passed a practical test for one of the ratings listed on the current flight instructor certificate, or an additional flight instructor rating; or

b. Has presented to an authorized FAA Flight Standards Inspector a record of training students showing that, during the preceding 24 calendar months, the flight instructor has endorsed at least five students for a practical test for a certificate or rating, and at least 80 percent of those students passed that test on the first attempt;

c. Or has a record showing that, within the preceding 24 calendar months, the flight instructor served as a company check pilot, chief flight instructor, company check airman, or flight instructor in a Part 121 or Part 135 operation, or in a position involving the regular evaluation of pilots;

d. Or has a graduation certificate showing that, within the preceding 3 calendar months, the person has successfully completed an approved flight instructor refresher course (FIRC) consisting of ground or flight training, or a combination of both.

29. What are the limits of a flight instructor certificate with a sport pilot rating? (14 CFR 61.415)

If I hold a flight instructor certificate with a sport pilot rating, I must hold any rating I give, and I am subject to the following limits:

a. May not provide ground or flight training in any aircraft for which I do not hold:

- A sport pilot certificate with applicable category and class privileges and make and model privileges or a pilot certificate with the applicable category and class rating; and

- Applicable category and class privileges for my flight instructor certificate with a sport pilot rating.

b. May not provide ground or flight training for a private pilot certificate with a powered parachute or weight-shift-control aircraft rating unless I hold:

- At least a private pilot certificate with the applicable category and class rating;

- Applicable category and class privileges for your flight instructor certificate with a sport pilot rating.

c. May not conduct more than 8 hours of flight training in any consecutive 24-hour period.

- Given that student the flight training required for solo flight privileges required by this part; and

- Determined that the student is prepared to conduct the flight safely under known circumstances, subject to any limitations listed in the student's logbook that I consider necessary for the safety of the flight.

- Student pilot's certificate and logbook for a solo cross-country flight, unless I have determined the student's flight preparation, planning, equipment, and proposed procedures are adequate for the proposed flight under the existing conditions and within any limitations listed in the logbook that I consider necessary for the safety of the flight.

- Student pilot's certificate and logbook for solo flight in Class B, C, and D airspace areas, at an airport within Class B, C, or D airspace and to from, through or on an airport having an operational control tower, unless I have—

  - Given that student ground and flight training in that airspace or at that airport; and

  - Determined that the student is proficient to operate the aircraft safely.

- Logbook of a pilot for a flight review, unless I have conducted a review of that pilot in accordance with the requirements of §61.56.

e. May not provide flight training in an aircraft unless I have at least 5 hours of flight time in a make and model of light-sport aircraft within the same set of aircraft as the aircraft in which I am providing training.

f. May not provide training to operate a light-sport aircraft in Class B, C, and D airspace, at an airport located in Class B, C, or D airspace, and to, from, through, or at an airport having an operational control tower, unless I have the endorsement specified in §61.325, or are otherwise authorized to conduct operations in this airspace and at these airports.

g. May not provide training in a light-sport aircraft with a V_H greater than 87 knots CAS unless I have the endorsement specified in §61.327, or are otherwise authorized to operate that light-sport aircraft.

h. Must perform all training in an aircraft that complies with the requirements of §91.109.

i. If I provide flight training for a certificate, rating or privilege, I must provide that flight training in an aircraft that meets the following:

- The aircraft must have at least two pilot stations and be of the same category and class appropriate to the certificate, rating or privilege sought.

- For single-place aircraft, presolo flight training must be provided in an aircraft that has two pilot stations and is of the same category and class appropriate to the certificate, rating, or privilege sought.

30. How do you obtain privileges to provide training in an additional category or class of light-sport aircraft? (14 CFR 61.419)

If I hold a flight instructor certificate with a sport pilot rating and want to provide training in an additional category or class of light-sport aircraft I must—

a. Receive a logbook endorsement from the authorized instructor who trained me on the applicable areas of operation specified in §61.409 certifying I have met the aeronautical knowledge and flight proficiency requirements for the additional category and class flight instructor privilege I seek;

b. Successfully complete a proficiency check from an authorized instructor other than the instructor who trained me (CFI 2*) on the areas specified in §61.409 for the additional category and class flight instructor privilege I seek;

c. Complete an application for those privileges on an 8710-11 form and present this application to the authorized instructor (CFI 2*) who conducted the proficiency check;

d. Receive a logbook endorsement from the instructor who conducted the proficiency check (CFI 2*) certifying I am proficient in the areas of operation and authorized for the additional category and class flight instructor privilege.

* Be sure to check current regulations because the FAA may change the CFI 2 requirement to a DPE, in the near future.

31. May you exercise the privileges of a flight instructor certificate with a sport pilot rating if you hold a flight instructor certificate with another rating? (14 CFR 61.429)

If I hold a current and valid flight instructor certificate, a commercial pilot certificate with an airship rating, or a commercial pilot certificate with a balloon rating, and I seek to exercise the privileges of a flight instructor certificate with a sport pilot rating, I may do so without any further showing of proficiency, subject to the following limits:

a. I am limited to the aircraft category and class ratings listed on my flight instructor certificate, commercial pilot certificate with an airship rating, or commercial pilot certificate with a balloon rating, as appropriate, when exercising my flight instructor privileges and the privileges specified in §61.413.

b. I must comply with the limits specified in §61.415 and the recordkeeping requirements of §61.423.

c. If I want to exercise the privileges of my flight instructor certificate, commercial pilot certificate with an airship rating, or commercial pilot certificate with a balloon rating, as appropriate, in a category, class, or make and model of light-sport aircraft for which I am not currently rated, I must meet all applicable requirements to provide training in an additional category or class of light-sport aircraft specified in §61.419.

An FAA examiner will determine whether an applicant exhibits instructional knowledge of the elements in planning of instructional activity. The applicant will be required to develop a lesson plan for any one of the required maneuvers. The following is an example of a lesson plan for a 90-minute flight instruction period.

Student .... **Date** ....

Lesson   Normal Takeoff

Objective   To familiarize the student with normal takeoffs and landings in calm wind while doing patterns at the nontowered airport.

Content   Determine that the wind is calm.

Determine the pattern direction for this wind condition.

Normal takeoffs and landings with rectangular patterns.

Schedule

Preflight Discussion	:10
Instructor Demonstration	:25
Student Practice	:45
Postflight Critique	:10

Equipment   Chalkboard or notebook for preflight discussion

Instructor's Actions   Preflight—Discuss lesson objective.

Inflight—Demonstrate elements. Demonstrate normal takeoffs, rectangular pattern, and normal approach and landing. Coach student practice.

Postflight   Critique student performance and assign study material.

Student's Actions   Preflight—Discuss lesson objective and resolve questions.

Inflight—Review previous maneuvers including slow flight.
Perform each new maneuver as directed.

Postflight—Ask pertinent questions.

Completion Standards   Student should demonstrate competency in normal takeoffs, rectangular pattern, and normal landings. Student should recognize and take prompt corrective action to abort takeoffs or landings and do an appropriate go-around if the landing approach is not appropriate or in question.

The following lists from the various FAA and other publications of aviation regulations and procedures are meant to help you find the "sport-pilot-specific" resources and references within these available handbooks and manuals. For the FAA regulations and procedures published in books such as ASA's *FAR/AIM*, the FAA makes changes throughout the year and therefore we have provided an online resource for them.

These study guides tell you what to study, as well as what you can ignore as a Sport Pilot flying light-sport aircraft. The FAA's publications are written with a general aviation audience in mind, so much of their information is not relevant to your intended operations—and therefore not necessary for you to study. You may find it helpful to cross off or otherwise note what FAA material does not apply to you as a sport pilot, as defined in this appendix. This is one method by which your FAA publications can be geared more specifically to you.

A study guide for two other helpful resources is provided here in this Appendix: the FAA's *Pilot's Handbook of Aeronautical Knowledge*, and ASA's *Visualized Flight Maneuvers Handbook for High Wing Aircraft*. Within these study lists, watch for the abbreviations for weight-shift control (WSC) and powered parachute (PPC) that will help you focus-in on what areas to study, depending upon the aircraft in which you will be taking your checkride. Note that vintage or older LSA are often referred to in these books as standard category airplanes (such as the Piper J-3, etc.). Also, weight-shift control and powered parachute pilots will need to study additional reference materials as these aircraft categories are not specifically addressed in the FAA publications at this time.

FAR/AIM Online Sport Pilot Study Guide

Go to the ASA website, at this address, **www.asa2fly.com/F2FCKRIDE** for the study guide to help you through these two very weighty FAA publications. You can download the PDF file located there and read it onscreen or print it out using Adobe Reader software.

This online reference is a comprehensive checklist of regulations and aeronautical information for the sport pilot. It lists what affects sport pilots, and provides specific areas to study for. All sport pilots and sport instructors need to be familiar with the rules and procedures; however, some will be more applicable than others, depending on your intended operations.

Your examiner will tailor the practical test for your aircraft type, equipment, and limitations. A powered parachute with no instruments flying out of a large field will be tested differently than a pilot flying a high speed airplane with a full panel of flight, navigation, and engine instruments. Use your best judgment in determining which areas to study for your particular situation; use the Practical Test Standards as a guide. Ask your recommending instructor or the examiner what areas on this list you will be tested on.

Chapter 1 Aircraft Structure

This is a short chapter that deals specifically with the airplane category. WSC and PPC pilots can look at the "Wings" section, and review the *Landing Gear* and *Powerplant*. Specifics on the WSC/PPC wings and fuselage should be covered with your instructor, and through the *Learn to Fly* and *Preflight* DVDs.

Chapter 3 Aerodynamics of Flight

PPC Overview—The increased speeds, stalls, and spins are not applicable to PPC and can be ignored.

WSC Overview—The spins are not applicable to WSC and can be ignored.

Page 3-7—PPC can ignore *Ground Effect* because the wing is too high above the ground to be affected by ground effect.

Page 3-10—PPC are statically and dynamically stable. You may ignore Page 3-11 starting with *Longitudinal Stability* through Page 3-17, column 1, then pick it back up again on Page 3-17, *Aerodynamic Forces In Flight Maneuvers*.

Pages 3-18 and 3-19—PPC and WSC can ignore *Slipping Turns* and *Skidding Turns*.

Page 3-24—PPC and WSC can ignore the *Corkscrew Effect*.

Page 3-26—*Load Factors in Airplane Design* is for standard category aircraft. S-LSA and E-LSA will have similar load limits but they are specified in the POH.

Page 3-28—PPC can ignore *Load Factors and Stalling Speeds*.

Page 3-29—PPC all Stalls and Spins can be ignored.

Page 3-29—WSC all Spins can be ignored.

Page 3-30—*Chandelles and Lazy Eights* can be ignored for all sport pilots.

Page 3-30—PPC ignore *VG Diagram*.

Page 3-33—WSC and PPC ignore *Effect of Load Distribution*.

Page 3-35—*High Speed Flight* can be ignored by all, through end of Chapter 3.

Chapter 4 Flight Controls

PPC and WSC ignore this entire chapter.

Appendix

Chapter 5 Aircraft Systems

Pages 5-1 and 5-2 apply to four-stroke engines. Two strokes combine the intake/compression stroke and the power/exhaust strokes without valves to accomplish the same objective.

Page 5-4—Ignore *Adjustable Pitch Propeller*.

Page 5-5—*Mixture Control*, most LSA have ground adjustable jets, where standard category/vintage LSA do use mixture controls.

Page 5-9 through 5-11—Ignore *Superchargers and Turbosuperchargers*. Only a few 4-stroke LSA engines have turbo or superchargers. Study only if your aircraft has this system.

Page 5-15—*Fuel Grades,* most LSA use auto gas except standard category. Most modern LSA use auto gas.

Page 5-16—*Oil Systems* is for 4-stroke only; 2-stroke is different.

Pages 5-19 through 5-22—*Electrical Systems* is more complicated with more accessories, but basically the same general systems for LSA. Study only if your aircraft has an electric system (battery, main switch/key/ electric starter).

Page 5-22—*Hydraulic System* is only for aircraft with these types of systems.

Pages 5-22 and 5-23—WSC and PPC ignore *Nose and Tail Wheel*.

Page 5-23—Ignore *Autopilot* through the end of Chapter 5.

Chapter 6 Flight Instruments

This section covers more detail than the typical LSA systems have. Some powered parachutes have no flight instruments and can ignore this section completely. Study only the instruments you have.

Page 6-1—*Pitot Static Flight Instruments*, lower speed aircraft may not have a separate static line and port, they just read the ambient static pressure.

Page 6-9—Ignore *Gyroscopic Flight Instruments* section through Page 6-14, unless your aircraft has these instruments (not typical on LSA).

Chapter 8 Weight and Balance

Page 8-2—PPC and WSC ignore *Balance, Stability, and Center of Gravity* through end of chapter.

Chapter 9 Aircraft Performance

Page 9-5—for PPC straight-and-level flight; the PPC is trimmed at the minimum total drag or slightly faster to relate *this* explanation for the single-speed PPC. PPC ignore the slower and faster speeds explanations.

Page 9-10—PPC ignore *Ground Effect*.

Page 9-18—PPC ignore *Performance Speeds*. WSC and airplane ignore the speeds not applicable to you.

Page 9-19—*Performance Charts* section through Page 9-13; LSA will not have as detailed performance data or details as presented here. Most likely there will be one situation at sea level standard conditions and maximum gross weight where the takeoff distance and/ or distance over a 50-foot obstacle is included. Reviewing these charts reveals there are great differences in takeoff distances, distance over a 50-foot obstacle with down wind takeoffs, high density altitude, uphill/rough field, etc.

Page 9-20 *Density Altitude* and Page 9-28 *Crosswind Component Charts*— These are both important for sport pilots to study, understand and use.

Page 9-31—Ignore *Transport Category Airplane Performance* through the end of Chapter 9.

Chapter 11 Weather Reports, Forecasts, and Charts

The FAA covers significantly more weather reports, forecasts, and charts than needed for the sport pilot; however, the more weather information you gather, the better an evaluation you can make. There is a great difference between a sport pilot flying a powered parachute around the pattern, to light-sport airplanes cruising at 120 knots and going on long cross-country trips. Many pilots flying around in the pattern observe the weather only and feel this is an acceptable weather analysis—experienced pilots do this and it works most of the time. However, knowing how hard the wind is blowing 3,000 feet above you, plus what the wind is predicted to do during the time of your flight, should be your minimum preflight weather analysis in addition to observing the sky for local flights. The high performance cross-country pilot does need more analysis and should study most areas in this chapter.

The "Weather to Fly for Sport Pilots" is the time-proven system for sport pilots and should be used by all to evaluate the weather to make the important go/no go decision. The following reports are particularly useful for all sport pilots:

Page 11-3—*Weather Briefings—Standard/Abbreviated/Outlook,* note that it's a good idea to call 1-800-WX-BRIEF and get the report from an aviation specialist.

Page 11-4—*Aviation Routine Weather Report* (METARs) provides the conditions at specific locations. This report helps you find out if your airport is fogged in or blown out before you drive there. These are now decoded on the internet so you do not need to memorize the coding as discussed in the book.

Page 11-9—*Terminal Aerodrome Forecasts* (TAFs) provides the predicted conditions at specific locations. This report gives you the predictions for the airport being fogged in or blown out in the near future. These are now decoded on the internet so you do not need to memorize the coding as discussed in the book.

Page 11-13—*Winds and Temperature Aloft Forecast* (FD, a great tool for predicting winds above and in the near future, and the best tool for determining wind limitations for LSA.

Page 11-18—*Significant Weather Prognostic Charts* are used to predict the big picture for fronts approaching and isobars/wind.

Chapter 13 Airspace

Note that the minimum visibility for sport pilots is 3 statute miles and sport pilots may not fly higher than 10,000 feet MSL maximum altitude, which takes precedence over the airspace weather minimums listed in this chapter.

Chapter 14 Navigation

Pages 14-3 to 14-16—*Measurement of Direction* is necessary only if the aircraft you're flying has a magnetic compass in it. Many LSA use a GPS instead of a magnetic compass for measurement of direction.

Pages 14-17 to 14-25—Ignore *Radio Navigation* section unless you have this equipment in your aircraft.

Chapter 15 Aeromedical Factors

Page 15-10—Ignore *Night Vision* to end of Chapter 15.

High Wing Aircraft (#ASA-VFM-HI)

Be sure to review your specific aircraft's POH because you will need to make some adjustments or modifications in the information presented in this part of the appendix to account for the specific engine, instruments, and performance of your airplane, trike, or PPC.

Pages 1–3—*Aircraft Review and Familiarization*. Airplanes must modify to eliminate the gear down/up speeds, engine systems, operations and instruments to include only those used for the practical. WSC must modify to eliminate the flap and gear down/up speeds, modify engine systems, operations and instruments to include only those used for the practical. The control systems and weight and balance must also be modified for weight-shift. PPC must modify to eliminate all speeds, modify engine systems, operations and instruments to include only those used for the practical. The control systems must also be modified and the weight and balance.

Preflight Operations, Starting and Taxiing sections—All must be modified for LSA airplanes, WSC, and PPC as appropriate. Modify all additional sections for specific type of aircraft.

Page 10—*Crosswind Takeoff and Climb*, airplane and WSC only.

Pages 10 through 15—*Soft Field and Short field Takeoff and Climb*, airplane only.

Page 17—*Shallow and Medium Turns,* PPC do shallow turns only.

Page 22—*Eights on Pylons*, ignore.

Page 24—*Maneuvering During Slow Flight*, airplane and WSC only.

Page 25—*Power Off Stalls*, Airplane and WSC only.

Page 26—*Power On Stalls,* airplane only

Pages 28 through 30—*Crossed Controlled Stalls, Elevator Trim Stalls, Secondary Stalls*, ignore.

Page 31—*Steep Turns*, airplane and WSC only.

Pages 32 to 37—*Steep Spirals, Chandelles, Lazy Eights*, ignore.

Page 38—*Spins*, ignore. (Airplanes, read spin awareness Page 39.)

Page 43—*Forward Slip,* airplane only.

Pages 46 and 47—*Soft and Short Field Approach and Landing*, airplane only.

Page 48—*Power-off 180° Accuracy Approach and Landing*, ignore.

Pages 51 to 53—*Private, Commercial, and Flight Instructor Checklists*, use your sport pilot practical test checklist.

Notes

Notes

Notes

Notes